MPRE

Welcome Letter
Quick Reference Guide

Substantive Outline
Lecture Handout
Final Review Outline
Legal Terminology List

Practice Exam One
Practice Exam Two

NCBE®, MBE®, MEE®, MPT®, MPRE®, and UBE® are trademarks of the National Conference of Bar Examiners. All other trademarks are the property of their respective companies.

The material herein is intended to be used in conjunction with the myThemis Portal™ in order to provide basic review of legal subjects and is in no way meant to be a source of or replacement for professional legal advice.

ISBN 978-1-949634-87-7

Welcome to the Themis MPRE Review course. We are excited that you have chosen Themis to help you pass the MPRE.

As you begin preparing for the MPRE, we want to offer you some tips for success:

- There are two modes of learning with Themis Bar Review—Directed Study and Flex Study.
    - In Directed Study mode, you will study according to a structured, sequential daily task schedule.
    - In Flex Study mode, you may choose to complete tasks in any order, at your own pace.
    - You may alternate between these two modes of study; any work completed in Flex Study mode will be reflected in your Directed Study calendar.

- Regardless of which mode of studying you prefer, we recommend a structured approach to your studies:
    - Review the *Quick Reference Guide* on the next page.
    - Go to ThemisBar.com to launch the free MPRE Review course.
    - Read the MPRE substantive outline.
    - Watch the on-demand MPRE lecture, following along with the interactive handout, and answer a series of Assessment Questions after each video chapter to ensure that you have mastered the material.
    - Test your MPRE knowledge with our Test Bank of multiple-choice practice questions, carefully reviewing the model answers.
    - Use your results on the practice questions and Assessment Quiz 2 (or AQ2) questions to identify areas of potential weakness for review. You can see these results by clicking on "Course Progress" and then "MPRE PQs" or "AQ2."
    - Finally, take the 30-question Practice Exams (accessible in this book and online) and the 60-question Simulated MPRE (online only), and carefully read the analysis of each question (available online) to help reinforce important points of law.

Although we will be in touch during the course, feel free to reach out directly to our experienced staff attorneys via the **Message Center**™. This *online* communication center is your source for course announcements, tips, and strategies, and is your means to submit questions about the course or the materials. In addition, you may email us any time or call us weekdays between 9 AM and 6PM ET.

Finally, we strongly encourage you to visit www.ncbex.org/exams/mpre for a complete explanation of MPRE registration procedures and exam-day policies.

Good luck!

Themis Bar Review
info@themisbar.com
(888) 843-6476

MPRE: Quick Reference Guide

Getting Started

To access your Themis MPRE Review, follow these three easy steps:

1. Log in to your Themis account at www.Themisbar.com. There is a **Sign In** button at the top right of the home page.
2. Your MPRE Course is located in the **Free Programs** area of the Account Summary page.
3. If your MPRE Course is currently accessible, you'll see a blue **Launch** button. Click it to access the online MPRE content. If it is not yet accessible, you will see the anticipated availability date.
4. Upon initial launch of your course, you will be prompted to select the date you are taking the MPRE. This will allow your assignments to calibrate correctly.

Directed Study

Directed Study mode activates approximately two weeks prior to the MPRE. Directed Study controls your daily assignments. The calendar recalculates every day based on the tasks you have completed. Each task activates as you complete the previously assigned one, keeping you on track to complete your preparation before the MPRE.

Flex Study

Flex Study mode allows you the freedom to choose your own preparation path. On the left navigation bar, you will see a list of the types of tasks to complete in your course: Outlines, Lectures, Practice Questions, and Practice Exams.

Outlines

The online outline is identical to the outline in your MPRE book. It allows you to move to a particular topic or section of the outline with the Table of Contents feature. Additionally, you can use the keyword search feature to find specific concepts within the outline.

To complete the outline tasks, be sure to click the **Mark As Complete** button.

Lecture, Handout, and Assessment Questions

Upon selecting a chapter of the lecture, click play to start the video. The lecture handout is available by clicking the Handout link located to the right of the video player screen. If it is the first time you are watching a chapter, there will be an **Assessments** link to the right of the video player screen. Click this link upon completion of the chapter.

Assessment questions are a series of questions designed by Themis to determine your understanding of the material and to assist in retention of the concepts. These questions must be completed for each chapter in order for the lecture task to be marked as complete.

Practice Questions

In Directed Study, practice questions are presented in Interactive Mode. In Flex Study, you have the option to complete your practice questions sessions in Interactive or Test Mode. Interactive Mode allows you to see immediately whether your answer is right or wrong along with an explanation. Test Mode allows you to complete the session before issuing a score report and answer explanations.

Once you have completed a session, you may access (and re-access) the task to review the questions.

Simulated Exams

Your MPRE Review course includes two 30-minute Practice Exams, which can be taken online or offline using this book, and a full 60-question Simulated MPRE, which can be taken online (to mimic actual MPRE testing conditions). If you complete the Practice Exams offline, we recommend uploading your results so that you receive your performance reports.

MPRE
Substantive Outline

MULTISTATE PROFESSIONAL RESPONSIBILITY EXAM (MPRE)

Table of Contents

MULTISTATE PROFESSIONAL RESPONSIBILITY EXAM (MPRE)

I. INTRODUCTION

A. FORMAT AND CONTENT OF MPRE

The Multistate Professional Responsibility Exam (MPRE) is a standardized exam created by the National Conference of Bar Examiners (NCBE).

1. Model Rules of Professional Conduct

The MPRE tests the Model Rules of Professional Conduct (Model Rules or MRPC) promulgated by the American Bar Association (ABA) in 1983, and amended several times since. The Model Rules consist of specific rules with explanatory comments. This outline references the 2002 version of the Model Rules, as amended. The Model Rules serve as a standard for adoption by states, but are not in and of themselves binding. With the exception of California, all states have adopted the basic organizational structure of the Model Rules.

2. Code of Judicial Conduct

The MPRE also tests the ABA Model Code of Judicial Conduct (CJC), which establishes the standard for ethical conduct of judges, and consists of broad canons and specific rules, which are further explained by corresponding comments. The CJC applies to full-time judges, including magistrates, justices of the peace, court commissioners, special masters, referees, and administrative law judges. Part-time and retired judges are required to comply with some of the limitations on outside and political activities. This outline references the 2007 version of the CJC. CJC questions make up between 6 and 10 percent of the questions on the MPRE.

3. Other Applicable Authorities

To the extent that questions of professional responsibility arise in the context of procedural or evidentiary issues, such as the availability of litigation sanctions or the scope of the attorney-client evidentiary privilege, the Federal Rules of Civil Procedure and the Federal Rules of Evidence are assumed to apply, unless otherwise stated. In addition, constitutional issues, especially First Amendment issues, may be involved, in which case the U.S. Constitution governs.

4. Exam Format

The MPRE is administered in March, August, and November of each year and consists of 60 multiple-choice questions given over the span of two hours. A minimum score on the MPRE is required for admission to the state bar in most states.

Each question on the MPRE provides a factual situation along with a specific question and four possible answer choices. You should choose the best answer from the four possible answer choices. There is no penalty for guessing, so guessing on an answer about which you are unsure is statistically better for you than not answering the question at all.

> **EXAM NOTE:** Remember not to focus solely on the "yes" or "no" component contained in many answers. Be sure to read the entire answer, as the explanations or qualifiers are generally very important in determining the correct answer.

B. DEFINITIONS OF KEY WORDS AND PHRASES USED ON THE MPRE

In taking the MPRE, you should read each question carefully, paying close attention to the following key words or phrases, which are critical in determining the correct answer and have specific definitions for purposes of the MPRE.

1. Subject to Discipline

The phrase "subject to discipline" asks whether the conduct would subject the lawyer to discipline under the Model Rules or a judge to discipline under the CJC. This phrase corresponds to the mandatory language "shall" (i.e., "must") in the Model Rules and CJC.

Example: A lawyer **shall** not charge an unreasonable fee. MRPC 1.5(a). A lawyer who charges an unreasonable fee is subject to discipline.

For a lawyer, discipline can range from private or public censure for less serious offenses to suspension and permanent disbarment for the most serious offenses or a pattern of less serious offenses.

2. May or Proper

The words "may" or "proper" ask whether the conduct is professionally appropriate (i.e., conduct that is not subject to discipline, not inconsistent with the preamble, comments, or text of the Model Rules or CJC, and not inconsistent with generally accepted principles of the law of lawyering).

Example: A lawyer **may** reveal information relating to the representation of a client to the extent the lawyer reasonably believes necessary to prevent reasonably certain death or substantial bodily harm. MRPC 1.6(b)(1). A lawyer who reveals such information has behaved in a professionally appropriate manner.

3. Subject to Litigation Sanction

The phrase "subject to litigation sanction" asks whether the conduct would subject the lawyer or the lawyer's law firm to a fine, fee forfeiture, disqualification, punishment for contempt, or other sanction by a legal tribunal.

Example: A lawyer who files a frivolous pleading may be subject to sanctions imposed by the court, which can include the payment of reasonable expenses incurred by the other party in responding to the pleading. Fed. R. Civ. P. 11(c)(4).

4. Subject to Disqualification

The phrase "subject to disqualification" asks whether the conduct would subject the lawyer or the lawyer's law firm to disqualification as counsel in a civil or criminal matter.

Example: A lawyer who represents a client in a civil action may be subject to disqualification due to a conflict of interest with another current client. MRPC 1.7(a).

5. Subject to Civil Liability

The phrase "subject to civil liability" asks whether the conduct would subject the lawyer or the lawyer's law firm to civil liability, such as a claim arising from malpractice, misrepresentation, or breach of fiduciary duty.

Example: A lawyer may be liable to a client for professional negligence if the lawyer fails to diligently pursue a matter. MRPC 1.3; Restatement (Third) of the Law Governing Lawyers § 16 cmt. a.

6. **Subject to Criminal Liability**

The phrase "subject to criminal liability" asks whether the conduct would subject the lawyer to criminal liability for participation in or aiding and abetting criminal acts, such as insurance or tax fraud, destruction of evidence, or obstruction of justice.

> **Example:** A lawyer who knowingly prepared a material false document for submission by a client may be subject to criminal liability. Restatement (Third) of the Law Governing Lawyers § 8.

7. **Bar, State Bar, or Appropriate Disciplinary Authority**

A reference to discipline by the "bar," "state bar," or "appropriate disciplinary authority" means the appropriate agency in the jurisdiction with the authority to administer the standards for admission to practice and for maintenance of professional competence and integrity.

8. **Certified Specialist**

Identification of a lawyer as a "certified specialist" means that the lawyer has been so certified by the appropriate agency in the jurisdiction in which the lawyer practices.

C. DEFINITIONS OF KEY WORDS AND PHRASES USED IN MODEL RULES

1. **Entities and Persons**

    a. **Tribunal**

    A "tribunal," in addition to encompassing a court, includes an arbitrator in a binding arbitration proceeding, and a legislative body, administrative agency, or other entity that acts in an adjudicative capacity. An entity acts in an adjudicative capacity when a neutral official, after the presentation of evidence or legal argument by a party or parties, reaches a binding legal judgment that directly affects a party's interest in a particular matter. MRPC 1.0(m).

    b. **Law firm**

    A "law firm" (or "firm") is any association of lawyers authorized to practice law, and includes a partnership or professional corporation as well as lawyers employed in a legal services organization or the legal department of a corporation or other organization. MRPC 1.0(c).

    Whether two or more lawyers constitute a firm depends on the specific facts. Factors such as how they hold themselves out to the public, the terms of any formal agreement, and access to information about clients are relevant in determining the existence of a law firm. The mere sharing of office space by lawyers coupled with occasional consultation or assistance is ordinarily insufficient to result in the lawyers being treated as a firm. In addition, the determination of whether two or more lawyers are a firm for purposes of one rule is not necessarily conclusive with respect to another rule. For example, a lawyer whose representation of a party would violate the conflict-of-interest rule because of another lawyer's representation of the opposing party might not be subject to the rule that imputes to the lawyer information known by the other lawyer. MRPC 1.0, cmt. 2.

    A lawyer practicing law as a sole proprietorship also falls within the definition of a "law firm." MRPC 1.0(c).

c. Partner

A "partner" is a member of a partnership, a shareholder in a law firm organized as a professional corporation, or a member of an association authorized to practice law. MRPC 1.0(g).

2. Writings

A "writing" encompasses any tangible or electronic record of a communication or representation, including a photograph, audio- or video recording, and electronic communications. A writing can be signed by any means, including an electronic sound, symbol, or process that is attached to or logically associated with the writing and is executed or adopted by a person with the intent to sign the writing. MRPC 1.0(n).

3. Informed Consent

In order to obtain a person's "informed consent" to a proposed course of conduct, the lawyer must communicate adequate information about the material risks of the proposed course of conduct, as well as reasonably available alternatives. The lawyer is not required to inform a person of facts or implications already known to the person, and can take into account the person's legal knowledge and representation by another lawyer, but the lawyer bears the risk as to adequacy of the information. Generally, consent may not be assumed from a person's silence, but may be inferred from a person's conduct. MRPC 1.0(e), cmts. 6, 7. For purposes of the MPRE, the term "consent after consultation" has the same meaning as "informed consent."

4. Confirmed in Writing

While the Model Rules require that a person's informed consent be "confirmed in writing," the informed consent need not take the form of a document signed by the person. In such circumstances, the consent can be given orally and a writing can be prepared by the lawyer as a confirmation of the oral consent. If it is not possible to obtain or transmit the writing at the time the informed consent is given, the lawyer must obtain and transmit it within a reasonable time thereafter, but may immediately act in reliance on the consent. MRPC 1.0(b), cmt. 1.

5. Knowledge and Belief

"Belief" (or "believes") indicates that the person actually supposed the fact in question to be true. "Knowingly" (or "known," or "knows") denotes actual knowledge of the fact in question. Each is subjective in nature, but each may be inferred from the circumstances.

By contrast, "reasonable" (or "reasonably") used in relation to a lawyer's conduct denotes the conduct of a reasonably prudent and competent lawyer, an objective standard.

When the phrase "reasonable belief" (or "reasonably believes") is used, the lawyer is required to believe the matter in question (a subjective standard) and the circumstances must be such that the belief is reasonable (an objective standard).

When the phrase "reasonably should know" is used, a lawyer of reasonable prudence and competence would ascertain the matter in question (an objective standard). MRPC 1.0(a),(f),(h),(i),(j).

6. Screened

Screening requires the isolation of the lawyer from any participation in the matter through the timely imposition of procedures that are reasonably adequate under the circumstances to protect information that the isolated lawyer is obligated to protect. MRPC 1.0(k).

7. Fraud

"Fraud" (or "fraudulent") is conduct that is fraudulent under the substantive or procedural law of the applicable jurisdiction and has a purpose to deceive. It does not include negligent misrepresentation. For disciplinary purposes, it is not necessary that anyone relied upon or suffered damages from the misrepresentation. MRPC 1.0(d), cmt. 5.

8. Substantial

"Substantial," when used in reference to degree or extent, indicates a material matter of clear and weighty importance. MRPC 1.0(l).

II. REGULATION OF THE LEGAL PROFESSION

A. INHERENT POWERS OF COURTS TO REGULATE LAWYERS

As the practice of law directly affects the administration of justice, courts have the inherent power to regulate the legal profession.

1. State Courts

State courts regulate all aspects of the practice of law within their jurisdiction; each state has its own bar association and rules of professional conduct. The highest court in a state generally oversees the promulgation of legal ethics rules and also supervises the discipline of lawyers in the state. Most states base their rules of professional conduct on the ABA Model Rules, but the ABA, a voluntary association of lawyers, has no direct regulatory authority over lawyers and no authority to discipline. Membership in a state bar association is voluntary in some states and mandatory in others. Legislative enactments can also affect the practice of law in a state, as for example, in defining the extent of the attorney-client privilege.

2. Federal Courts

Each federal court has its own bar and a lawyer must be admitted to the bar of a federal court in order to practice before it. Each federal court has the inherent authority to regulate lawyers who appear before it. *Chambers v. NASCO, Inc.*, 501 U.S. 32, 43(1991); *Ex parte Burr*, 22 U.S. (9 Wheat.) 529 (1824).

3. Right to Counsel

The Sixth Amendment Right to Counsel does not negate "the authority of trial courts to establish criteria for admitting lawyers to argue before them." *United States v. Gonzalez-Lopez*, 548 U.S. 140, 151 (2006).

B. ADMISSION TO THE PROFESSION

A license is required before engaging in the practice of law. States license lawyers to practice law within their jurisdiction. The state has an interest in maintaining the integrity of the legal profession to protect the public from those who are incompetent or unscrupulous.

1. Requirements for Admission

States impose educational, knowledge, and character requirements on applicants for admission to the practice of law. A lawyer must not assist in the admission of an unqualified applicant. MRPC 8.1.

a. Education

Most states require graduation from an ABA-accredited law school for admission to practice. A few states require only a state accreditation, and California even makes provisions for students from unaccredited law schools.

b. Knowledge

A bar examination is administered in each state, although a waiver is still allowed in a few states for graduates of select, in-state law schools. Many states permit a lawyer in good standing in the bar of another state to gain permanent admission (admission "on motion") without the need for a bar examination or with only a limited examination. Some states condition eligibility on comity, requiring that a state in which the lawyer is currently admitted provide a similar privilege to lawyers from the state in which the request for admission on motion has been made.

c. Character

Past conduct may be considered in determining whether an applicant has the requisite good character and general fitness necessary to practice law. Mere conviction of a crime is not necessarily sufficient to deny admission to the bar. The crime must generally involve moral turpitude (intentional dishonesty for personal gain) or violence. A false statement or the concealment of a fact in response to an inquiry by the bar examiners' committee would be enough to deny an applicant admission, even if the action about which the applicant lied or concealed did not involve moral turpitude. MRPC 8.1.

d. No residence requirements

Local residence and U.S. citizenship may **not** be imposed as a condition on the right to practice law in a state. *In re Griffiths*, 413 U.S. 717 (1973) (U.S. citizenship requirement violates the Equal Protection Clause); *Supreme Court of New Hampshire v. Piper*, 470 U.S. 274 (1985) (In-state residency requirement violates the Privileges and Immunities Clause of Article IV). Some courts have upheld the requirement of the maintenance of an in-state office if this requirement is imposed on all lawyers. *Tolchin v. Supreme Court of the State of N.J.*, 111 F.3d 1099 (3d Cir. 1997); *Parnell v. Supreme Court of Appeals of W. Va.*, 110 F.3d 1077 (4th Cir. 1997); *See also Schoenefeld v. New York*, 2011 U.S. Dist. LEXIS 100576 (2011) (New York rule that imposed the maintenance of an in-state office only on nonresidents unconstitutional).

2. Application Process

a. Prohibited behavior

An applicant for admission to the bar is prohibited from:

i) Knowingly making a false statement of material fact in connection with the application;

ii) Failing to disclose a fact necessary to correct a misapprehension known by him to have arisen in the matter; or

iii) Failing to respond to a lawful demand by an admissions authority in connection with the application (unless such fact is protected by the rules governing confidential communications).

MRPC 8.1.

b. Fifth Amendment privilege

An applicant for admission to the bar may invoke the Fifth Amendment privilege against self-incrimination but must do so openly rather than simply leaving out requested information. MRPC 8.1, cmt. 2.

c. Violations prevent admission

Violation of the provisions of the Model Rules may prevent admission. If the applicant has been admitted, the applicant is subject to discipline as a lawyer for having violated the provisions. MRPC 8.1, cmt. 1.

d. Information from others

Bar authorities seek information as to an applicant's fitness to practice law from the applicant and from other people. A person who is a member of the bar is subject to the same rules as those impacting the applicant. If a lawyer is asked about an applicant and fails to disclose a fact necessary to correct a misapprehension or to disclose any material fact requested in connection with the application, the lawyer is subject to discipline under the Model Rules. MRPC 8.1, cmt. 1. This rule, however, does not require the lawyer to disclose information that is otherwise protected by the confidentiality provisions of the Model Rules or the attorney-client privilege.

> **Example:** An attorney is asked to write a letter of recommendation for a client's nephew for admission to the bar. The attorney has had no direct contact with the nephew, but the client has assured the attorney that the nephew is industrious and honest. The attorney is not permitted to write the letter based on the client's assurance. The attorney must make an independent investigation and write the letter only if the attorney is then satisfied that the nephew is qualified.

A question on a bar application such as, "Have you ever been a party to any legal action or proceeding?" must be answered truthfully and completely, even if the action was dismissed or the judgment eventually expunged.

C. REGULATION AFTER ADMISSION

1. Grounds of Misconduct

It is professional misconduct for a lawyer to:

i) Violate or attempt to violate any of the Model Rules, knowingly assist or induce another to do so, or to do so through the acts of another. MRPC 8.4(a).

ii) Commit a criminal act that reflects adversely on the lawyer's honesty or fitness as a lawyer in other respects. MRPC 8.4(b).

iii) Engage in conduct involving dishonesty, fraud, deceit, or misrepresentation, regardless of whether the conduct is criminal. MRPC 8.4(c).

iv) Engage in conduct prejudicial to the administration of justice, regardless of whether the conduct is criminal or dishonest in nature. MRPC 8.4(d).

v) State or imply an ability to influence improperly a government agency or official. MRPC 8.4(e).

vi) Knowingly assist a judge or judicial officer in conduct that is a violation of applicable rules of judicial conduct or other law. MRPC 8.4(f).

vii) Engage in conduct that the lawyer knows or reasonably should know is harassment or discrimination on the basis of race, sex, religion, national origin, ethnicity, disability, age, sexual orientation, gender identity, marital status, or socioeconomic status in conduct related to the practice of law. MPRC 8.4(g).

A lawyer does not have to be engaged in the practice of law to violate the Model Rules and be subject to professional discipline.

Example: An attorney is a member of the bar in Delaware and is also licensed as a stockbroker in New York. In his application for renewal of his stockbroker's license in New York, the attorney knowingly filed a false financial statement. The attorney is subject to professional discipline as a lawyer in Delaware because his actions involved dishonesty or misrepresentation in violation of MRPC 8.4(c).

a. Commission of a criminal act that reflects adversely on a lawyer's fitness as a lawyer

Some matters of personal morality, such as adultery and comparable offenses, have no specific connection to fitness for the practice of law. Although a lawyer is personally answerable to the entire criminal law, a lawyer should be professionally answerable only for offenses that indicate lack of those characteristics relevant to law practice. Offenses involving violence, dishonesty, breach of trust, or serious interference with the administration of justice are in that category. A pattern of repeated offenses, even ones of minor significance when considered separately, can indicate indifference to legal obligation. MRPC 8.4(a), cmt. 2.

2. Misconduct Committed by Others Associated With Law Firm

In general, a lawyer is only subject to discipline for her own conduct and is not subject to discipline for the conduct of a partner, associate, or subordinate merely because both belong to the same law firm. MRPC 5.1., cmt. 7.

Compare civil liability: A lawyer who is practicing law as a partner in a partnership may have civil liability for the conduct of another lawyer-partner.

a. Misconduct ordered or ratified

A lawyer is subject to discipline for a violation of the Model Rules committed by another lawyer if the lawyer: (i) orders the misconduct or (ii) ratifies the misconduct with knowledge of the specific conduct. A lawyer is also subject to discipline for ordering or ratifying conduct by a non-lawyer employed by, retained by, or associated with the lawyer that would constitute a violation of the Model Rules if engaged in by a lawyer. MRPC 5.1(c), 5.3(c).

Example: A lawyer employed an agent to monitor accidents and other events likely to produce legal work in order to solicit business on the lawyer's behalf (e.g., a runner, capper). The agent initiated in-person contact with prospective clients who have recently been involved in an accident. This conduct constitutes a violation of Model Rule 7.3. The lawyer is subject to discipline. (Note: Employment of runners or cappers is a criminal violation in some states.)

b. Manager's responsibility for firm's preventive measures

A lawyer who has managerial authority over the professional work of a law firm, such as a partner of a partnership or the head of a corporation's legal department, or a lawyer with intermediate managerial responsibilities, such as the head of the litigation branch of a law firm, must make reasonable efforts to ensure the firm has measures in place that give reasonable assurance that the conduct of all lawyers in the firm, as well as that of non-lawyers employed by, retained by, or associated with the firm, conforms to the Model Rules. MRPC 5.1(a), 5.3(a). What constitutes reasonable measures depends on the size and kind of firm.

> **EXAM NOTE:** The obligations of a partner are tested frequently in the context of paralegals or other non-lawyers violating a Model Rule without the lawyer's knowledge. The outcome depends on whether the firm had procedures in place to prevent such violations. If a question indicates that a subordinate engaged in misconduct without the lawyer's knowledge, check to see if preventative measures, such as employee training, were taken.

c. Direct supervisor's responsibility for supervised person's conduct

A lawyer with direct supervisory authority over the work of another lawyer in the firm or a non-lawyer employed by the firm must make reasonable efforts to ensure that the supervised person's conduct conforms to the Model Rules. MRPC 5.1(b).

> **EXAM NOTE:** Supervisory obligations are frequently tested in situations in which non-lawyers are not properly instructed of the need to maintain confidential communications.

d. Failure to remediate known misconduct

A lawyer with managerial authority in a law firm or a lawyer with direct supervisory authority over another lawyer or non-lawyer employed by the firm is subject to discipline for misconduct about which the managerial or supervisory lawyer knows at a time when the consequences of the misconduct can be avoided or mitigated, but the managerial or supervisory lawyer fails to take reasonable remedial action. MRPC 5.1(c); 5.3(c).

> **EXAM NOTE:** This is a frequently tested area on the MPRE. Often the issue will involve whether the supervisor could have prevented the misconduct. If the supervisor could not have prevented the subordinate's misconduct, then the subordinate's misconduct is not attributed to the supervisor unless the supervisor learned of the action while it was still possible to take remedial action to mitigate the consequences of the misconduct.

e. Duties of subordinate lawyer

A subordinate lawyer must conform to the Model Rules even if acting under the direction of a supervising lawyer. MRPC 5.2. The subordinate lawyer is not in violation of the Model Rules, however, if the subordinate lawyer acts in accordance with the supervising lawyer's reasonable resolution of an arguable question of professional duty. MRPC 5.2(b). If an ethical issue can only be reasonably answered in one specific way, it does not constitute an arguable question. MRPC 5.2, cmt. 2. Also, in order to know whether a supervising lawyer's resolution is in fact reasonable, the subordinate lawyer has a responsibility to undertake his own analysis of the law applicable to his conduct.

> **Example:** An associate attorney disagreed with his supervising attorney as to their responsibility to respond to a request for production of documents. The request is ambiguous and after careful consideration of the rules, the associate attorney follows his supervisor's direction not to produce certain documents. A court subsequently finds that the refusal to produce the documents constituted a violation of the Model Rules. The supervising attorney is subject to discipline, but the associate attorney is not.

3. Misconduct Outside of the State or Jurisdiction

A lawyer is subject to discipline for misconduct in any jurisdiction in which the lawyer is admitted to practice, even if the misconduct occurred outside of that jurisdiction. The lawyer may be subject to discipline in both the jurisdiction where admitted and the jurisdiction where the misconduct occurs. MRPC 8.5(a).

a. Choice of law

For conduct relating to a proceeding pending before a tribunal, the lawyer is subject only to the rules of the jurisdiction in which the tribunal sits unless the rules of the tribunal, including its choice of law rule, provide otherwise. As to all other conduct, a lawyer is subject to the rules of the jurisdiction in which the conduct occurred. MRPC 8.5(b), cmt. 4.

b. Multiple jurisdictions

If a lawyer's conduct involves significant contacts with more than one jurisdiction, the lawyer is not subject to discipline so long as the lawyer's conduct conforms to the rules of a jurisdiction in which the lawyer reasonably believes the predominant effect will occur. In determining a lawyer's reasonable belief with regard to conflict of interest, a written agreement between a lawyer and client that reasonably specifies a jurisdiction will be considered if the agreement was obtained with the client's informed consent confirmed in the agreement. In addition, if two or more jurisdictions proceed against a lawyer for the same conduct, both should seek to apply the same ethical rules. MRPC 8.5(b), cmts. 5, 6.

4. Sanctions for Misconduct

The Model Rules do not set forth particular sanctions for misconduct by a lawyer. Sanctions are set by individual states, federal courts, or agencies, and can range from private or public censure for less serious offenses to suspension and permanent disbarment for the most serious offenses or a pattern of less serious offenses. The burden of proving misconduct is on the jurisdiction's disciplinary authority.

5. Other Consequences

In addition to disciplinary sanctions for violation of a rule of professional conduct, a lawyer may also face other consequences. Among such consequences are litigation sanctions imposed by a court or other tribunal, such as contempt, fine, fee forfeiture, or disqualification, as well as civil and criminal liability. A lawyer may be subject to civil or criminal liability even when the lawyer's conduct does not violate a rule of professional conduct. MRPC 8.4, cmt. 2.

D. PEER RESPONSIBILITY FOR REPORTING MISCONDUCT

A lawyer generally must report misconduct by another lawyer to the appropriate professional authority (e.g., bar disciplinary agency) when the lawyer has actual knowledge of the misconduct. This duty applies with regard to any other lawyer, even a lawyer who is not a member of the lawyer's firm. MRPC 8.3.

1. Substantial Matter

The duty to report is limited to matters that raise a substantial question as to the lawyer's honesty, trustworthiness, or professional fitness. A substantial question is one involving a material matter of clear and weighty importance. MRPC 1.0(l), 8.3(a).

2. Confidential Communications

The duty to report misconduct by another lawyer does not require disclosure of information otherwise protected by Model Rule 1.6 (see § IV.C., Professional Obligation of Confidentiality, *infra*) or of information gained by a lawyer or judge while participating in an approved lawyers assistance program. MRPC 8.3(c). Such an obligation, however, may be imposed by the rules of the lawyers assistance program or by other law. MRPC 8.3 cmt. 5.

3. Knowledge Required

The duty to report does not arise until the lawyer has **actual knowledge** of the misconduct. Actual knowledge may be inferred from the circumstances and includes learning of the misconduct from a reliable source when there is independent corroboration. MRPC 1.0(f), 8.3(a).

4. Judicial Misconduct

A lawyer who knows that a judge has committed a violation of applicable rules of judicial conduct that raises a substantial question as to the judge's fitness for office must inform the appropriate authority. MRPC 8.3(b).

5. Sanctions for Failure to Report Misconduct

If a lawyer fails to report misconduct by another lawyer or judge, the lawyer is subject to discipline. MRPC 8.4(a).

6. Defamation Action

To protect the reporting lawyer from a retaliatory defamation action by the lawyer engaged in misconduct, a privilege against defamation applies to the required reporting of another lawyer's misconduct. Restatement (Third) of the Law Governing Lawyers §§ 5, cmt. i; 57 cmt. c.

E. UNAUTHORIZED PRACTICE OF LAW

A lawyer is subject to discipline for practicing in a jurisdiction in which the lawyer is not admitted to practice. MRPC 5.5(a); 8.5(a). Lawyers are also obligated to ensure that only authorized persons engage in the practice of law and are subject to discipline for assisting non-lawyers in the unlicensed practice of law. MRPC 5.5(b).

Only lawyers are subject to discipline under the Model Rules, but non-lawyers (as well as lawyers) may be subject to civil and criminal penalties for the unauthorized practice of law.

1. Not Admitted to Practice in a Jurisdiction

a. Unauthorized practice

In general, a lawyer may not practice law in a jurisdiction where the lawyer is not admitted to practice, or assist another in doing so. MRPC 5.5(a). Except as permitted by a jurisdiction's laws or ethics rules, a lawyer who is not admitted to practice in a jurisdiction must not establish an office or other systematic and continuous presence in the jurisdiction for the practice of law in that jurisdiction or hold out to the public or otherwise represent that the lawyer is admitted to practice law in the jurisdiction. MRPC 5.5(b).

b. Exceptions permitting temporary practice

Under certain circumstances, a lawyer who is admitted to practice in another United States jurisdiction, and **not disbarred or suspended from practice in any jurisdiction**, may provide legal services on a temporary basis in a second jurisdiction where the lawyer is not admitted to practice. MRPC 5.5(c).

Note: A lawyer who is admitted to practice in a jurisdiction but who is not authorized to practice in that jurisdiction (e.g., is on inactive status) does not qualify for these exceptions or the exceptions for permanent practice discussed at c, *infra*. MRPC 5.5, cmt. 7.

1) In association with a local lawyer

A lawyer admitted in a jurisdiction may provide legal services in another jurisdiction on a temporary basis if the services are undertaken in association with a lawyer who is admitted to practice in the second jurisdiction and who actively participates in the matter. MRPC 5.5(c)(1).

2) Authorized by law or order to appear *pro hac vice*

A lawyer admitted in a jurisdiction may provide legal services in another jurisdiction on a temporary basis if the services are in—or reasonably related to a pending or potential proceeding before a tribunal in—any jurisdiction, if the lawyer or a person the lawyer is assisting is authorized by law or order to appear in such proceeding or reasonably expects to be so authorized. MRPC 5.5(c)(2). Such authority may be granted pursuant to formal rules governing admission *pro hac vice* (meaning "for this turn only") or pursuant to informal practice of the tribunal. A lawyer admitted to practice in a jurisdiction who seeks to appear before a tribunal in another jurisdiction in which the lawyer is not admitted to practice must comply with any court rule or other law of the other jurisdiction that requires the lawyer to obtain admission *pro hac vice* before appearing. MRPC 5.5, cmt. 9.

> Note that a lawyer rendering services in a jurisdiction on a temporary basis does not violate the Model Rules if the lawyer engages in conduct in anticipation of a proceeding or hearing in a jurisdiction in which the lawyer is authorized to practice law or in which the lawyer reasonably expects to be admitted *pro hac vice*. Examples of such conduct include meetings with the client, witness interviews, and document review.
>
> Additionally, a lawyer admitted only in another jurisdiction may engage in conduct temporarily in a jurisdiction in connection with pending litigation in another jurisdiction in which the lawyer is or reasonably expects to be authorized to appear, including taking depositions in the unadmitted jurisdiction. MRPC 5.5, cmt. 10.
>
> The Model Rules also permit an unadmitted lawyer to provide legal services so long as the unadmitted lawyer works in association with a lawyer who is admitted, and the admitted lawyer actively participates in the matter. Thus, a subordinate lawyer may conduct research, review documents, or attend meetings with witnesses in support of the lawyer with responsibility for the litigation. MRPC 5.5, cmt. 11.

3) Mediation or arbitration arising out of practice in admitted jurisdiction

An unadmitted lawyer may provide legal services in a jurisdiction on a temporary basis if the services are in or reasonably related to a pending or potential arbitration, mediation, or other alternative dispute resolution proceeding in the jurisdiction or elsewhere, if the services arise out of or are reasonably related to the lawyer's practice in a jurisdiction in which the lawyer is admitted to practice and are not services for which the forum requires *pro hac vice* admission. MRPC 5.5(c)(3).

4) Other temporary practice arising out of practice in admitted jurisdiction

Under a catch-all exception in the Model Rules, an unadmitted lawyer may provide legal services in a jurisdiction on a temporary basis if the services are not otherwise covered by the other exceptions and arise out of or are reasonably related to the lawyer's practice in a jurisdiction in which the lawyer is admitted to practice. MRPC 5.5(c)(4).

c. Exceptions permitting permanent practice

1) Lawyer is providing services only to his employer

A lawyer who is admitted in another United States jurisdiction, and not disbarred or suspended from practice in any jurisdiction, may provide legal services through an office or other systematic and continuous presence in a second jurisdiction where the lawyer is not admitted to practice if the lawyer is only providing legal services to the lawyer's employer or its organizational affiliates and the forum does not require *pro hac vice* admission for such services. MRPC 5.5(d)(1). This rule permits an in-house corporate lawyer or a government lawyer to provide legal advice to an employer without having to be admitted to practice. If such a lawyer litigates a matter in the jurisdiction, however, the lawyer typically should seek *pro hac vice* admission. Additionally, the exception does not authorize the provision of personal legal services to the employer's officers or employees. MRPC 5.5, cmt. 16.

2) Federal or local law authorizes such practice

A lawyer who is admitted in another United States jurisdiction, and not disbarred or suspended from practice in any jurisdiction, may provide legal services through an office or other systematic and continuous presence in a second jurisdiction where the lawyer is not admitted to practice if the services that the lawyer is providing are authorized to be provided by federal law or other law or rule of the second jurisdiction. MRPC 5.5(d)(2).

Note that a lawyer who is admitted to practice in one jurisdiction and practices law in another jurisdiction where the lawyer is not admitted under one of the exceptions discussed above is subject to the disciplinary rules of **both** jurisdictions. MRPC 5.5, cmt. 19; 8.5(a).

3) Foreign lawyer

These exceptions also apply to a person who is a lawyer in good standing in a foreign country. If the foreign lawyer is performing services for an employer or its organizational affiliates, the advice as to U.S. federal or state law must be based on advice of a lawyer who is licensed and authorized by the applicable jurisdiction to give such advice. MRPC 5.5(d)(1),(2).

2. Assisting Non-Lawyers in the Unauthorized Practice of Law

a. In general

A lawyer must not assist a person who is not admitted to practice in a jurisdiction in the unauthorized practice of law. MRPC 5.5(a). While the definition of the practice of law is established by law and varies from one jurisdiction to another, conducting an investigative interview does not constitute the practice of law, while meeting with clients and giving them legal advice clearly does.

The non-lawyer who engages in the unauthorized practice of law can be subject to civil and criminal penalties, but is not subject to discipline under the Model Rules. A lawyer who engages in the unauthorized practice of law or assists a non-lawyer in unauthorized practice may be subject to civil and criminal penalties and is also subject to discipline under the Model Rules.

b. Employment of paraprofessionals

The Model Rules permit a lawyer to employ the services of paraprofessionals and delegate functions to them, so long as the lawyer supervises the delegated work and retains responsibility for it. MRPC 5.5, cmt. 2; 5.3.

c. Providing professional advice to non-lawyers whose employment requires legal knowledge

The Model Rules do not prohibit a lawyer from providing professional advice and instruction to non-lawyers whose employment requires legal knowledge (e.g., claims adjusters, employees of financial or commercial institutions, social workers, accountants, and persons employed in government agencies). Lawyers may also advise independent non-lawyers, such as paraprofessionals, who are authorized by the law of a jurisdiction to provide particular law-related services. MRPC 5.5, cmt. 3.

d. Assistance to non-lawyers proceeding *pro se*

A lawyer may counsel non-lawyers who wish to proceed *pro se* (represent themselves) in a legal matter. MRPC 5.5, cmt. 3. (Note: While an individual who is not a lawyer may represent himself, a legal entity, such as a corporation, generally may not act *pro se* in a legal matter through an employee who is not a lawyer. Restatement (Third) of the Law Governing Lawyers § 4 cmt. d, e.)

F. FEE DIVISION WITH NON-LAWYERS

The Model Rules prohibit fee sharing by lawyers with non-lawyers **except when**:

i) Fees are paid into a **lawyer's estate** or to one or more specified persons over a reasonable period of time as a death benefit according to an operating agreement;

ii) A lawyer who purchases the practice of a deceased, disabled, or disappeared lawyer pays to that lawyer's estate or other representative the agreed-upon purchase price;

iii) Fees are shared with law firm personnel via a **compensation or retirement plan**, even though it is based on a profit-sharing arrangement; and

iv) A lawyer shares court-awarded legal fees with a non-profit organization that employed, retained, or recommended employment of the lawyer in the matter.

MRPC 5.4(a).

> **Example:** A law firm is organized as a professional corporation with five lawyer-shareholders. It is improper for a widow, whose husband was a lawyer-shareholder in the law firm until his death three years ago, to continue to hold her husband's shares in the law firm until their ten-year old child completes a college education. By contrast, the law firm can properly pay fees to the husband's estate or to the widow over a reasonable period of time as a death benefit according to an operating agreement, or could pay an agreed-upon purchase price to the husband's estate for his shares.

G. THE LAW FIRM AND OTHER FORMS OF PRACTICE

1. Definition

For purposes of the Model Rules, a "law firm" is a lawyer or lawyers in a law partnership, professional corporation, sole proprietorship or other association authorized to practice law, or lawyers employed in a legal services organization or the legal department of a corporation or other organization. MRPC 1.0(c). Whether two or more lawyers constitute a firm under the Model Rules depends on the specific facts. Thus, if two practitioners share office space and occasionally consult or assist each other, they ordinarily would not be regarded as constituting a firm. If, however, they hold themselves out to the public in a way that suggests that they are a firm or conduct themselves as a firm, they would be regarded as a firm for purposes of the Model Rules. The terms of any formal agreement between associated lawyers would be relevant in determining whether they constitute a firm, as would be the fact that they have mutual access to information concerning the clients they serve. MRPC 1.0, cmt. 2.

2. Fee Splitting Within a Firm

Lawyers in the same law firm, by agreement, may legitimately share or split fees earned by any of them. Fees may even be shared with a lawyer who has retired from the firm. MRPC 1.5, cmt. 8.

3. Limitations on Association With Non-Lawyers

The Model Rules limit the extent to which lawyers may form partnerships or associate with non-lawyers. MRPC 5.4.

a. Partnership

A lawyer is **not** permitted to form a partnership with a non-lawyer if any of the activities of the partnership consist of the practice of law. MRPC 5.4(b).

b. Professional corporation

A lawyer is **not** permitted to practice with or in the form of a professional corporation or association authorized to practice law for a profit, if:

  i) A non-lawyer owns any interest therein (except that a fiduciary representative of the estate of a lawyer may hold the stock or interest of the lawyer for a reasonable time during administration);

  ii) A non-lawyer is a corporate director or officer thereof or occupies a position of similar responsibility in any form of association other than a corporation; or

  iii) A non-lawyer has the right to direct or control the professional judgment of a lawyer.

MRPC 5.4(d).

Example: A law firm is organized as a professional corporation with five lawyer-shareholders. It would be improper for the office manager, who is not a member of the bar, to serve as the executive vice president of the law firm.

c. Third party refers client or pays fee

A lawyer must not permit a person who recommends, employs, or pays the lawyer to render legal services for another to direct or regulate the lawyer's professional judgment in rendering such legal services. MRPC 5.4(c). See also, MRPC 1.8(f) (lawyer may accept compensation from third party so long as there is no interference with lawyer's independent professional judgment and client gives informed consent).

4. **Responsibilities Regarding Law-Related Services**

a. **"Law-related services"**

Lawyers may provide "law-related services," which are defined by the Model Rules as services that might reasonably be performed in conjunction with and in substance are related to the provision of legal services, and that are not prohibited as unauthorized practice of law when provided by a non-lawyer. MRPC 5.7(b). Some examples of law-related services include providing title insurance, financial planning, accounting, trust services, real estate counseling, legislative lobbying, economic analysis, social work, psychological counseling, tax preparation, and patent, medical, or environmental consulting. MRPC 5.7, cmt. 9. Under certain circumstances, the lawyer providing law-related services is subject to the Model Rules with regard to such services, even though a non-lawyer performing such services would not be subject to the rules.

1) **Provision of law-related services is not distinct from legal services**

A lawyer is subject to the Model Rules with respect to the provision of law-related services, if such services are provided by the lawyer in circumstances that are not distinct from the lawyer's provision of legal services to clients. MRPC 5.7(a)(1).

> **Example:** An attorney assists a client with drafting a will and also provides financial planning advice as part of his estate planning services. The attorney is subject to the Model Rules with regard to both his legal services in drafting the will and his provision of law-related financial planning services.

2) **Lawyer fails to take reasonable measures to assure that person obtaining law-related services knows that protections of client-lawyer relationship do not exist**

A lawyer is subject to the Model Rules with respect to the provision of law-related services by an entity controlled by the lawyer individually or with others if the lawyer fails to take reasonable measures to assure that a person obtaining the law-related services knows that the services are not legal services and that the protections of the client-lawyer relationship do not exist. MRPC 5.7(a)(2). The burden is on the lawyer to show that the lawyer has taken reasonable measures under the circumstances to communicate the desired understanding. Thus, a sophisticated user of law-related services, such as a publicly-held corporation, may require a lesser explanation than someone unaccustomed to making distinctions between legal services and law-related services. MRPC 5.7, cmt. 7.

b. **Business transactions with a client**

Note that other Model Rules may be applicable to a lawyer's provision of law-related services. The conflict of interest rules (MRPC 1.7 through 1.11, discussed *infra*) may apply. For example, if a client-lawyer relationship exists between a lawyer and a person who is referred by a lawyer to a separate law-related service entity controlled by the lawyer, individually or with others, the lawyer must comply with Model Rule 1.8(a), which details the requirements a lawyer must meet when entering into a business transaction with a client. In addition, the promotion of law-related services must also in all respects comply with MRPC 7.1 through 7.3, dealing with advertising and solicitation.

5. Sale of Law Practice

A lawyer who ceases the practice of law entirely or ceases to practice in an area of the law (e.g., divorce, criminal defense) may obtain compensation for the reasonable value of the practice. A withdrawing partner of a law firm may receive similar compensation. MRPC 1.17, cmt. 1.

Note that this rule does not apply to a transfer between lawyers of legal representation that is unrelated to the sale of a practice. MRPC 1.17, cmt. 15.

a. Requirements

A lawyer or law firm may sell or purchase a law practice or an area of a law practice, including goodwill, if:

i) The seller **ceases to practice** law entirely, or in the area of practice sold, within a geographic area or jurisdiction;

ii) Written **notice is given to the clients** regarding the proposed sale, the clients' right to seek other counsel, and the fact that consent to the transfer of files will be presumed if no action is taken by a client within 90 days. If a client cannot be given notice, the representation of that client may be transferred to the purchaser only on entry of an order so authorizing by a court having jurisdiction. The seller may disclose to the court in camera information relating to the representation only to the extent necessary to obtain an order authorizing the transfer of a file.

iii) The **entire** practice or area of practice is **sold to one or more lawyers** or law firms; and

iv) Client **fees are not increased** due to the sale.

MRPC 1.17.

The seller is also obligated to exercise competence in identifying a purchaser qualified to assume the practice. MRPC 1.17, cmt. 11; see also MRPC 1.1.

b. Sale of entire practice or area of practice

The requirement that all of the private practice, or all of an area of practice, be sold is met if the seller, in good faith, makes the entire practice, or the area of practice, available for sale to the purchasers. The fact that a number of the seller's clients decide not to be represented by the purchasers and take their matters elsewhere, does not result in a violation of the rule. MRPC 1.17, cmt. 2.

c. Situations in which seller may still practice or return to practice

1) Seller may work for a public agency, legal services to poor, or in-house counsel to a business

The requirement that the seller cease to engage in the private practice of law does not prohibit employment as a lawyer on the staff of a public agency or a legal services entity that provides legal services to the poor, or as in-house counsel to a business. MRPC 1.17, cmt. 3.

2) Sale is only of an area of practice

If only an area of practice is sold and the lawyer remains in the active practice of law, the lawyer must cease accepting any matters in the area of practice that has been sold, either as counsel or co-counsel or by assuming joint responsibility for a matter in connection with the division of a fee with another lawyer.

> **Example:** An attorney has a substantial number of estate planning matters and a substantial number of probate administration cases. The attorney sells the estate planning part of his practice but remains in the practice of law by concentrating on probate administration. This is proper, so long as the attorney does not thereafter accept any estate planning matters.

3) Return to private practice due to unanticipated circumstances

A return to private practice as a result of an unanticipated change in circumstances does not necessarily result in a violation of the rule. For example, a lawyer who has sold the practice to accept an appointment to judicial office does not violate the requirement that the sale be attendant to cessation of practice if the lawyer later resumes private practice upon being defeated in a contested or a retention election for the office or resigns from a judiciary position. MRPC 1.17, cmt. 2.

d. Obligations of the purchaser

The purchaser is required to undertake **all** client matters in the practice or practice area, subject to client consent and conflict of interest constraints. MRPC 1.17, cmt. 6. Thus, a purchaser cannot merely limit representation to those cases that generate large fees. Note also that the purchaser has an obligation under the Model Rules to undertake the purchased representation competently. MRPC 1.17, cmt. 11; see also MRPC 1.1. In addition, the purchase may not be financed by an increase in the fees charged to the clients of the practice. The purchaser must honor existing arrangements between the seller and the client as to fees and the scope of the work. MRPC 1.17, cmt. 10.

H. CONTRACTUAL RESTRICTIONS ON PRACTICE

1. Restrictions in Partnership or Employment Agreements

A lawyer must not participate in offering or making a partnership, shareholders, operating, employment, or other similar type of agreement that would restrict the right of a lawyer to practice after termination of the relationship, except for an agreement concerning benefits upon retirement. MRPC 5.6(a).

> This rule does not apply to prohibit restrictions that may be included in the terms of the sale of a law practice pursuant to MRPC 1.17.

2. Restrictions in Settlement Agreements

A lawyer must not make or offer an agreement in which a restriction on the lawyer's right to practice is part of the settlement of a client controversy. MRPC 5.6(b).

> Note that this rule **prohibits** a lawyer from agreeing not to represent other persons in connection with settling a claim on behalf of a client.

III. THE CLIENT-LAWYER RELATIONSHIP

The Model Rules limit the conduct of lawyers in their relationships with their clients in an attempt to protect the integrity of the judicial system.

A. ACCEPTANCE OR REJECTION OF CLIENTS

1. Acceptance in General

In general, a lawyer is not under a duty to accept representation of any client. A lawyer is generally not required to have a good cause for refusing to accept representation of a client, or even to tell a potential client the lawyer's reasons for declining to represent a client. See MPRC 6.2., cmt. 1.

2. Exception for Court Appointments

A lawyer does have a duty to accept **court appointments**, so long as no good cause exists to decline. MRPC 6.2. Good cause to decline representation exists if: (i) the lawyer could not handle the matter competently; (ii) if the representation would result in an improper conflict of interest (as for example, when the client or the cause is so repugnant to the lawyer as to be likely to impair the client-lawyer relationship or the lawyer's ability to represent the client); or (iii) if acceptance would be unreasonably burdensome, for example, when it would impose a financial sacrifice so great as to be unjust. MRPC 6.2, cmt. 2.

Note that an appointed lawyer has the same obligations to the client as retained counsel, including the obligations of loyalty and confidentiality, and is subject to the same limitations on the client-lawyer relationship, such as the obligation to refrain from assisting the client in violation of the Model Rules.

3. Undertaking Representation

Once a lawyer undertakes representation, the full range of obligations and duties to a client exists. The lawyer is both a fiduciary and agent of the client.

a. Reasonable belief of representation

The client-lawyer relationship begins when the client **reasonably believes** the relationship exists. No formal writing or agreement is required. No payment of a fee is necessary.

> On the exam, look for casual conversations between a lawyer and a potential client. If the facts indicate the client **reasonably believes** the relationship exists, then it does.

b. Duty to reject

A lawyer has a duty to reject representation when doing so would violate a rule of ethics or law, or when the lawyer's physical or mental condition materially impairs the lawyer's ability to represent the client. MRPC 1.16(a)(1), (2). A lawyer should not accept representation in a matter unless it can be performed competently, promptly, without improper conflict of interest and to completion. MRPC 1.16, cmt. 1.

B. SCOPE, OBJECTIVE, AND MEANS OF THE REPRESENTATION

The Model Rules confer on the client the ultimate authority to determine the purposes to be served by legal representation within the limits imposed by the law and the lawyer's professional obligations. MRPC 1.2, cmt. 1. In general, a lawyer must abide by a client's decisions concerning the objectives of representation. MRPC 1.2(a). The lawyer generally controls the means by which the objectives of representation are to be pursued and may take such actions as are impliedly authorized to carry out the representation, but the lawyer must reasonably consult with the client. MRPC 1.2, 1.4.

1. **Decisions Made by Lawyer**

   a. **Procedural tactics**

   The lawyer has the authority to make most of the decisions relating to the strategy and methods for achieving the client's goals (e.g., manner and scope of cross-examination, choosing a theory of the case). MRPC 1.2(a). The Model Rules require that the lawyer reasonably consult with the client about the means by which the client's objectives are to be accomplished and keep the client reasonably informed about the status of the matter. MRPC 1.4. If a disagreement between the lawyer and the client cannot be resolved, the lawyer may withdraw or the client may fire the lawyer. See MRPC 1.16.

   b. **Limiting client objectives**

   A lawyer may limit the scope of the representation if the limitation is **reasonable under the circumstances** and if the client provides **informed consent**. MRPC 1.2(c). The terms on which representation is undertaken may exclude specific means that might otherwise be used to accomplish the client's objectives, including actions that the client thinks are too costly or that the lawyer regards as repugnant or imprudent. MRPC 1.2, cmt. 6.

2. **Decisions Made by Client**

   The client makes decisions regarding the objectives and goals of the representation. As the client's agent, the lawyer must abide by those decisions (within some constraints), but has the authority to determine how best to achieve those objectives. MRPC 1.2(a).

   a. **Scope of representation**

   The lawyer and client can negotiate the scope of the representation, including the duration of the relationship (e.g., through the first appeal) or the subject matter of the representation (e.g., only the tax aspects of a real estate transaction). MRPC 1.2(c), cmt. 6.

   > A client has no constitutional right to compel his lawyer to assert issues if the lawyer decides not to press those issues as a matter of the lawyer's professional judgment. *Jones v. Barnes*, 463 U.S. 745 (1983).

   b. **Advanced authorization**

   A client may authorize the lawyer to take specific action on the client's behalf without further consultation. Unless there has been a material change in circumstance, the lawyer may rely on such authorization, subject to the lawyer's duty to keep the client reasonably informed about the status of the matter. MRPC 1.2, cmt. 3.

   > There is no requirement in the Model Rules that the client's advanced authorization be in writing.

   The client may withdraw the authorization at any time. MRPC 1.2, cmt. 3.

   c. **Acceptance of settlement**

   Generally, a lawyer must communicate all bona fide offers of settlement to the client, and the ultimate decision as to whether to accept rests with the client. An exception exists when the client has authorized the lawyer to accept or to reject the offer. MRPC 1.2(a), cmt. 3, 1.4(a), cmt. 2.

1) Unauthorized settlements

A lawyer who agrees to a settlement without the client's consent and authorization is subject to discipline, but the opposing party may enforce the agreement if the lawyer acted with apparent authority. MRPC 1.2(a), 1.4(a)(1). *See* § 5. Apparent Authority, *below*.

d. Taking an appeal

The decision to take an appeal rests with the client. Restatement (Third) of the Law Governing Lawyers § 22(1); *Jones v. Barnes*, 463 U.S. 745 (1983).

e. Criminal cases

1) Client testimony

The decision as to whether the client will testify in a criminal case is the client's. MRPC 1.2(a).

2) Right to trial by jury

Waiving the right to a jury trial (or waiving other fundamental rights) is exclusively the client's decision to make. MRPC 1.2(a).

3) Entry of plea

The decision as to the plea to be entered is exclusive to the client. MRPC 1.2(a).

3. Client Under Disability

To the extent possible, a lawyer with a client with diminished capacity to make decisions must maintain an ordinary client-lawyer relationship. The client's diminished capacity may be due to a mental impairment, age (i.e., minority), or other factor. MRPC 1.14(a).

a. Protective action, including appointment of a guardian

When the lawyer reasonably believes that the client has diminished capacity, is at risk of substantial physical, financial, or other harm unless action is taken, and cannot adequately act in her own interest, the lawyer may take reasonably necessary protective action, including consulting with individuals or entities that have the ability to take action to protect the client and, in appropriate cases, seeking the appointment of a guardian *ad litem*, conservator, or guardian to act on behalf of the client. MRPC 1.14(b).

b. Revealing confidential information about client under disability

Information that relates to the representation of a client with diminished capacity is protected by the confidentiality provisions of MRPC 1.6. Thus, generally, unless authorized to do so, the lawyer may not disclose such information. When taking protective action, including seeking the appointment of a guardian, however, the lawyer is impliedly authorized to reveal information about the client, even if the client directs otherwise, but only to the extent reasonably necessary to protect the client's interests. MRPC 1.14(c). The lawyer should determine whether it is likely that the person or entity consulted with will act adversely to the client's interests before discussing matters related to the client. MRPC 1.14, cmt. 8.

c. Emergency legal assistance

In an emergency when the health, safety, or financial interest of a person with seriously diminished capacity is threatened with imminent and irreparable harm, a lawyer may take legal action on behalf of such person even if the person is unable to establish a client-lawyer relationship or to make or express considered judgments about the matter, when the person or another acting in good faith on that person's behalf has consulted with the lawyer. The lawyer should not act, however, unless the lawyer reasonably believes that the person has no other lawyer, agent, or other representative available, and the lawyer should only take legal action to the extent reasonably necessary to maintain the status quo or otherwise avoid imminent and irreparable harm. The lawyer has the same duties as the lawyer would to a client, including the duty of confidentiality, and should not normally seek compensation for emergency actions taken for a non-client. MRPC 1.14, cmt. 9, 10.

4. **Prohibition on Counseling Crimes or Fraud**

A lawyer is prohibited from counseling or assisting the client in conduct the lawyer knows to be criminal or fraudulent. If the lawyer does advise or assist with a crime or fraud, the lawyer is subject to discipline as well as criminal or civil liability. A lawyer is permitted, however, to discuss the legal consequences of any proposed course of conduct with a client and may counsel or assist a client to make a good faith effort to determine the validity, scope, meaning, or application of the law. MRPC 1.2(d).

If the client's course of action has already begun and is continuing, the lawyer is required to avoid assisting the client and must withdraw from the representation. MRPC 1.2, cmt. 10; 1.16(a). In certain cases, withdrawal alone may be insufficient and the lawyer may have to give notice of the fact of withdrawal and publicly disaffirm any opinion, document, or affirmation previously provided to the client. MRPC 1.2, cmt. 10; 4.1.

5. **Apparent Authority**

A lawyer's act is considered to be that of the client in proceedings before a tribunal or in dealings with a third person if the tribunal or third person reasonably assumes that the lawyer is authorized to do the act on the basis of the client's (and not the lawyer's) manifestations of such authorization. Restatement (Third) of the Law Governing Lawyers § 27. Simply retaining a lawyer confers broad apparent authority on the lawyer unless other facts apparent to the third person show that the lawyer's authority is narrower. By retaining the lawyer, the client implies that the lawyer is authorized to act for the client in matters relating to the representation and reasonably appropriate under the circumstances to carry out the representation.

Example: At the suggestion of a judge, the attorneys for both parties to a civil action agree to waive additional discovery and to begin the trial immediately. The judge does not know that the client of one of the attorneys has instructed its lawyers in writing not to bring cases to trial without specified discovery, some of which the attorney has not yet accomplished in the case. Although the attorney lacked actual authority to waive discovery here, the attorney had apparent authority, from the point of view of the judge, and the judge may hold the client to the immediate trial date. The client, however, may seek a discretionary release from the waiver from the judge, and may be able to obtain damages from the attorney for acting beyond the scope of her specific authority.

Authority arising from retention does not extend to matters, such as approving a settlement, that are reserved for client decision. When a lawyer purports to enter a settlement binding on the client but lacks authority to do so, the burden of inconvenience resulting if the client repudiates the settlement is properly left with the opposing party, who should know that settlements are normally subject to approval by the client and who has no manifested contrary indication from the client. The opposing party can protect itself by obtaining clarification of the lawyer's authority. Restatement (Third) of the Law Governing Lawyers § 27, cmt. d. *See* § 2.b.1, Unauthorized settlements, *above*.

> **Example:** An attorney represents a client in a civil action in which the court has ordered the lawyers from both sides to appear at a pre-trial conference with authority to settle the case or to arrange for a person so authorized to attend. The client was not informed of the court's order and has not authorized the attorney to approve any settlement. The attorney, without disclosing her lack of authority, attends the pre-trial conference and agrees to a settlement with the opposing party. The client is not bound by this settlement and the attorney is subject to disciplinary sanctions, including contempt of court, and may be liable to the opposing party for damages.

6. **Attribution of Knowledge and Notice**

   a. **Lawyer's knowledge**

   Information that is imparted to a lawyer during and related to the representation of a client is attributed to the client for purposes of determining the client's rights and liabilities with regard to matters in which the lawyer represents the client, unless such rights or liabilities require proof of the client's personal knowledge or intentions or the lawyer's legal duties preclude disclosure of such information to the client. Restatement (Third) of the Law Governing Lawyers § 28(1).

   1) **Exception—transactions not within scope of representation**

   A client is not charged with a lawyer's knowledge with regard to a transaction in which the lawyer does not represent the client. Restatement (Third) of the Law Governing Lawyers § 28, cmt. b.

   2) **Exception—other lawyers within the firm**

   The knowledge of a lawyer not personally engaged in representing a client, but in the same firm, is not attributed to the client unless the lawyer acquiring the knowledge is aware that the information is relevant to the firm's representation of the client. Restatement (Third) of the Law Governing Lawyers § 28, cmt. b.

   3) **Exception—criminal liability**

   A lawyer's knowledge is not attributed to the client to establish the client's criminal liability, but evidence of the lawyer's knowledge might be admissible to show what the client knew. Restatement (Third) of the Law Governing Lawyers § 28, cmt. b.

   b. **Notification to a lawyer**

   In the absence of applicable law otherwise, a third person may give notification to a client in a matter in which the client is represented by a lawyer by giving notification to the client's lawyer, unless the third person knows of circumstances reasonably indicating that the lawyer's authority to receive notification has been abrogated. Restatement (Third) of the Law Governing Lawyers § 28(2).

C. WITHDRAWAL OR TERMINATION OF REPRESENTATION

1. Mandatory Withdrawal

a. Resulting violation

A lawyer is required to withdraw from representation and subject to discipline if failure to do so would result in violating ethics rules or other law. MRPC 1.16(a)(1). Note that the lawyer is not obliged to withdraw simply because the client suggests a course of conduct that would result in such a violation, but only if the client demands such conduct. MRPC 1.16, cmt. 2.

b. Lawyer's health

A lawyer is required to withdraw when his physical or mental condition materially impairs his ability to represent the client. MRPC 1.16(a)(2).

c. Discharge

Generally a client has an absolute right to discharge a lawyer at any time, with or without cause. The lawyer is required to withdraw from the representation upon being discharged, unless ordered by the court to continue representation. MRPC 1.16(c), cmt. 4.

1) Limitations on client's ability to discharge lawyer

a) Client with severely diminished capacity

If the client has severely diminished capacity, the client may lack the legal capacity to discharge the lawyer. The lawyer may take reasonably necessary protective action to protect the client's interests. MRPC 1.16, cmt. 6.

b) Client with court-appointed lawyer

If the lawyer has been appointed to represent a client, the ability of the client to discharge the lawyer may be restricted by statute. At the least, the client should be advised as to the consequences of a discharge, which may include a court concluding that the appointment of a successor counsel is unjustified, and requiring the client to continue *pro se*. MRPC 1.16, cmt. 5.

2. Permissive Withdrawal

a. No harm to client

A lawyer may generally withdraw from representation for any reason if it can be done without material adverse effect on the interests of the client. MRPC 1.16(b)(1).

b. When acceptable even with harm

Even when there is material adverse effect on the client's interests as a result, the lawyer may withdraw in the following circumstances:

i) The client persists in a course of action involving the lawyer's services that the lawyer reasonably believes is **criminal or fraudulent**. MRPC 1.16(b)(2).

ii) The lawyer learns that previous services of the lawyer have been used by the client to **perpetrate a crime or fraud**. MRPC 1.16(b)(3).

iii) The client insists on a course of action that the lawyer finds **repugnant or with which the lawyer has a fundamental disagreement**. MRPC 1.16(b)(4).

iv) The client fails substantially to fulfill an obligation to the lawyer regarding the lawyer's services (e.g., paying the lawyer's reasonable fees) and has been given reasonable warning that the lawyer will withdraw unless the obligation is met. MRPC 1.16(b)(5).

v) The representation will result in an **unreasonable financial burden** on the lawyer. MRPC 1.16(b)(6).

vi) The client has made **representation unreasonably difficult** for the lawyer. MRPC 1.16(b)(6).

vii) Other good cause exists. MRPC 1.16(b)(7).

3. Order to Continue Representation

A lawyer attempting to withdraw must continue representing the client if ordered to do so by a tribunal, even if there is otherwise good cause for terminating the representation. MRPC 1.16(c).

4. Withdrawal—Notice and Permission

An appointed lawyer generally must obtain the permission of the appointing authority in order to withdraw. In addition, a lawyer in a matter pending before a court may be required by statute or rule to give the court notice of withdrawal and obtain permission of the court before doing so. MRPC 1.16(c), cmt. 3.

5. Duties to Client Upon Termination

Upon termination of the representation, the lawyer must take steps to the extent reasonably practicable to protect the client's interests, such as giving reasonable notice to the client, allowing time for employment of other counsel, surrendering property to which the client is entitled, and refunding any advance payment of fee or expense that has not been earned or incurred. The lawyer may retain papers relating to the representation to the extent permitted by law. MRPC 1.16(d).

Even if the lawyer has been unfairly discharged by the client, the lawyer must take all reasonable steps to mitigate the consequences to the client.

6. Fees Upon Termination

Even though the client-lawyer relationship is terminated at discharge, the lawyer is generally entitled to fees already earned but not yet paid. If the lawyer is discharged for cause, the right to such fees may be forfeited. MRPC 1.16, cmt. 4.

a. Fixed or hourly fees

When the fee arrangement is fixed or hourly, the lawyer can recover in quantum meruit for the value of the services rendered, although a cap on the lawyer's recovery may apply.

b. Contingent fees

Courts are split as to how to allocate contingency fees. Some allocate a reasonable value of services, others allow the agreed upon percentage even when another lawyer did the work, and still others deny any fee recovery.

c. Securing fees through retention of papers

The lawyer may retain papers as security for a fee only to the extent permitted by law. MRPC 1.16, cmt. 9.

D. FEES AND EXPENSES

1. Reasonable Fees

A lawyer is prohibited from charging a fee that is unreasonable. In addition, a lawyer is prohibited from entering into an agreement for an unreasonable fee or collecting such a fee. MRPC 1.5(a).

a. Basis of fee

Among the factors that may be considered when determining the reasonableness of a lawyer's fees are the following:

1) Difficulty of case

Factors impacting the difficulty of the case may be considered when evaluating the fee, such as the time, labor, novelty, and skill necessary to perform the services, as well as the time limitations imposed by the client or the specific circumstances surrounding the case. MRPC 1.5(a)(1), (5).

2) Other employment likely precluded

The likelihood that the lawyer's representation will preclude other employment for the lawyer, either due to the time requirements or potential conflicts that may arise, may be considered, but only if the client is aware of these limitations. MRPC 1.5(a)(2).

3) Nature of the relationship and the fee arrangement

Whether the fee is fixed or contingent, pre-paid or hourly, may be considered, as well as the way in which the particular client-lawyer relationship had been developed or evolved over time. MRPC 1.5(a)(6), (c).

4) Expertise of the lawyer

A seasoned, well-known lawyer may be able to charge more for the same service than a new lawyer without specific expertise. MRPC 1.5(a)(7).

5) Amount at issue and results obtained

The amount at issue (e.g., the recovery sought by the plaintiff) can be considered when a lawyer is setting the fee. In addition, the amount of the fee can depend on the results obtained by the lawyer. MRPC 1.5(a)(4).

6) Fee charged in locality

The customary fee charged for similar services in a given locality may also be considered. MRPC 1.5(a)(3).

2. Contingent Fees

Except for criminal cases and certain domestic relations cases as discussed below, lawyers may charge a fee contingent on the outcome of the case. **Contingent fee arrangements must be in writing and be reasonable.**

a. When prohibited

1) Criminal cases

Because no pool of recovery money is produced from a criminal matter, a lawyer is prohibited from charging a contingent fee to a criminal defendant. MRPC 1.5(d)(2).

2) Domestic relations cases

A lawyer may not charge a fee in a domestic relations case when the fee is contingent on obtaining a divorce or on the amount of support recovered. MRPC 1.5(d)(1). A contingent fee may be charged with respect to legal representation to recover post-judgment balances due under support, alimony or other financial orders. MRPC 1.5, cmt. 4.

> **Example:** An attorney's standard retainer contract in divorce cases provides for the payment of a fee of one-fourth of the amount of alimony or property settlement secured by the attorney. The attorney declines to represent clients who do not agree to this provision. Such a provision violates MRPC 1.5(d)(1) because it calls for a contingent fee based on the amount of support recovered in a domestic relations case.

b. Reasonableness requirement

Contingent fees, like any other fees, must be reasonable under the circumstances. MRPC 1.5, cmt. 3. The fee itself must be reasonable and it must be reasonable under the circumstances to charge any form of contingent fee.

c. Writing requirement

A contingent fee arrangement must be in writing, and must include the:

i) **Signature** of the client;

ii) Calculation methodology of the fee; and

iii) Details of the calculation for **deductions for expenses**, including whether such expenses are to be deducted before or after the contingency fee is calculated.

The agreement must clearly set out any expenses for which the client will be liable even though the client is not the prevailing party. At the conclusion of a contingent fee matter, the lawyer must provide the client with a written statement stating the outcome of the matter and, if there is a recovery, showing the remittance to the client and the method of its determination. MRPC 1.5(c).

d. Local law

Applicable local law may further limit contingency fee arrangements, such as by imposing a ceiling on the percentage allowed. MRPC 1.5, cmt. 3.

3. Terms of Payment

a. Payment in advance vs. retainer

A lawyer may require payment in advance of services rendered as long as the lawyer returns any portion that is ultimately unearned because the representation is terminated. MRPC 1.5, cmt. 4; 1.16(d). If the lawyer charges a retainer fee (i.e., money paid solely to ensure the availability of the lawyer), the lawyer generally does not have to refund the fee if the representation ends, unless the parties agree otherwise.

b. Property as payment

Property is generally an acceptable form of payment, but the payment is subject to requirements of MRPC 1.8(a) (*see* V.D.1. Business transactions with client, *infra*). Payment in the form of a proprietary interest in the cause of action or subject matter of the litigation must also comply with MRPC 1.8(i) (*see* V.C.1. Proprietary interest in causes of action, *infra*).

c. No agreement to curtail services

A lawyer may not make an agreement with a client the terms of which might induce the lawyer improperly to curtail services for the client or perform them in a way contrary to the client's interest. MRPC 1.5, cmt. 5. Thus, a lawyer may not enter into an agreement under which services are to be provided only up to a stated amount when it is foreseeable that more extensive services will likely be required, unless the situation is adequately explained to the client. Otherwise, the client might have to bargain for further assistance in the midst of a proceeding or transaction. However, it is proper to define the extent of services in light of the client's ability to pay.

4. Reasonable Expenses

Expenses for which the client is charged also cannot be unreasonable. MRPC 1.5(a). A lawyer may seek reimbursement for the cost of services performed in-house, such as copying, or for other expenses incurred in-house, such as telephone charges, either by charging a reasonable amount to which the client has agreed in advance or by charging an amount that reasonably reflects the cost incurred by the lawyer. MRPC 1.5, cmt. 1.

5. Fee Splitting

Although lawyers within a firm can legitimately share fees with each other (even after retirement), fee sharing with lawyers not within the same firm or with non-lawyers is restricted. MRPC 1.5(e).

a. Lawyers from different firms

Fee splitting among lawyers at different firms is permitted if all three of the following conditions are met:

   i)   The **fee is in proportion** to the services rendered by each lawyer **or joint responsibility** is assumed for the representation;

   ii) The **client agrees in writing** to the fee splitting arrangement; and

   iii) The **total fee charged must be reasonable** (such that a client is not charged more just because additional lawyers are working on the case).

MRPC 1.5(e).

If all of these requirements are met, the lawyers can submit one bill to the client and then divide the fee.

b. Referral fees

A lawyer is generally prohibited from giving anything of value to anyone for recommending the lawyer's services. MRPC 7.2(b). (See § X.B., *infra*, for exceptions to this prohibition.) A lawyer paying a fee to a referring lawyer in return for a referral violates this rule. However, the referring lawyer is entitled to be reasonably compensated for any work he did prior to the referral, such as interviewing the client. MRPC 1.5, cmt. 1.

c. Former partner

Fees may be shared with former partners and associates of the primary lawyer in a matter pursuant to a profit sharing or retirement plan.

d. Minimum fee schedule

Minimum fee schedules once imposed on lawyers by state bars are no longer lawful because their anti-competitive nature violates the Sherman Act, and are thus not enforceable. *Goldfarb v. Virginia State Bar*, 421 U.S. 773 (1975).

6. Modification of Fee Agreement

A fee agreement may be modified during a lawyer's representation of a client, but the modified agreement must be reasonable under the circumstances at the time of the modification. Additionally, if the lawyer proposes the modification, then the lawyer must communicate the modification to the client and the client must accept it for it to be effective. ABA Formal Opinion 11-458; MRPC 1.5(b).

a. Periodic, incremental increases

If, at the commencement of the representation, a client was informed of a lawyer's policy of making periodic, incremental increases in the lawyer's hourly rate and the client accepted the policy at that time, such increases are generally permissible unless they are unreasonable.

b. Change in basic nature or significant increase

A change in the basic nature of a fee arrangement or a significant increase in the lawyer's compensation is generally unreasonable unless there has been an unanticipated change in circumstances.

c. Enforceability of modified fee agreement

Since a client-lawyer relationship is in part a fiduciary relationship, a modification of the fee arrangement beyond a reasonable time after the beginning of the representation may be avoided by a client unless the lawyer is able to establish that the modified contract is fair and reasonable to the client. Restatement (Third) of the Law Governing Lawyers § 18(a). In addition, some jurisdictions may require that the modification be supported by consideration.

7. Communication With Client

A lawyer must generally communicate to a client the basis or rate of the lawyer's fee before, or within a reasonable time after, the commencement of the representation. An exception exists if the lawyer charges a regularly represented client on the same basis or rate as previously charged. A lawyer must also communicate to the client any changes in the basis or rate of the lawyer's fee. MRPC 1.5(b).

a. Scope and expenses

In addition to the fee itself, the scope of the lawyer's representation and the expenses for which the client will be responsible must also be communicated to the client in a timely fashion. MRPC 1.5(b), cmt. 2.

b. No writing requirement

While it is advisable to provide the client with at least a memorandum of the lawyer's fee in order to reduce the possibility of a misunderstanding, the Model Rules do not specifically require that the lawyer's communication regarding fees and expenses be in written form, with the exception of a contingency fee (see 2.c., Writing requirement, *supra*). MRPC 1.5(b), cmt. 2.

8. Fee Disputes

a. Arbitration or mediation

If a procedure has been established for resolution of fee disputes, such as an arbitration or mediation procedure established by the bar, the lawyer must comply with the procedure when it is mandatory, and, even when it is voluntary, the lawyer should conscientiously consider submitting to it. MRPC 1.5, cmt. 9.

b. Retention of funds in trust account pending dispute resolution

If a lawyer receives funds on behalf of a client from which the lawyer's fees are to be paid, and the client disputes the amount of the fee, the lawyer may retain the disputed amount in a client trust account until the dispute is resolved. The lawyer must promptly distribute all undisputed funds to the client. MRPC 1.15(e).

IV. PRIVILEGE AND CONFIDENTIALITY

A. DUTY VERSUS PRIVILEGE IN GENERAL

The principle of client-lawyer confidentiality is given effect by related areas of the law: (i) attorney-client privilege, (ii) the work product doctrine, and (iii) the ethical duty of confidentiality. Attorney-client privilege and work-product doctrine apply in judicial and other legal proceedings in which a lawyer may be called as a witness or otherwise required to produce evidence with regard to a client. The duty of client-lawyer confidentiality applies in situations other than those in which evidence is sought from the lawyer through legal compulsion. It applies not only to matters communicated in confidence by a client but also to all information relating to the representation of the client, from any source. A lawyer may not disclose such information except as authorized or required by the Model Rules or by other law. A court cannot order the revelation of material subject to the attorney-client privilege, but may order the disclosure of information protected by the duty of confidentiality that is not subject to that privilege.

> **EXAM NOTE:** Be certain to understand the difference between the duty of confidentiality and the evidentiary attorney-client privilege. Remember that only client-driven confidential communication is covered by the privilege. The duty of confidentiality also covers third party-driven communication, lawyer observation, and all information relating to the representation.

B. ATTORNEY-CLIENT PRIVILEGE

A confidential communication between a client and her lawyer is privileged if it is made for the purpose of obtaining or providing legal assistance for the client. The evidentiary attorney-client privilege covers the client's communication to a lawyer whom the client reasonably believes represents the client, and only when the circumstances indicate a desire by the client for confidentiality. This privilege applies in judicial and other proceedings in which a lawyer may be called as a witness or otherwise required to produce evidence concerning a client. MRPC 1.6, cmt. c.

1. **Elements**

   a. **Confidential**

   The communication must be intended to be confidential in order to be privileged. A communication made in the presence of a third party generally is not privileged, but a communication that is made in the reasonable belief that it is being made in confidence that is overheard by a third party is privileged. In addition, the presence of, or communication by or through, a representative of the client or the lawyer does not destroy the attorney-client privilege.

   1) **Waiver and disclosure**

   A client may waive the privilege directly or by disclosure of the information communicated. The Federal Rules of Evidence address the effect that a litigation-related disclosure of protected information has on the waiver of the attorney-client privilege, drawing a distinction between an intentional disclosure and an unintentional disclosure. The rule applies to confidential communications as well as material protected by the work-product doctrine. Fed. R. Evid. 502.

   a) **Inadvertent disclosure—no waiver**

   When made during a federal proceeding, the inadvertent disclosure of privileged communication or information does not waive the privilege if the holder of the privilege:

   i)   Took reasonable steps to prevent disclosure; and

   ii) Promptly took reasonable steps to rectify the error.

   Fed. R. Evid. 502(b). In determining whether the holder took reasonable steps to prevent disclosure, factors such as the number of documents to be reviewed, the time constraints for production, or the existence of an efficient records-management system may be relevant.

   b) **Intentional disclosure—limitation on the scope of waiver**

   When made during a federal proceeding, the intentional disclosure of privileged material operates as a waiver of the attorney-client privilege. The waiver extends to undisclosed information only in those unusual situations in which (i) the disclosed and undisclosed material concern the same subject matter and (ii) fairness requires the disclosure of related information because a party has disclosed information in a selective, misleading, and unfair manner. Fed. R. Evid. 502(a).

   c) **Effect of disclosure made in a state proceeding**

   When privileged material is disclosed in a state proceeding and the state and federal laws are in conflict as to the effect of the disclosure, the disclosure does not operate as a waiver in a subsequent federal proceeding if the disclosure (i) would not be a waiver had it been made in a federal proceeding or (ii) is not a disclosure under the law of the state where it was made. In other words, the federal court must apply the law that is most protective of the privilege. This rule does not apply if the state court has issued an order concerning the effect of the disclosure; in such a case, the state-court order would be controlling. Fed. R. Evid. 502(c).

d) Controlling effect of a federal confidentiality order

A federal court may order that the privilege or protection is not waived by disclosure connected with the pending litigation (i.e., a confidentiality order). In such a case, the disclosure does not constitute a waiver in any other federal or state proceeding. Fed. R. Evid. 502(d).

e) Parties' agreement

An agreement between the parties regarding the effect of a disclosure binds only the parties unless the agreement is incorporated into a court order. Fed. R. Evid. 502(e).

b. Communication

The communication must be for the purpose of obtaining or providing legal advice or representation, but the lawyer does not need to give advice or agree to the representation for the privilege to exist.

1) Non-privileged statements

A statement made to a lawyer that is not about legal advice or services sought by the client is not privileged. This includes statements regarding the fact of employment, the identity of the client, and the fee arrangements for the representation. If providing such information would divulge a confidential communication or incriminate the client, then it may be protected.

Furthermore, the attorney-client privilege does not protect disclosure of the underlying facts. A client cannot be compelled to answer the question "What did you say to your lawyer?" but cannot refuse to reveal a fact within her knowledge merely because she told that fact to her lawyer. *Upjohn Co. v. United States*, 449 U.S. 383 (1981) (quoting *Philadelphia v. Westinghouse Electric Corp.,* 205 F.Supp. 830, 831 (E.D. Pa. 1962)).

Finally, communications are not privileged when they are made to a lawyer who is acting in a capacity other than as a lawyer, such as a business partner, or witness to a will.

2) Corporate client

When a lawyer represents a corporation, some states limit the privilege to communications received by the lawyer from a member of the "control group" of the corporation (employees in a position to control or take a substantial part in a decision). *See, e.g., Consolidation Coal Co. v. Bucyrus-Erie Co.*, 432 N.E.2d 250 (Ill. 1982). However, in cases in which federal law controls, the privilege extends to communications by a non-control-group employee about matters within the employee's corporate duties made for the purpose of securing legal advice for the corporation. *Upjohn Co. v. United States*, 449 U.S. 383 (1981) (protecting communications by lower-level employees who were directed by their superiors to communicate with the corporation's lawyer).

c. Client holds privilege

The client holds the privilege, and is the only one who may waive it. The lawyer, however, must assert the privilege on the client's behalf to protect the client's interests.

d. Indefinite duration

Unless waived, the attorney-client privilege continues indefinitely, even if the lawyer's representation is terminated. The privilege generally survives the client's death.

2. Exceptions

The attorney-client privilege does not protect these confidential communications:

i) Communications made to enable or aid the commission of what the client knew or should have known was a crime or fraud;

ii) Communications relevant to a dispute between lawyer and client or former client (e.g., client's malpractice allegation, lawyer's compensation or reimbursement claim);

iii) Communications relevant to a dispute between parties who claim through the same deceased client; and

iv) Communications between former co-clients who are now adverse to each other.

3. Work Product Doctrine

Documents prepared by a lawyer for her own use in anticipation of litigation, including summaries of or notes regarding a witness's statement, are protected under the "work product" doctrine. Generally, these documents are subject to discovery only if the party seeking disclosure (i) demonstrates a substantial need for the information, and (ii) cannot obtain the information by any other means without undue hardship. The mental impressions, conclusions, and trial tactics of a lawyer are protected from discovery, regardless of another party's need for the information or inability to otherwise obtain it. Fed. R. Civ. P. 26(b)(3).

C. PROFESSIONAL OBLIGATION OF CONFIDENTIALITY

1. General Rule

Under the Model Rules, a lawyer is prohibited from disclosing information relating to the representation of a client, unless the client gives informed consent, the disclosure is impliedly authorized in order to carry out the representation, or other specific exceptions (discussed below) apply. MRPC 1.6(a).

a. Protected information

The ethical duty of confidentiality applies not only to confidential client communications, but also to **all information relating to the representation, regardless of the source**, including lawyer observations and third-party communications. Information that relates to a representation may be acquired before, during, or after the representation and is confidential so long as it is not generally known. MRPC 1.6, cmt. 3; Restatement (Third) of the Law Governing Lawyers § 59, cmt. (b),(c).

b. Prohibition on disclosure of information that could reasonably lead to discovery of protected information

The prohibition also applies to disclosures by a lawyer that do not in themselves reveal protected information but could reasonably lead to the discovery of such information by a third person. A lawyer's use of a hypothetical to discuss issues relating to the representation is permissible so long as there is no reasonable likelihood that the listener will be able to ascertain the identity of the client or the situation involved. MRPC 1.6, cmt. 4.

Note that legal strategies about the representation would be covered by both the ethical duty of confidentiality and the work product doctrine.

c. Prohibition on use of information to client's disadvantage

A lawyer must not use information relating to representation of a client to the disadvantage of the client unless the client gives informed consent, except as permitted or required by the Model Rules. MRPC 1.8(b).

2. Duty of Confidentiality to Prospective Client

a. Prospective client

A person who consults with a lawyer about the possibility of forming a client-lawyer relationship with respect to a matter is a prospective client. MRPC 1.18(a). Whether communications (written, oral, or electronic) constitute a consultation depends on the circumstances.

Example: An attorney is preparing to file a class action suit against a large pharmaceutical company, alleging that an asthma medication causes kidney failure. The attorney runs a television advertisement inviting members of the public who have taken the medication to call him. After seeing the ad, a woman calls the attorney and tells him about her experiences taking the medication. The woman has likely "consulted" with the attorney.

Contrast: An attorney advertises his personal injury practice on television, including a statement that he "fights for the rights of victims." After seeing the ad, a mother telephones the attorney, tells him that her son has been taking a particular asthma medication for two years, and asks if it is true that the drug causes kidney failure. It is unlikely that this conversation would be considered a "consultation."

A person who communicates information unilaterally to a lawyer, without any reasonable expectation that the lawyer is willing to discuss the possibility of forming a client-lawyer relationship, is **not** a "prospective client." Moreover, a person who communicates with a lawyer for the purpose of disqualifying the lawyer is not a "prospective client."

b. Confidentiality

Even if no client-lawyer relationship is formed, a lawyer who has learned information from a prospective client is not generally permitted to use or reveal that information, except to the extent as would be permitted by the Model Rules with regard to a former client. MRPC 1.18(b).

3. Duty of Confidentiality to Former Client

With respect to a former client, a lawyer is not permitted to reveal information relating to the representation except when permitted or required by the Model Rules. The lawyer also cannot use such information to the disadvantage of the former client except when permitted or required by the Model Rules or the information has become generally known. The former client can waive this requirement through informed consent, confirmed in writing. MRPC 1.9(c), cmt. 9.

4. Acting to Preserve Confidentiality

A lawyer must make reasonable efforts to prevent the inadvertent or unauthorized disclosure of, or unauthorized access to, information relating to the representation of a client. A lawyer must consider the sensitivity of information and take reasonable precautions to safeguard confidential information of a client against unauthorized access by third parties, and even from inadvertent or unauthorized disclosure by the lawyer or other persons who are participating in the representation of the client or who are subject to the lawyer's supervision. Factors considered in determining the reasonableness of the lawyer's efforts to prevent the access or disclosure include:

i) The sensitivity of the information;

ii) The likelihood of disclosure if additional safeguards are not employed;

iii) The cost and difficulty of utilizing additional safeguards; and

iv) The extent to which the safeguards would adversely affect the lawyer's ability to represent clients (e.g., by making certain software exceedingly difficult to use).

MRPC 1.6(c), cmts. 18, 19.

a. Transmission of communications

When transmitting a communication that includes information relating to a client's representation, the lawyer must take reasonable precautions to prevent the information from coming into the hands of unintended recipients. This duty does not require that the lawyer use special security measures if the communication method affords a reasonable expectation of privacy. A client may require the lawyer to implement special security measures not otherwise required or may give informed consent to the use of a means of communication that would otherwise be prohibited. MRPC 1.6, cmt. 19.

b. Use of e-mail

The transmission by e-mail of information about a client's representation is proper under the Model Rules. A lawyer has a reasonable expectation of privacy with regard to the use of e-mail. *See* ABA Formal Opinion 99-413.

D. CLIENT-AUTHORIZED DISCLOSURE

1. Informed Consent by the Client

The lawyer may reveal confidential information if the client gives informed consent. MRPC 1.6(a).

2. Implied Authority

a. Disclosure necessary to carry out representation

A lawyer may disclose information relating to the representation of a client if such disclosure is impliedly authorized in order to carry out the representation. MRPC 1.6(a). A client's instructions or special circumstances can limit such authority. MRPC 1.6, cmt. 5.

b. Within a firm

Lawyers in a firm may, in the course of the firm's practice, disclose to each other information relating to a client of the firm, unless the client has instructed that particular information be confined to specified lawyers. MRPC 1.6, cmt. 5. Disclosure may also be made to non-lawyers in a firm when necessary to carry out the representation. The firm must have procedures in place (including training) to ensure that non-lawyers do not violate the duty of confidentiality. MRPC 5.3.

E. EXCEPTIONS TO CONFIDENTIALITY

In addition to client-authorized disclosure, the Model Rules permit disclosure in several other specific circumstances.

1. **Reasonably Certain Death or Substantial Bodily Harm**

   A lawyer may reveal confidential information concerning the representation of a client to the extent the lawyer reasonably believes disclosure is necessary to prevent reasonably certain death or substantial bodily harm. MRPC 1.6(b)(1).

   a. **"Reasonably certain"**

   Substantial bodily harm or death is reasonably certain to occur if it will be suffered imminently **or** if there is a present and substantial threat that a person will suffer such harm or death at a later date if the lawyer fails to take action necessary to eliminate the threat. MRPC 1.6, cmt. 6.

   > Harm or death need not be imminent, but merely reasonably certain to occur if the lawyer does not disclose.

   b. **Applicable no matter who causes the harm**

   This exception applies even if a third party—not the client—is the cause of the potential substantial bodily harm or death.

   c. **Applicable no matter what brings about the harm**

   This exception applies even if the substantial bodily harm or death would result from an unintentional act or natural causes.

   d. **Lawyer has discretion**

   The Model Rules allow, but do not require, disclosure under these circumstances.

   > **Example:** An attorney has been hired by a client to represent the client in a civil commitment proceeding. The client tells the attorney that she intends to commit suicide the next day, and the attorney believes that the client will carry out this threat. It would be proper for the attorney to disclose the client's intentions to the proper authorities, because there is a present and substantial threat that the client will suffer harm or death if the attorney fails to take action necessary to eliminate the threat. MRPC 1.6, cmt. 6.

2. **Substantial Financial Harm to Another Based on Client's Fraud or Crime**

   A lawyer may reveal confidential information concerning the representation of a client to the extent the lawyer reasonably believes it necessary to prevent the client from committing a crime or fraud that is reasonably certain to result in substantial injury to the financial interests or property of another and in furtherance of which the client has used or is using the lawyer's services. MRPC 1.6(b)(2). Disclosure is also permitted to prevent, mitigate, or rectify substantial injury to the financial interests or property of another that is reasonably certain to result or has resulted from the client's commission of a crime or fraud in furtherance of which the client has used the lawyer's services. MRPC 1.6(b)(3).

   a. **Discretionary with lawyer**

   Disclosure is discretionary by the lawyer, but no matter what, the lawyer may not counsel or assist the client in conduct the lawyer knows is criminal or fraudulent. MRPC 1.6, cmt. 7.

   b. **Not applicable when person who has committed crime or fraud then employs lawyer**

   The exceptions do not apply when a person who has committed a crime or fraud thereafter employs a lawyer for representation concerning that offense.

3. Securing Legal Advice About Lawyer's Compliance With Model Rules

A lawyer's duty of confidentiality does not prohibit a lawyer from obtaining confidential legal advice about the lawyer's responsibility to comply with the Model Rules. MRPC 1.6(b)(4). Generally, disclosing information to obtain such advice would be impliedly authorized for the lawyer to carry out the representation. Even if not impliedly authorized, the Model Rules allow such disclosure. MRPC 1.6, cmt. 9.

4. Controversy Between Lawyer and Client or Arising From Lawyer's Representation of Client

A lawyer may reveal confidential information concerning the representation of a client to the extent the lawyer reasonably believes it necessary to establish a claim or defense on behalf of the lawyer in a controversy between the lawyer and the client, to establish a defense to a criminal charge or civil claim against the lawyer based on conduct in which the client was involved, or to respond to allegations in any proceeding concerning the lawyer's representation of the client. MRPC 1.6(b)(5).

Example: A client disputes a fee owed to his attorney for representation in a criminal defense matter. The attorney is permitted to prove the services rendered in the defense action in order to collect the fee.

5. Compliance With Other Law or Court Order

A lawyer may reveal confidential information concerning the representation of a client to the extent the lawyer reasonably believes it necessary to comply with other law or a court order. MRPC 1.6(b)(6). Unless the client provides informed consent to do otherwise, the lawyer should assert on behalf of the client all non-frivolous claims that the order is not authorized by other law or that the information sought is protected against disclosure by attorney-client privilege or other applicable law. MRPC 1.6, cmt. 15.

6. Detecting Conflicts of Interest

A lawyer may reveal confidential information relating to the representation of a client to the extent the lawyer reasonably believes it necessary to detect and resolve conflicts of interest arising from the lawyer's change of employment or from changes in the makeup or ownership of a firm, but only if the revealed information would not compromise the attorney-client privilege or otherwise prejudice the client. MRPC 1.6(b)(7). Once substantive discussions regarding a change in the employment relationship have begun, lawyers and law firms may disclose limited information, ordinarily including no more than the identity of the persons and entities involved in a matter, a brief summary of the general issues involved, and information about whether the matter has terminated. MRPC 1.6, cmt. 13.

V. CONFLICTS OF INTEREST

Lawyers owe clients a basic duty of loyalty and independent professional judgment. MRPC 1.7, cmt. 1. When a lawyer's independent professional judgment is potentially compromised by a non-client interest (i.e., a conflict of interest exists), the lawyer may be in breach of his duty of loyalty. A conflict of interest may arise between the lawyer and the client, between clients (including former, prospective, and current clients) and between current clients and third parties.

A. AS AFFECTED BY LAWYER'S PERSONAL INTEREST

1. In General

A lawyer must not represent a client if the representation of the client may be materially limited by the lawyer's own interests, unless: (i) the lawyer reasonably believes that the lawyer will be able to provide competent and diligent representation to the affected client; (ii) the representation is not prohibited by law; and (iii) the affected client gives informed consent, confirmed in writing. MRPC 1.7.

Note that both subjective and objective standards apply in determining reasonable belief; both the specific lawyer's subjective belief and a disinterested lawyer's reasonable belief are required in the analysis of whether the representation would be materially limited by the lawyer's own interests.

2. Related Lawyers

A lawyer related to another lawyer (e.g., parent, child, sibling, or spouse) may not represent a client in a matter in which the related lawyer is representing another party, unless each client gives informed consent. Disqualification arising from a close family relationship is personal and ordinarily is not imputed to members of firms with whom the lawyers are associated. MRPC 1.7, cmt. 11.

3. Sexual Relations With Client

A lawyer is prohibited from engaging in sexual relations with a client, **unless** a consensual sexual relationship existed between the lawyer and client when the client-lawyer relationship commenced. MRPC 1.8(j). The rule does not permit the client to waive the conflict through informed consent. The conflict is personal to the lawyer and is not imputed to others in the lawyer's firm. MRPC 1.8(k). If the client is an organization, the lawyer for the organization (whether inside counsel or outside counsel) is prohibited from having a sexual relationship with a constituent of the organization (e.g., employee of a corporation) who supervises, directs, or regularly consults with the lawyer with regard to the organization's legal matters. MRPC 1.8, cmt. 19.

B. LAWYER AS WITNESS

Due to the potential conflict between the interests of a client and the interest of a lawyer in testifying truthfully, a lawyer generally is disqualified from representing a client if the lawyer is likely to be a necessary witness in the action (i.e., the advocate-witness rule).

1. Circumstances Under Which Lawyer May Testify

A lawyer is not permitted to act as an advocate at a trial in which the lawyer is likely to be a necessary witness unless:

i) The testimony relates to an uncontested issue;

ii) The testimony relates to the nature and value of legal services rendered in the case; or

iii) Disqualification of the lawyer would work substantial hardship on the client.

MRPC 3.7(a).

2. Other Lawyers in Firm

A lawyer is generally permitted to act as an advocate in a trial in which another lawyer in the lawyer's firm is likely to be called as a necessary witness. If, however, the testifying lawyer herself would be prohibited from testifying by Rule 1.7 or 1.9 (regarding conflicts with current or former clients), the lawyer herself, as well as other lawyers in the firm would be precluded from representing the client by Rule 1.10 (regarding imputed disqualification) unless the client gives informed consent, confirmed in writing. MRPC 3.7(b).

C. ACQUIRING AN INTEREST IN LITIGATION

1. Proprietary Interest in Causes of Action

A lawyer must not obtain a proprietary interest in the cause of action or subject matter of litigation in which a client is represented, except when: (i) the lawyer acquires a lien granted by law to secure payment of a fee; or (ii) the lawyer contracts for a reasonable contingent fee, provided the case is not a criminal or matrimonial/domestic matter. MRPC 1.8(i).

> When a lawyer acquires by contract a security interest in property other than that recovered through the lawyer's efforts in the litigation, such an acquisition is a business or financial transaction with a client and is subject to the requirements of MRPC 1.8(a) (*see* V.D.1. Business transactions with client, *infra*). MRPC 1.8(i), cmt. 16.

2. Financial Assistance

Financial assistance to a client is prohibited with respect to pending or planned litigation, except that a lawyer is permitted to advance litigation costs (including the expenses of medical examination and the costs of obtaining and presenting evidence) to the client. MRPC 1.8(e). Although the client usually remains ultimately liable for them, repayment may be made contingent on the outcome of the case. Lawyers representing indigent clients may advance court costs and litigation expenses regardless of whether repayment is required. MRPC 1.8(e), cmt. 10.

D. ENTERING INTO BUSINESS TRANSACTIONS WITH CLIENT

1. Business Transactions With Client

A lawyer must not enter into a business transaction with a client or knowingly acquire any interest adverse to a client, unless the terms are fair and reasonable to the client, the client is advised in writing of the desirability of seeking independent counsel and is given an opportunity to do so, and the client consents in writing to the transaction and its terms after a full written disclosure of the terms and the lawyer's role in the transaction. MRPC 1.8(a).

The rule does not apply to standard commercial transactions between the lawyer and the client for products or services that the client generally markets to others, for example, banking or brokerage services, medical services, products manufactured or distributed by the client, and utilities' services. MRPC 1.8, cmt. 1.

2. Literary or Media Rights

A lawyer is prohibited from negotiating for literary or media rights relating to representation of a client **prior to the conclusion of the representation.** MRPC 1.8(d). The rule does not prohibit a lawyer representing a client in a transaction concerning literary property from agreeing that the lawyer's fee will consist of a share in ownership in the property, if the arrangement does not result in an unreasonable fee and meets the rules regarding business transactions with a client.

3. Soliciting Gifts

A lawyer may not solicit a substantial gift or prepare an instrument (such as a will, trust agreement, or deed) that gives a substantial gift to the lawyer or a person related to the lawyer, unless the client is related to the donee. Related persons include a spouse, child, grandchild, parent, grandparent, or other relative or individual with whom the lawyer or the client maintains a close, familial relationship. MRPC 1.8(c), cmts. 6, 7

Note that a lawyer may accept an unsolicited gift from a client, if the transaction meets general standards of fairness. For example, a simple gift such as a present given at a holiday or as a token of appreciation is permitted. If a client offers the lawyer a more substantial gift, the rule does not prohibit the lawyer from accepting it, but such a gift may be voidable by the client under the doctrine of undue influence, which treats client gifts as presumptively fraudulent. MRPC 1.8(c), cmt. 6.

4. **Promise to Limit Malpractice Recovery**

A lawyer is prohibited from making an agreement prospectively limiting malpractice liability to a client, **unless** the client is represented by an independent lawyer in making the agreement. MRPC 1.8(h)(1).

> Merely advising a client to seek the counsel of an independent lawyer is **not** sufficient to satisfy this exception to the prohibition on an agreement to limit a malpractice recovery. The client must be represented by such a lawyer in making the agreement. Also note that this provision does not require that the agreement be in writing or that the client sign the agreement.

An agreement to submit a future malpractice dispute to arbitration is permitted when the client is informed as to the scope and the effect of the arbitration clause. MRPC 1.8(h), cmt. 14.

E. **CONFLICTING INTERESTS AMONG CLIENTS**

1. **Current Clients**

   a. **General rule**

   A lawyer must not represent a client if doing so would be directly adverse to the interests of another current client or there is a significant risk that the representation of the client will be materially limited by the lawyer's responsibilities to the current client, unless: (i) the lawyer reasonably believes that the lawyer will be able to provide competent and diligent representation to each affected client; (ii) the representation is not prohibited by law; (iii) the representation does not involve the assertion of a claim by one client against another client represented by the lawyer in the same litigation or other proceeding before a tribunal; **and** (iv) each affected client gives informed consent, confirmed in writing. MRPC 1.7.

   b. **Directly adverse**

   Under no circumstances may a lawyer represent **opposing** parties in the same lawsuit. Absent informed consent in writing, a lawyer also may not act as an advocate in one matter against a person the lawyer represents in some other matter, even if the matters are wholly unrelated. MRPC 1.7, cmt. 6.

      1) **Transactional matters**

      Directly adverse conflicts can also arise in transactional matters. Thus, if a lawyer represents the potential buyer of a business in negotiations with the seller, the lawyer cannot undertake the representation of the seller in an unrelated matter without the informed consent of each client, confirmed in writing. MRPC 1.7, cmt. 7.

      2) **Unrelated matters**

      A directly adverse conflict may arise when a lawyer is required to cross-examine a client who appears as a witness in an unrelated lawsuit involving another client, as when the testimony will be damaging to the client who is represented in the lawsuit. Simultaneous representation in unrelated matters of clients whose interests are only economically adverse, however, such as representation of competing economic enterprises (two baseball teams, for example) in unrelated litigation, does not ordinarily constitute a conflict of interest and thus may not require consent of the respective clients. MRPC 1.7, cmt. 6.

c. Material limitation

Even if clients are not directly adverse, a conflict of interest exists if there is a significant risk that a lawyer's ability to consider, recommend, or carry out an appropriate course of action for the client will be materially limited as a result of the lawyer's other responsibilities or interests. Thus, if a lawyer is asked to represent several persons seeking to form a partnership, the lawyer is likely to be materially limited in her ability to recommend or advocate all possible positions that each partner might take because of the lawyer's duty of loyalty to the others. The mere possibility of subsequent harm, though, does not require disclosure and consent. The lawyer must evaluate the likelihood that a difference in interests will occur and, if so, whether it will materially interfere with the lawyer's independent professional judgment in considering alternatives that reasonably should be pursued on behalf of the client. MRPC 1.7, cmt. 8.

d. Reasonable belief

Both subjective and objective standards apply in determining reasonable belief. The specific lawyer's subjective belief and a disinterested lawyer's reasonable belief are each required in the analysis of whether the representation would be adverse or materially limited by the lawyer's responsibilities to another client.

e. Settlements involving co-parties

A lawyer representing co-parties may make an aggregate settlement only if each client consents in writing after full consultation and disclosure by the lawyer, including disclosure of the nature and extent of all claims and pleas, and the participation of each party in the settlement. MRPC 1.8(g).

f. Class actions—unnamed members

Unnamed members of a class in a class-action lawsuit are generally not treated as clients of the lawyer who represents the class for purposes of directly adverse rule. Generally, the lawyer for a class is also not required to obtain the consent of an unnamed member of that class before representing a client who is suing that unnamed class member in an unrelated matter. Similarly, the lawyer who represents an unnamed class member in an unrelated matter is typically not required to obtain that class member's consent before representing an opponent in the class action. MRPC 1.7, cmt. 25.

2. Conflicts Between Current and Former Clients

The duty of loyalty to a client extends beyond the duration of the representation and can limit a lawyer's ability to represent other clients or use information obtained in representing the client.

a. Representation materially adverse to former client

A lawyer who has previously represented a client in a matter must not subsequently represent another person in the same or a substantially related matter in which that person's interests are materially adverse to the interests of the former client, unless the former client gives informed consent, confirmed in writing. MRPC 1.9(a).

1) Scope of a matter

The scope of a "matter" for purposes of determining a conflict depends on the facts of each particular situation or transaction. If a lawyer has been directly involved in a specific transaction, subsequent representation of other clients with materially adverse interests in that transaction is clearly prohibited. If the lawyer commonly handled a type of problem for a former client, though, the lawyer is not prohibited from later representing another client in a factually different problem of the same type even though the subsequent representation involves a position adverse to the prior client. MRPC 1.9, cmt. 2.

2) "Substantially related"

Matters are "substantially related" if they involve the same transaction or legal dispute, or if there is a substantial risk that confidential factual information as would normally have been obtained in the prior representation would materially advance the client's position in the subsequent matter. Thus, a lawyer who learned extensive private financial information about a business client in the ordinary course of representing that client may not subsequently represent that person's spouse in seeking a divorce. Whether a matter is "substantially related" is not determined by the lawyer's actual knowledge of confidential information, but by whether a lawyer engaged in providing the services provided by the lawyer ordinarily would have learned such information (i.e., an objective test). Information that has been disclosed to the public or to other parties adverse to the former client generally will not be disqualifying. MRPC 1.7, cmt. 3.

b. Information obtained in former representation

A lawyer who has formerly represented a client in a matter or whose present or former firm has formerly represented a client in a matter is not permitted to reveal information relating to the representation to the disadvantage of the former client except when permitted or required by the Model Rules. In addition, a lawyer is not permitted to use such information except when the Model Rules so require or permit, or the information has become generally known. The former client can waive this requirement through informed consent, confirmed in writing. MRPC 1.9(c), incl. cmt. 9.

c. Lawyer switches private firms

1) Limitations on lawyer

A lawyer is not permitted to represent knowingly a person in the same or a substantially related matter in which a firm with which the lawyer was formerly associated had previously represented a client whose interests are materially adverse to that person and about whom the lawyer had acquired confidential information that is material to the matter. The former client may give informed consent, confirmed in writing, to permit such representation, however. MRPC 1.9(b).

2) Limitations on former firm

If a lawyer has terminated an association with a firm, the firm is not prohibited from subsequently representing a person with interests materially adverse to those of a client represented by the formerly associated lawyer and not currently represented by the firm, unless: (i) the matter is the same or substantially related to that in which the formerly associated lawyer represented the client; and (ii) any lawyer remaining in the firm has confidential information that is material to the matter. MRPC 1.10(b). A client may give informed consent, in writing, to overcome a disqualification.

d. Government lawyers

1) Former government lawyers

The Model Rules prohibit a former government lawyer from representing a client in a matter in which the lawyer participated **personally and substantially** as a government lawyer, unless the appropriate government agency gives its informed consent, confirmed in writing, to the representation. MRPC 1.11(a).

> Note that the prohibition applies regardless of whether the lawyer is adverse to the government in attempting to represent the new client. Thus, a lawyer who has pursued a claim on behalf of the government may not pursue the same claim on behalf of a subsequent private client after the lawyer has left government service, except when the government agency gives its informed, written consent.

2) Disqualification of former government lawyer's firm

If a former government lawyer is disqualified from representation, no lawyer in the firm with which the former government lawyer is associated may knowingly undertake or continue representation in the matter unless: (i) the disqualified lawyer is timely screened from any participation in the matter and gets no part of any fee from the matter; and (ii) written notice is promptly given to the appropriate government agency to enable it to ascertain whether the lawyer and firm are in compliance with the conflict rules. MRPC 1.11(b).

3) Use of confidential information obtained during government service

a) General rule

Except as the law may otherwise expressly permit, a government lawyer who acquires information that the lawyer knows is confidential government information about a person may not later represent a private client whose interests are adverse to that person in a matter in which the information could be used to that person's material disadvantage. MRPC 1.11(c).

b) Confidential government information

"Confidential government information" means information that has been obtained under governmental authority and which, at the time the rule is applied, the government is prohibited by law from disclosing to the public or has a legal privilege not to disclose and which is not otherwise available to the public. MRPC 1.11(c).

c) Former government lawyer's firm

A firm with which a former government lawyer is associated may undertake or continue representation in a matter in which that lawyer is disqualified due to possession of confidential government information only if the disqualified lawyer is timely screened from any participation in the matter and gets no part of the fee from the representation. MRPC 1.11(c).

4) Current government lawyer

a) General conflict rules apply

Except as law may otherwise expressly permit, a lawyer currently serving as a government employee is subject to the general ethics rules relating to current and former clients. In addition, the government lawyer is not permitted to participate in a matter in which the lawyer participated personally and substantially while in private practice or non-governmental employment, unless the appropriate government agency gives its informed, written consent.

b) Negotiation for private employment

A current government lawyer is not generally permitted to negotiate for private employment with any person who is involved as a party or as lawyer for a party in a matter in which the lawyer is participating personally and substantially. MRPC 1.11(d)(ii). There is an exception that allows for a lawyer serving as a law clerk to negotiate for private employment, but only after the law clerk has notified the judge or other adjudicative officer for whom the clerk works. MRPC 1.12(b).

5) Meaning of "matter"

For purposes of determining a conflict by a former or current government lawyer, the Model Rules define the term "matter" as including: (i) any judicial or other proceeding, application, request for a ruling or other determination, contract, claim, controversy, investigation, charge, accusation, arrest or other particular matter involving a specific party or parties; and (ii) any other matter covered by the conflict of interest rules of the appropriate government agency. MRPC 1.11(e).

3. Conflicts Involving Prospective Clients

a. General rule

In general, a lawyer may not represent a client with interests materially adverse to those of a prospective client in the same or a substantially related matter if the lawyer received information from the prospective client that could be significantly harmful to that person in the matter. MRPC 1.18(c).

b. Exceptions

1) Informed consent

Representation is permissible if the affected and prospective clients each give informed consent, confirmed in writing. MRPC 1.18(d).

2) Limited exposure, screening, and notice

Representation is also permissible if: (i) the lawyer who received the information took reasonable measures to avoid exposure to more disqualifying information than was reasonably necessary to determine whether to represent the prospective client; (ii) the disqualified lawyer is timely screened from any participation in the matter and gets no part of the fee; and (iii) written notice is promptly given to the prospective client.

c. Disqualification of firm

If a lawyer is disqualified from representation in a conflict involving a prospective client, no lawyer in a firm with which that lawyer is associated may knowingly undertake or continue representation in such a matter.

d. Duty of confidentiality

A lawyer may not use or reveal information learned during a discussion with a prospective client to the extent that use or revelation would be prohibited under the rules for former clients. MRPC 1.18(b). Note that the attorney-client privilege may also apply to a confidential communication by the prospective client.

F. INFLUENCE BY PERSONS OTHER THAN CLIENT

1. Responsibility to Third Party

A lawyer must not represent a client if there is a significant risk that the representation of the client will be **materially limited** by the lawyer's responsibilities to a third person (e.g., as a guardian) unless:

i) The lawyer reasonably believes that the lawyer will be able to provide competent and diligent representation to the client;

ii) The representation is not prohibited by law; and

iii) The client gives consent after consultation, confirmed in writing.

MRPC 1.7(a),(b).

2. Payment From a Third Party

A lawyer may not accept payment for representation from someone other than the client, **unless**: (i) the client gives informed consent; (ii) there is no interference with the lawyer's professional judgment; and (iii) client-lawyer confidentiality is preserved. MRPC 1.8(f).

> **EXAM NOTE:** A common exam question involves a parent paying for representation of a son or daughter. Remember that a competent child, not the parent, is the client whose expressed interests govern.

3. Organization as Client

a. Lawyer's Representation of Organization

A lawyer employed or retained to represent an organization (e.g., corporation) represents the organization acting through its duly authorized constituents (e.g. employees, officers, directors). An organizational lawyer owes the duties of loyalty and confidentiality to the organization. MRPC 1.13(a).

1) Duty to constituents of organization

In dealing with an organization's constituents (e.g., directors, officers, employees, members, shareholders), a lawyer must explain the identity of the client when the lawyer knows or reasonably should know that the organization's interests are adverse to those of the constituents with whom the lawyer is dealing. MRPC 1.13(f).

2) Representing both the organization and an employee

A lawyer may represent both the organization and its constituents (e.g., employees) as long as no other conflict exists. If the organization's consent to the dual representation is required, the consent must be given by an appropriate official within the organization other than the individual who is to be represented, or by the shareholders. MRPC 1.13(g).

b. Rectifying misconduct

Upon learning of an action (or intent to act or refusal to act) by a person associated with the organization (e.g., employee, officer, director) that will **likely cause substantial injury to the organization**, the lawyer must proceed as is reasonably necessary in the best interest of the organization.

1) Reporting misconduct

a) To authority within the organization

Unless the lawyer reasonably believes that it is not necessary in the best interest of the organization to do so, the lawyer must refer the matter to higher authority in the organization, including, if warranted by the circumstances to the highest authority that can act on behalf of the organization as determined by applicable law.

b) To authority outside the organization

If the lawyer has reported to the highest authority that can act on behalf of the organization and that authority insists on or fails to address in a timely and appropriate manner an action, or a refusal to act, that is **a clear violation of law** and the lawyer reasonably believes that the violation is reasonably certain to result in substantial injury to the organization, then the lawyer may reveal information relating to the representation, but only if and to the extent the lawyer reasonably believes necessary to prevent the substantial injury. MRPC 1.13(c).

If the lawyer was engaged to investigate a violation of the law or defend the organization against a claim arising out of a violation of the law, the lawyer is prohibited from revealing information related to the lawyer's representation. MRPC 1.13(d).

2) If lawyer is discharged or forced to withdraw for reporting misconduct

A lawyer who reasonably believes that he has been discharged because of his actions in reporting misconduct pursuant to the Model Rules, or who withdraws under circumstances that require or permit him to take action under the Model Rules, must proceed as he reasonably believes necessary to assure that the organization's highest authority is informed of the lawyer's discharge or withdrawal. MRPC 1.13(e).

3) Sarbanes-Oxley Act (SOX) requirements

a) Lawyer's duty under SOX

Under the Sarbanes-Oxley Act (SOX), 17 CFR §§ 205.1-205.7, the Securities and Exchange Commission (SEC) established rules of professional conduct for securities lawyers. Securities lawyers practice before the SEC and represent an issuer of securities (publicly-traded corporation). SOX § 307 obligates securities lawyers to report any evidence of **reasonably likely material violations of federal or state securities laws** to the chief legal officer or both the chief legal officer and chief executive officer within the corporation.

Note that the SEC rule requires that the violation merely be "reasonably likely," whereas MRPC 1.13 requires actual knowledge of a material violation.

b) Chief legal officer's duty under SOX

The chief legal officer is required to investigate to determine if a material violation did occur, is ongoing, or is about to occur, and must take reasonable steps to advise the corporation to adopt an appropriate response, unless the lawyer reasonably believes that there is no such violation. Instead of investigating, the chief legal officer may refer the issue to a qualified legal compliance committee, if one already exists.

c) Report to corporate officers is futile or officers fail to respond

If the securities lawyer reporting the matter reasonably believes it would be futile to report the issue to the chief legal officer or chief executive officer or, after doing so, reasonably believes that they have not provided an appropriate response within a reasonable time, the lawyer must report the issue to one of the following: (i) the audit committee of the board of directors; (ii) a committee made up entirely of outside (independent, non-officer) directors; or (iii) the entire board of directors.

d) Direct reporting to the SEC

A securities lawyer may report a material violation directly to the SEC without the consent of the client in order to: (i) prevent the client from committing a violation that will cause substantial injury to the corporation or its shareholders; (ii) prevent the client from committing or suborning perjury; or (iii) to mitigate or remedy a financial injury to the client or shareholders.

e) Compliance with or failure to comply with SOX

A securities lawyer cannot be subject to professional discipline or civil liability for reporting to the SEC or complying with the terms of SOX.

A securities lawyer who does not comply with the terms of SOX is subject to civil penalties and may be denied the privilege of practicing before the SEC.

G. IMPUTED DISQUALIFICATION

1. Imputation of Conflicts Generally

In general, if one lawyer in a firm is prohibited by the conflict of interest rules from representing a client, that prohibition applies to all other lawyers in the firm.

a. Waiver by the client

Such a disqualification may be waived by the affected client if: (i) the lawyer reasonably believes that she will be able to provide competent and diligent representation to the affected client; (ii) the representation is not prohibited by law; (iii) the representation does not involve the assertion of a claim by one client against another client represented by the lawyer in the same litigation or other proceeding before a tribunal; and (iv) the affected client gives informed consent, confirmed in writing. MRPC 1.10(c); 1.7.

b. No imputation of conflicts for involvement of non-lawyer employees

The rule of imputed disqualification does not prohibit representation by others in a law firm when the person prohibited from involvement in a matter is a non-lawyer (e.g., paralegal, legal secretary). Such persons, however, must generally be screened from any personal participation in the matter to avoid communication to others in the firm of confidential information that both the non-lawyers and the firm have a legal duty to protect. If a nonlawyer employee in fact conveys confidential information learned about a client in one firm to lawyers in another, a prohibition on representation by the second firm is warranted. (Note that a similar approach is required when a lawyer is prohibited from involvement in a matter because of events before the individual became a lawyer, such as involvement in a matter as a law student.) MRPC 1.10, cmt. 4; Restatement (Third) of the Law Governing Lawyers § 123, cmt. f.

2. Exception: Lawyer Changes Firms

If a lawyer switches firms and has a conflict of interest because of the lawyer's previous representation of a client or the prior law firm's previous representation of a client pursuant to MRPC 1.9, the disqualified lawyer's conflict is not imputed to the new law firm if:

i) The disqualified lawyer is timely screened from any participation in the matter and is apportioned no part of the fee;

ii) Written notice is promptly given to any affected former client so that the client can determine if there has been compliance with the Model Rules; and

iii) Certifications of compliance with the Model Rules and with the screening procedures are provided to the former client by the screened lawyer and by a partner at the firm at reasonable intervals, upon written request by the former client, and if the screening procedures are terminated.

MRPC 1.10(a)(2).

Note that if all of the above requirements are met, the former client's consent is not required.

a. Contents of notice

The notice provided to the affected former client must describe the screening procedures used, state compliance with the confidentiality provisions of the Model Rules by the disqualified lawyer and the firm, indicate that review before a tribunal may be available, and provide that the firm will respond promptly to any written questions or objections by the client about the screening procedures. MRPC 1.10(a)(2)(ii).

b. Fee restriction

The requirement that the disqualified lawyer not be apportioned any part of the fee does not prohibit the lawyer from receiving a salary or partnership share that is established by prior independent agreement. The disqualified lawyer may not receive compensation that is directly related to the matter from which the lawyer is disqualified. MRPC 1.10, cmt. 8.

3. Exception: Personal Interest

If the prohibition is based on a **personal interest** of the disqualified lawyer and does not present a **significant risk of materially limiting the representation of the client** by the remaining lawyers in the firm, the disqualified lawyer's conflict is not imputed to the firm. MRPC 1.10(a)(1). Disqualification arising from a close family relationship, for example, is considered personal and ordinarily is not imputed to members of the firm with whom the lawyer is associated. MRPC 1.7, cmt. 11.

4. Sexual Relationship with a Client

If a lawyer is involved in a sexual relationship with the client, the Model Rules provide that the resulting conflict is personal to the lawyer and is not imputed to others in the lawyer's firm. MRPC 1.8(k).

H. CONFLICTS BASED ON LAWYER'S SERVICE AS ARBITRATOR, MEDIATOR, OR JUDGE

1. General Rule

A lawyer may not represent anyone in connection with a matter in which the lawyer participated **personally and substantially** as a judge or other adjudicative officer, law clerk, arbitrator, mediator or other neutral third party, unless all parties to the proceeding give informed consent, confirmed in writing. MRPC 1.12(a). A judge who was a member of a multi-member court, and then returned to private practice, would not be prohibited from representing a client in a matter pending in the court, but in which the former judge did not participate. Similarly, the fact that a former judge exercised administrative responsibility in a court would not prevent him from acting as a lawyer in a matter in which the judge had previously exercised remote or incidental administrative responsibility that did not affect the merits of the case. MRPC 1.12, cmt. 1.

2. Exception

An arbitrator selected as a **partisan** of a party in a multi-member arbitration panel is not prohibited from subsequently representing such party. MRPC 1.12(d).

3. Disqualification of Firm

If a lawyer is disqualified for having participated personally and substantially as a judge or other adjudicative officer, law clerk, arbitrator, mediator or other third-party neutral, no lawyer in a firm with which that lawyer is associated may knowingly undertake or continue representation in the matter unless: (i) the disqualified lawyer is timely screened from any participation in the matter and gets no part of the fee; and (ii) written notice is promptly given to the parties and any appropriate tribunal to enable them to determine if the ethics rules have been met. MRPC 1.12(c).

4. Negotiation for Employment

A lawyer who is participating personally and substantially as a judge or other adjudicative officer, arbitrator, mediator or other third-party neutral may not negotiate for employment with any person who is involved as a party or lawyer for a party in the matter. A lawyer serving as a law clerk may negotiate for employment with a party or lawyer involved in a matter in which the clerk is participating personally and substantially, but only after the lawyer has notified the judge or other adjudicative officer for whom the lawyer works. MRPC 1.12(b).

VI. COMPETENCE, LEGAL MALPRACTICE, AND OTHER LIABILITY

A. PROFESSIONAL COMPETENCE

A lawyer is obligated to provide competent representation to a client and must possess the legal knowledge, skill, thoroughness, and preparation reasonably necessary for the representation. MRPC 1.1.

1. **Knowledge and Skill**

   a. **In general**

   Factors relevant to determining whether a lawyer has the requisite knowledge and skill in a particular matter include the relative complexity and specialized nature of the matter, the lawyer's general experience, the lawyer's training and experience in the field in question, the preparation and study the lawyer is able to give the matter and whether it is feasible to refer the matter to, or associate or consult with, a lawyer of established competence in the field in question. MRPC 1.1, cmt. 1. In some cases, all that is necessary in a case is the proficiency of a general practitioner. Expertise in a particular field of law may be required in some circumstances, however.

   b. **Competency through preparation or association**

   A lawyer may accept representation when the requisite level of competence can be achieved by reasonable preparation. This also applies to a lawyer who is appointed as counsel for an unrepresented person. MRPC 1.1, cmt. 4. Competent representation can also be provided through the association with a lawyer of established competence in the field. MRPC 1.1, cmt. 2.

   c. **Emergencies**

   In an emergency, a lawyer may give advice or assistance in a matter in which the lawyer does not have the skill ordinarily required if referral to or consultation or association with another lawyer would be impractical. Assistance should be limited, however, to what is reasonably necessary under the circumstances. MRPC 1.1, cmt. 3.

2. **Thoroughness and Preparation**

   Whether a lawyer is properly prepared is determined by the degree of complexity and consequence of the matter. Major litigation and complex transactions ordinarily require more extensive treatment than matters of lesser complexity and consequence. A lawyer's responsibility to prepare may further be limited by an agreement between the lawyer and client as to the scope of the representation. MRPC 1.1, cmt. 5.

3. **Retaining or Contracting With Other Lawyers**

   Before a lawyer retains or contracts with lawyers outside the lawyer's own firm to provide or assist in the provision of legal services to a client, the lawyer should obtain informed consent from the client and must reasonably believe that the other lawyers' services will contribute to the competent and ethical representation of the client. The reasonableness of the decision to retain or contract with other lawyers depends upon the circumstances, including the education, experience, and reputation of the other lawyers; the nature of the services assigned to the other lawyers; and the laws and professional conduct rules of the jurisdictions in which the services will be performed, particularly relating to confidential information. MRPC 1.1, cmt. 6

   When lawyers from more than one law firm are providing legal services to the client on a particular matter, the lawyers should consult with each other and the client about the scope of their respective representations and the allocation of responsibility among them. MRPC 1.1, cmt. 7.

4. **Maintaining Competence**

   To maintain the requisite knowledge and skill, a lawyer should make efforts to keep abreast of changes in the law and its practice, including the benefits and risks associated with relevant technology, engage in continuing study and education, and comply with all continuing legal education requirements to which the lawyer is subject. MRPC 1.1, cmt. 8.

5. Lacking Competence

A lawyer lacking the necessary knowledge or experience must:

i) **Decline or withdraw** from representing the client;

ii) **Become competent** without unreasonable delay; or

iii) **Associate** with competent counsel.

A lawyer should not accept representation in a matter unless it can be performed competently. MRPC 1.16, cmt. 1.

A lawyer can accept representation of a client when the lawyer reasonably believes that she can become competent without unreasonable delay without disclosing her lack of competency to the client.

A lawyer who represents a client incompetently is subject to the punishment determined by the disciplinary tribunal, regardless of causation or any financial loss to the client.

A client cannot consent to the less than competent representation. Even if the client does "consent" (perhaps because the lawyer's services are offered at a low fee or because of friendship), the lawyer providing incompetent services is subject to discipline.

B. DILIGENCE

A lawyer must act with reasonable diligence and promptness in representing a client. MRPC 1.3.

1. Dedication to Client's Interests

The lawyer must be dedicated and committed to the interests of the client despite obstruction or inconvenience to the lawyer. A lawyer is not bound, however, to press for every possible advantage that might be realized for a client. The lawyer's duty to act with reasonable diligence does not require the use of offensive tactics or prohibit treating all persons involved in the legal process with courtesy and respect. MRPC 1.3, cmt. 1.

2. Controlled Workload

A lawyer cannot justify a lack of diligence based on illness, subordinates, personal animosity, or the inability to balance other work. A lawyer must control her workload to ensure that all matters are handled competently. MRPC 1.3, cmt. 2.

3. Reasonable Promptness

A lawyer must act with reasonable promptness in representing a client. A client's interests can often be adversely affected by the passage of time or a change of conditions. Moreover, unreasonable delay can cause a client anxiety and undermine confidence in the trustworthiness of the lawyer. A lawyer's duty to act with reasonable promptness, however, does not prohibit the lawyer from agreeing to a **reasonable** request for a postponement that will not prejudice the lawyer's client. MRPC 1.3, cmt. 3.

4. Pursuing Matter to Completion

The lawyer should follow through on all matters until completion as outlined by the agreement between the lawyer and the client. Whether the lawyer is obligated to prosecute an appeal for a client depends on the agreed-upon scope of the representation. If there is any doubt about the status of the relationship, the lawyer should clarify it, preferably in writing. MRPC 1.3, cmt. 4.

> Misleading a client about the status of the lawyer's progress is its own violation separate from a diligence violation. MRPC 1.4, cmt. 7.

5. Duty of Solo Practitioner

In order to prevent neglect of client matters in the event of death or disability of a sole practitioner, the practitioner should prepare a plan, in conformity with applicable rules, that designates another competent lawyer to review client files, notify each client of the lawyer's death or disability, and determine whether there is a need for immediate protective action. MRPC 1.3, cmt. 5.

C. MALPRACTICE

1. Professional Discipline vs. Malpractice

a. Professional discipline

Professional discipline is a penalty that is imposed on a lawyer by the state disciplinary authority for violating a rule of professional responsibility (i.e., the Model Rules). While a complaint is initially brought to the state disciplinary authority by the aggrieved client or anyone with knowledge of the violation, it is prosecuted by the state disciplinary authority itself. The complaint is investigated by a grievance committee and if the committee finds merit to the charges, it will hold a hearing limited to the charges brought in the complaint. The accused lawyer is entitled to notice, counsel, and an opportunity to be heard, and also has the right to introduce evidence and cross-examine witnesses. The burden of proof is on the party prosecuting the matter. If the committee finds that the charges are warranted, it will recommend appropriate sanctions (e.g., private or public censure, suspension from practice, disbarment). The lawyer will have the right to review of the committee's decision by the highest court in the state.

> Keep in mind that, unlike a successful malpractice action, violation of a rule of professional responsibility does not require a finding that a client has been harmed. MRPC, Scope, cmt. 20.

b. Malpractice

In addition to professional discipline, a lawyer who violates an ethics rule may also potentially be subject to **civil liability** for malpractice. While sanctions for violation of the disciplinary rules are aimed at punishing a lawyer and protecting the public from future violations, damages for malpractice compensate an injured client or third party. A malpractice action is brought in a civil court and is prosecuted by the injured client or third party.

> The mere violation of a rule of professional responsibility does not automatically result in a finding of malpractice. It is not negligence per se. Violation of a rule is, however, generally treated as evidence that the lawyer's conduct violated the duty of care.

2. Malpractice Theories

Malpractice can be based on a variety of different legal theories including:

a. Breach of contract for not fulfilling a duty

A lawyer can be found liable for malpractice for breaching an express or implied agreement with a client. Restatement (Third) of the Law Governing Lawyers § 55.

b. Breach of the fiduciary relationship between the lawyer and the client

Malpractice can be found for a lawyer's breach of fiduciary duties owed to a client, such as loyalty, confidentiality, honesty, and fair dealing. Fiduciary duties may also arise when a lawyer acts in another capacity, such as trustee, executor, or escrow agent. Restatement (Third) of the Law Governing Lawyers §§ 48, cmt. d; 56, cmt. h.

c. Intentional tort

A lawyer may be liable for malpractice for intentional torts including fraud, intentional infliction of emotional distress, malicious prosecution, and abuse of process. Restatement (Third) of the Law Governing Lawyers § 56, cmts. f, g.

d. Negligence

Negligence is the most commonly asserted malpractice theory and is discussed immediately below in detail.

3. Malpractice Based on Negligence

A lawyer may be liable for malpractice based on negligence if the client establishes the elements of negligence, unless the lawyer has a valid defense. Restatement (Third) of the Law Governing Lawyers §§ 48-54.

a. Duty of care

A lawyer owes a duty of care to the client. The duty of care is generally the competence and diligence exercised by lawyers of similar experience under similar conditions. Unless properly disclaimed, a lawyer must exercise any special skill he has. If a lawyer represents to the client that he has specialized expertise, the lawyer is held to the standard of care of a specialist.

b. Breach of duty

c. Causation

The client must establish that but for the lawyer's breach the client's injury would not have occurred, and that it is reasonable to hold the lawyer responsible for the injury caused.

d. Actual damages

The client must demonstrate that she suffered actual damages, such as money that was lost as a result of losing the case due to the lawyer's actions.

e. Defenses

Comparative negligence, or, where recognized instead, contributory negligence, may serve as a defense to a malpractice action. Assumption of the risk may also be available, but is subject to consideration of a lawyer's fiduciary duties. A lawyer is not subject to liability for malpractice for failing to act in a manner that the lawyer reasonably believes is prohibited by law, court order, or a professional rule. Restatement (Third) of the Law Governing Lawyers § 54(1), cmt. d, e, h.

4. Vicarious Liability

a. Law firm liability

A law firm may be civilly liable for compensatory damages resulting from an injury caused by the wrongful conduct a principal (e.g., partner) or an employee of the firm who was acting in the ordinary course of the firm's business or with actual or apparent authority. Restatement (Third) of the Law Governing Lawyers § 58(1), cmt. f.

b. General partners liability

If the law firm is a general partnership, the partners are also jointly and severally liable with the firm. Restatement (Third) of the Law Governing Lawyers § 58(2), cmt. c.

Individual partners need not be named in a suit against the partnership in order to collect a judgment out of partnership assets. However, a judgment against a partnership is not a judgment against its partners. Unless there is also a judgment against the partner, a judgment against a partnership cannot be satisfied from a partner's assets, only from the partnership's assets. Revised Uniform Partnership Act § 307(a-c), inc. cmts. 2, 3.

Even though a partner is personally liable for a partnership obligation, a partnership creditor generally must exhaust the partnership's assets before levying on the partners' personal assets. Exceptions exist when the partnership is a debtor in bankruptcy, the partner has consented, or the partner is liable independent of the partnership, such as when the partner was the primary tortfeasor. In addition, a court may authorize execution against a partner's assets when the partnership's assets are clearly insufficient, exhaustion of the partnership's assets would be excessively burdensome, or it is otherwise equitable to do so. Revised Uniform Partnership Act § 307(d); Restatement (Third) of the Law Governing Lawyers § 58(2), cmt. g.

c. Other principals' liability

If the firm is a professional corporation, a limited liability partnership, or a limited liability company, a principal of the firm is typically not subject to vicarious liability, but can, of course, be liable for the principal's own negligence, which can include negligent supervision of another member or employee of the firm. A lawyer of a corporate law department or a governmental agency is not vicariously liable for damages cause by another lawyer in the department or agency. Restatement (Third) of the Law Governing Lawyers § 58(3), cmt. c.

5. Limiting Malpractice Recovery

A lawyer may not enter into an agreement with a client prospectively limiting malpractice liability to the client, unless the client is represented by another independent lawyer in making the agreement. MRPC 1.8(h)(1). *See* V.D.4. Promise to limit malpractice recovery, *supra*.

6. Settlement of Malpractice Claims

A lawyer may not settle a claim or potential claim for malpractice liability with an unrepresented client or former client unless that person is advised in writing of the desirability of seeking independent legal counsel with regard to the settlement and is given a reasonable opportunity to seek such advice. MRPC 1.8(h)(2).

7. Malpractice Insurance

As legal malpractice disputes have increased, most lawyers today carry professional liability or legal malpractice insurance. Oregon is the only state to specifically require lawyers to carry malpractice insurance, but many states, including Arizona, Colorado, Illinois, Massachusetts, Michigan, North Carolina, and Virginia, require lawyers to disclose their insurance status to the appropriate agency with the authority to administer the standards for admission to practice and for the maintenance of professional competence and integrity. A few states, including California, Ohio, and Pennsylvania, require disclosure directly to potential clients. Many clients, especially larger companies, require proof of professional liability insurance before they will enter into an engagement with any legal firm.

D. CIVIL LIABILITY TO NON-CLIENTS

1. Tort Liability

a. Inviting reliance of non-client

Under certain circumstances, a lawyer may owe a duty to a non-client when the non-client has been invited to rely on the opinion or legal services of the lawyer. A lawyer owes a duty to use care to a non-client when and to the extent that: (i) the lawyer or, with the lawyer's acquiescence, the lawyer's client, invites the non-client to rely on the opinion of the lawyer or the lawyer's provision of other legal services; (ii) the non-client so relies; and (iii) the non-client is not, under applicable tort law, too remote from the lawyer to be entitled to protection. (*See* § VIII.B.2, Lawyer as Evaluator, *infra*.) A lawyer may avoid liability by making clear that any opinion or representation is directed only to the client and should not be relied on by others. Restatement (Third) of the Law Governing Lawyers § 51(2).

b. Non-client enforcing a lawyer's duties to a client

Sometimes, a lawyer may owe a duty to a non-client when the lawyer knows that the client intends the lawyer's services to benefit the non-client. A lawyer will owe a duty to use care to a non-client when and to the extent that: (i) the lawyer knows that the client intends as one of the primary objectives of the representation that the lawyer's services benefit the non-client; (ii) such duty would not significantly impair the lawyer's performance of obligations to the client; and (iii) the absence of such duty would make enforcement of those obligations to the client unlikely. Restatement (Third) of the Law Governing Lawyers § 51(3).

> **Example:** An attorney is designated by an insurance company to defend the insured party in a civil suit. The attorney negligently fails to oppose a motion for summary judgment against the insured party, and the insurance company is then required to pay the subsequent adverse judgment. The insurance company has a claim against the attorney for any proximately caused loss. Both the insurance company and the insured party have a reasonable expectation under the insurance contract that the attorney's services will benefit both the insurer and the insured. No duty would arise, however, if it would significantly impair, under the circumstances of the representation, the attorney's obligations to the insured party.

c. Duty based on knowledge of a breach of fiduciary duty owed by a client

A lawyer representing a client in the client's capacity as a fiduciary may in some circumstances be liable to a beneficiary for failure to use care to protect that beneficiary. A lawyer will owe a duty to use care to a non-client when and to the extent that: (i) the lawyer's client is a trustee, guardian, executor, or fiduciary acting primarily to perform similar functions for the non-client; (ii) the lawyer knows that appropriate action by the lawyer is necessary with respect to a matter within the scope of the representation to prevent or rectify the breach of a fiduciary duty owed by the client to the non-client, when the breach is a crime or fraud or the lawyer has assisted or is assisting the breach; (iii) the non-client is not reasonably able to protect its rights; and (iv) such a duty would not significantly impair the performance of the lawyer's obligations to the client. Restatement (Third) of the Law Governing Lawyers § 51(4).

Example: An attorney represents a client in her capacity as the trustee of an express trust for the benefit of a beneficiary. The client tells the attorney that she intends to transfer trust funds into her personal account under circumstances that would constitute embezzlement under state law. The attorney tells the client that the transfer would be criminal, but the client transfers the funds, and shortly thereafter the attorney learns of this transfer. The attorney takes no steps to rectify the consequences, such as informing the beneficiary or the court to which the client, as trustee, is required to make an annual accounting. The state's professional responsibility rules do not forbid such disclosures. The funds are subsequently lost, to the beneficiary's detriment. The attorney is subject to liability to the beneficiary.

Example: Assume the same facts as above, except that the client falsely tells the attorney that the funds are being transferred to another account of the trust. Even though the attorney could have exercised diligence to determine that the client's assertion was false and did not do so, the attorney did not owe the beneficiary any duty to use care because the attorney did not **know** that appropriate action was necessary to prevent a breach of fiduciary duty by the client.

d. Defenses to specific tort actions

1) Defamation

A lawyer has an absolute defense to a defamation action for the publication of a matter relating to a non-client if:

i) The publication occurs in communications initiating or made during the course of legal proceedings or preliminary to a reasonably anticipated legal proceeding;

ii) The lawyer participates as counsel in the proceedings;

iii) The matter is published to someone who may be involved in the proceedings; and

iv) The publication has some relation to the proceedings.

Restatement (Third) of the Law Governing Lawyers § 57(1).

2) Wrongful use of civil proceedings or malicious prosecution

A lawyer representing a client in a civil proceeding or procuring the institution of criminal proceedings for a client is not liable to a non-client for wrongful use of civil proceedings or for malicious prosecution if the lawyer has probable cause for acting, or if the lawyer acts primarily to help the client obtain a proper adjudication of the client's claim in that proceeding. Restatement (Third) of the Law Governing Lawyers § 57(2).

3) Interference with contractual or prospective contractual relationship

A lawyer is not subject to liability for interference with a contractual or prospective contractual relationship if the lawyer acts to advance the client's objectives without using wrongful means, such as threatening an unfounded criminal prosecution. Generally, a lawyer does not incur civil liability for advising a client not to enter into a contract or to breach an existing contract, or for assisting a client in such a breach, for example, by sending a letter that states the client's intention not to perform the contract. If the lawyer has the purpose of promoting the client's welfare, then it is immaterial that the lawyer also hopes to benefit. Restatement (Third) of the Law Governing Lawyers § 57(3).

2. Liability for contracts entered on client's behalf

a. Undisclosed principal

Unless at the time of contracting the lawyer or third person disclaimed such liability, a lawyer is subject to liability to a third person on a contract the lawyer entered into on a client's behalf if the client's existence or identity was not disclosed to the third person. Restatement (Third) of the Law Governing Lawyers § 30(2).

b. Contracts for goods or services normally provided to lawyers

Unless at the time of contracting the lawyer or third person disclaimed such liability, a lawyer is subject to liability to a third person on a contract the lawyer entered into on a client's behalf if the contract is between the lawyer and a third person who provides goods or services used by lawyers and who, as the lawyer knows or reasonably should know, is relying on the lawyer's credit. Restatement (Third) of the Law Governing Lawyers § 30(2). Liability normally attaches unless the lawyer disclaims liability or the circumstances show that the third person did not rely on the lawyer's credit.

c. Liability for unauthorized acts

A lawyer is subject to liability to a third person for damages for loss proximately caused by the lawyer's acting without authority from the client if:

i) The lawyer tortiously misrepresents to the third person that the lawyer has authority to make a contract, conveyance, or affirmation on behalf of the client and the third person reasonably relies on such misrepresentation; or

ii) The lawyer purports to make a contract, conveyance, or affirmation on the client's behalf, unless the lawyer manifests that he does not warrant that he is authorized to act or the third person knows that the lawyer is not authorized to act.

Restatement (Third) of the Law Governing Lawyers § 30(3).

E. CRIMINAL LIABILITY

A lawyer is generally guilty of a crime committed in the course of representing a client to the same extent and on the same basis as a non-lawyer acting in a similar manner. In order to ascertain whether a lawyer's conduct constitutes a crime, the lawyer's compliance or failure to comply with the applicable rules of professional conduct is relevant. A lawyer who advises a client as to activities that constitute a crime is not criminally liable when the client commits the crime if the lawyer did not know of the client's intended use of the advice or the lawyer attempted to dissuade the client from committing the crime. Restatement (Third) of the Law Governing Lawyers § 8.

VII. LITIGATION AND OTHER FORMS OF ADVOCACY

A. AUTHORITY TO ACT FOR CLIENT

A lawyer is the client's advocate before a court or other tribunal. As discussed at III.B. Scope, Objective, and Means of the Representation, *supra*, the client controls the objectives of the representation within the limits imposed by law and the lawyer's professional obligations. MRPC 1.2. With respect to the means by which the client's objectives are to be pursued, the lawyer may generally take such action as she is impliedly authorized to take to carry out the representation. The Model Rules require the lawyer to reasonably consult with the client about the means to be used to accomplish the client's objectives. MRPC 1.2, 1.4. Depending on the importance of the action under consideration and the feasibility of consulting with the client, such consultation will generally be required before the action is taken. Sometimes, as during a trial when an immediate decision must be made, the exigency of the circumstances may require the lawyer to act without prior consultation of the client. The lawyer must still act reasonably to inform the client of actions the lawyer has taken on the client's behalf.

B. IMPARTIALITY, CIVILITY, COURTESY, AND DECORUM

1. Conduct Before the Tribunal

A lawyer must not engage in conduct intended to disrupt a tribunal. This duty applies to any proceeding of a tribunal, including a deposition. MRPC 3.5(d), cmt. 5.

2. Civility and Courtesy

As an advocate for his client, the lawyer's role is to present evidence and argument so that the cause may be decided according to law. As an advocate, a lawyer must refrain from abusive or unruly conduct. A lawyer may stand firm against abuse by a judge but should avoid reciprocating. MRPC 3.5, cmt. 4.

3. Avoiding Improper Influence

A lawyer must not seek to influence a judge, juror, prospective juror, or other official by means prohibited by law. MRPC 3.5(a).

C. CONDUCT IN THE COURSE OF LITIGATION

1. Duty to Avoid Frivolous Claims

a. In general

A lawyer is prohibited from bringing or defending a proceeding, or asserting or opposing an issue in a proceeding unless there is a basis in law and fact for doing so that is not frivolous. A good faith argument for an extension, modification, or reversal of existing law is not frivolous. MRPC 3.1.

This prohibition does not extend to situations other than legal proceedings in which a lawyer may represent a client. such as an appearance before legislative committee.

b. Frivolous

An action will be considered frivolous if the lawyer is unable either to make a good faith argument on the merits of the action taken or to support the action taken by a good faith argument for an extension, modification, or reversal of existing law. The filing of an action or defense or similar action taken for a client will not be considered frivolous merely because the facts have not first been fully substantiated or because the lawyer expects to develop critical evidence only through discovery. An action is also not frivolous merely because the lawyer believes that the client's position ultimately will not prevail. MRPC 3.1, cmt. 2.

c. Criminal defense

A lawyer for the defendant in a criminal proceeding, or the respondent in a proceeding that could result in incarceration, may nevertheless so defend the proceeding as to require that every element of the case be established beyond a reasonable doubt, even if there is not a factual or legal basis for challenging the element. MRPC 3.1.

d. Claims brought to embarrass, delay, or burden a third person

A claim that is brought merely to embarrass, delay, or burden a third person is a violation of the Model Rules. MRPC 4.4(a).

e. Rule 11 sanctions

Federal Rule of Civil Procedure (FRCP) 11 imposes sanctions for filing frivolous pleadings and motions (other than a discovery request or response) and taking frivolous positions.

By presenting to the court a pleading, written motion, or other paper, a lawyer certifies that to the best of his knowledge, information, and belief, formed after an inquiry reasonable under the circumstances: (i) the paper is not being presented for any improper purpose, such as to harass, cause unnecessary delay, or needlessly increase the cost of litigation; (ii) the claims, defenses, and other legal contentions are warranted by existing law or by a non-frivolous argument for extending, modifying, or reversing existing law or for establishing new law; (iii) the factual contentions have evidentiary support or, if specifically so identified, will likely have evidentiary support after a reasonable opportunity for further investigation or discovery; and (iv) the denials of factual contentions are warranted on the evidence or, if specifically so identified, are reasonably based on belief or a lack of information. "Presenting" a pleading under FRCP 11 includes "signing, filing, submitting, or later advocating" a position presented in the pleading. Fed. R. Civ. P. 11(b).

The standard for determining whether the lawyer conducted an objectively reasonable investigation into the factual and legal support for the claim or position is based on what a similarly-situated lawyer would have done under the circumstances. Many states have a similar procedural rule.

2. Duty to Expedite Litigation

a. In general

A lawyer must make reasonable efforts to expedite litigation consistent with the interests of the client. MRPC 3.2. In doing so, a lawyer must balance the duty to use legal procedures to the fullest benefit of the client with the duty not to abuse such procedures. MRPC 3.1, cmt. 1.

b. Test

A lawyer will not be subject to discipline under this standard if a competent lawyer acting in good faith would regard the course of action taken as having some substantial purpose other than delay. It is not reasonable to fail to expedite a matter if done for the purpose of frustrating an opposing party's attempt to obtain **rightful** redress or repose. Realizing a financial or other benefit from otherwise improper delay in litigation is **not** a legitimate interest of the client. MRPC 3.2, cmt. 1.

c. Postponement for personal reasons of lawyer

While a lawyer may sometimes properly seek a postponement for personal reasons, it is not proper for a lawyer to routinely fail to expedite litigation solely for the convenience of the advocates. MRPC 3.2, cmt. 1.

3. Duty of Candor to the Tribunal

A lawyer who is representing a client in the proceedings of a tribunal (*see* I.C.1.a. "Tribunal," above) has the duty of candor. This duty also applies when the lawyer is representing a client in an ancillary proceeding conducted pursuant to the tribunal's authority, such as a deposition. MRPC 3.3, cmt. 1.

The duty of candor applies through the conclusion of the proceeding, which is defined as when a final judgment in the proceeding has been affirmed on appeal or the time for review has passed. MRPC 3.3(c), cmt. 13. It applies even if compliance requires disclosure of information otherwise protected by the ethical duty of confidentiality. MRPC 3.3(c).

a. Statements about the law

A lawyer must not knowingly make a false statement of law to the court, but the lawyer is free to make non-frivolous arguments regarding the law that favor the client. MRPC 3.3(a)(1).

1) Duty to correct

A lawyer is also required to correct a false statement of law previously made to the tribunal by the lawyer. MRPC 3.3(a)(1).

2) Controlling adverse legal authority

A lawyer must disclose to the tribunal legal authority in the controlling jurisdiction known to the lawyer to be directly adverse to the position of the client and that was not disclosed by opposing counsel. MRPC 3.3(a)(2). The lawyer may argue against the authority and seek to have it overturned.

b. Factual statements

1) In general

The duty of candor also applies to factual statements made by the lawyer to the tribunal. A lawyer must not knowingly make a false statement of fact to a tribunal or fail to correct a false statement of material fact previously made to the tribunal by the lawyer. MRPC 3.3(a)(1). While a lawyer is responsible for pleadings and other documents prepared for litigation, the lawyer is not usually required to have personal knowledge of matters asserted in the pleadings and documents, which are generally assertions by the client, or by someone on the client's behalf, and not assertions of the lawyer. If an assertion purports to be on the basis of the lawyer's own knowledge (e.g., in an affidavit by the lawyer or in a statement made in open court), it may only be made when the lawyer knows the assertion is true or believes it to be true on the basis of a reasonably diligent inquiry. MRPC 3.3, cmt. 3.

2) Failure to disclose

A lawyer is not under a general duty to reveal facts unfavorable to the client, unless doing so is necessary to avoid assisting in a criminal or fraudulent act by the client. A lawyer who voluntarily offers adverse facts may be subject to discipline for breaching the duty of loyalty. Under certain circumstances, however, a failure to make a disclosure would be the equivalent of an affirmative misrepresentation. Thus, if the lawyer fails to correct what she knows to be a court's erroneous understanding of a fact, such failure would be improper.

a) Ex parte proceeding

In an ex parte proceeding (e.g., an application for a temporary restraining order), a lawyer **must** inform the tribunal of all material facts known to the lawyer that will enable the tribunal to make an informed decision, whether or not the facts are adverse to the lawyer's client. MRPC 3.3(d). Since there is no opposing counsel, there is no balance of presentation. The tribunal still has the purpose to obtain a just result and an affirmative responsibility to accord the absent party just consideration. The lawyer for the represented party thus has the duty to disclose any material facts known to the lawyer that the lawyer reasonably believes are necessary to an informed decision by the tribunal. MRPC 3.3, cmt. 14.

4. Duty of Fairness to Opposing Party and Counsel

a. Access to evidence

A lawyer must not unlawfully obstruct another party's access to evidence or unlawfully alter, destroy, or conceal a document or other material having potential evidentiary value. A lawyer must also not counsel or assist another person to do any such act. MRPC 3.4(a). This rule applies to evidentiary material generally, including computerized information. MRPC 3.4, cmt. 2.

b. Inducements to witnesses

A lawyer must not offer an inducement to a witness that is prohibited by law. MRPC 3.4(b).

1) Non-expert witnesses

If permitted by the law of the jurisdiction, a lawyer may properly pay a non-expert witness the statutory fee and reasonable expenses (e.g., travel, lodging, meals, lost wages) incurred as a result of testifying.

2) Expert witnesses

An expert witness may only be paid the rate reasonable in the industry for the expert's profession and reasonable expenses incurred as a result of testifying. Expert fees may not be contingent on the outcome of the matter. MRPC 3.4, cmt. 3.

c. Violation of rules of the tribunal

A lawyer must not knowingly disobey an obligation under the rules of a tribunal except for an open refusal based on an assertion that no valid obligation exists. MRPC 3.4(c).

d. Discovery

A lawyer is not permitted to make a frivolous discovery request or fail to make a reasonably diligent effort to comply with a legally proper discovery request by an opposing party. MRPC 3.4(d).

e. Undermining evidentiary rules at trial

At trial, a lawyer must not allude to matters that are irrelevant or are not supported by evidence that the lawyer reasonably believes will be admissible. MRPC 3.4(e). When addressing the jury, a lawyer is prohibited from alluding to evidence that is ruled inadmissible by the court. The lawyer is also prohibited from (i) asserting personal knowledge of facts in issue except when testifying as a witness, or (ii) stating a personal opinion as to the justness of a cause, the credibility of a witness, the culpability of a civil litigant, or the guilt or innocence of an accused. MRPC 3.4(e). The lawyer may make an argument about any of the above based on the evidence in the case, however.

f. Requesting that person not give relevant information to another party

A lawyer must not request a person **other than a client** to refrain from voluntarily giving relevant information to another party **unless**: (i) the person is a relative or an employee or other agent of the client; and (ii) the lawyer reasonably believes that the person's interests will not be adversely affected by refraining from giving such information. MRPC 3.4(f).

D. CLIENT FRAUD AND PERJURY BY A CLIENT OR WITNESS

1. Prohibition on Falsifying Evidence or Assisting in Witness Perjury

A lawyer must not falsify evidence, or counsel or assist a witness to testify falsely. MRPC 3.4(b).

2. Use of False Evidence

a. In general

A lawyer is prohibited from knowingly offering false evidence and may refuse to offer evidence that the lawyer reasonably believes is false. MRPC 3.3(a)(3). The term "knows" means actual knowledge of the fact in question. A person's knowledge may be inferred from circumstances. MRPC 1.0(f). In addition, a lawyer should resolve doubts about truthfulness in favor of the client, but cannot ignore an obvious falsehood. MRPC 3.3, cmt. 8.

> **EXAM NOTE:** Examiners frequently test the subtle distinction between knowing and reasonably believing that evidence is false. The prohibition against offering false evidence only applies if the lawyer **knows** that the evidence is false. A lawyer's reasonable belief that evidence is false does not preclude its presentation to the trier-of-fact.

b. Learning of false evidence after it has been offered

If a lawyer, the lawyer's client, or a witness called by the lawyer, has offered material evidence and the lawyer comes to know of its falsity, the lawyer must take **reasonable remedial measures**. MRPC 3.3(a)(3).

1) Reasonable remedial measures

Reasonable remedial measures can include confidentially advising the client of the lawyer's duty of candor and urging the client's cooperation with respect to the withdrawal or correction of the false statements or evidence. If that fails, the lawyer is required to take further remedial action. If withdrawal from the representation is not permitted or will not undo the effect of the false evidence, the lawyer must make such disclosure to the tribunal as is reasonably necessary to remedy the situation, even if doing so requires the lawyer to reveal information that otherwise would be protected as confidential by the Model Rules. MRPC 3.3, cmt. 10.

2) Tribunal's action

Once disclosed, the tribunal will determine what, if anything, should be done. It may make a statement about the matter to the trier-of-fact, order a mistrial, or may do nothing after finding that the matter is not material.

c. Criminal defendant

1) In general

Because of the special protections that have historically been provided to criminal defendants, the Model Rules do not permit a lawyer to refuse to offer the testimony of such a client when the lawyer **reasonably believes but does not know** that the testimony will be false. Unless the lawyer knows the testimony will be false, the lawyer must honor the client's decision to testify. MRPC 3.3, cmt. 9.

2) Lawyer knows testimony is or will be false

If a lawyer knows the client's testimony will be or was false, the lawyer is required to take remedial measures. The lawyer should confidentially attempt to dissuade the client from testifying falsely or attempt to persuade the client to correct the false statement. If the client refuses, the lawyer must take further remedial action. If withdrawal from the representation is not permitted or will not undo the effect of the false evidence, the advocate must make such disclosure to the tribunal as is reasonably necessary to remedy the situation, even if doing so requires the lawyer to reveal information that otherwise would be protected by the lawyer's duty of confidentiality. MRPC 3.3(b), cmt. 10.

3) Narrative required by local law

In some jurisdictions, courts have required lawyers to present the accused as a witness or to allow the accused to give a narrative statement if the accused so desires, even if the lawyer knows that the testimony or statement will be false. The Model Rules subordinate the lawyer's obligation to such local jurisdictional requirements. MRPC 3.3, cmt. 7.

d. Duration of obligation

The prohibition on knowingly offering false evidence and the duty to take reasonable remedial measure on learning of the falsity of evidence after it has been admitted applies through the conclusion of the proceeding, which is defined as when a final judgment in the proceeding has been affirmed on appeal or the time for review has passed. MRPC 3.3(c), cmt. 13. It applies even if compliance requires disclosure of information otherwise protected by the ethical duty of confidentiality. MRPC 3.3(c).

A lawyer is under no duty to reveal false evidence or perjury that is discovered after the conclusion of the proceedings. In a criminal case, a verdict of acquittal concludes the proceedings because the Double Jeopardy Clause of the Constitution prevents the state from retrying the defendant.

E. COMMUNICATIONS IN THE COURSE OF REPRESENTATION

1. Communicating With the Client

a. Requirements

Lawyers are required to communicate with their clients throughout the representation. A lawyer must: (i) promptly inform the client of any decision or circumstance with respect to which the client's informed consent is required by the Model Rules; (ii) reasonably consult with the client about the means by which the client's objectives are to be accomplished; (iii) keep the client reasonably informed about the status of the matter; (iv) promptly comply with reasonable requests for information from the client; and (v) consult with the client about any relevant limitation on the lawyer's conduct when the lawyer knows that the client expects assistance not permitted by the Model Rules or other law. MRPC 1.4(a). A lawyer must explain a matter to the extent reasonably necessary to permit the client to make informed decisions regarding the representation. MRPC 1.4(b).

> A lawyer who receives from opposing counsel an offer of settlement in a civil controversy or a proffered plea bargain in a criminal case must promptly inform the client of its substance unless the client has previously indicated that the proposal will be acceptable or unacceptable or has authorized the lawyer to accept or to reject the offer. MRPC 1.4, cmt. 2.

b. Withholding information from a client

There are some times when a lawyer may be justified in delaying transmission of information when the client would be likely to react imprudently to an immediate communication. Thus, a lawyer might withhold a psychiatric diagnosis of a client when the examining psychiatrist indicates that such disclosure would harm the client. MRPC 1.4, cmt. 7. Note that a lawyer may not withhold information to serve the lawyer's own interest or convenience or the interests or convenience of another person. In some instances, local rules or court orders governing litigation may provide that information supplied to a lawyer may not be disclosed to the client. A lawyer is required to comply with such rules or orders. See MRPC 3.4(c).

2. Improper Ex Parte Communication

During a proceeding a lawyer is not permitted to communicate ex parte (i.e., without the other party or that party's lawyer present) with persons serving in an official capacity in the proceeding, such as judges, masters, or jurors, unless authorized to do so by law or court order. MRPC 3.5(b).

a. Scope of rule

The rule includes **all forms of communication,** including written communications. Generally, if a copy of a written communication is also sent to the other party or that party's representative, the communication is not ex parte. Restatement (Third) of the Law Governing Lawyers § 113, cmt. 3.

b. Permitted communication

Only communications involving "housekeeping" matters, which do not involve the merits of the case, or emergency communications authorized by law or court order (such as emergency restraining orders) are permitted ex parte. A routine and customary request, such as a communication dealing with the scheduling of a hearing, is not prohibited, but a communication made for the purpose of having a matter assigned to a particular judge is prohibited. Restatement (Third) of the Law Governing Lawyers § 113, cmt. 3.

c. Communication with jurors

All out-of-court communication with jurors or members of the panel from which jurors will be chosen, before and during the proceeding, is prohibited. This includes all communication, even if it involves matters unrelated to the case. MRPC 3.5(b).

1) After juror's duties end

Contact with a juror or prospective juror after he has been discharged is permitted unless the jurisdiction prohibits such contact, the juror has made known to the lawyer a desire not to talk with the lawyer, or the communication involves misrepresentation, coercion, duress, or harassment. MRPC 3.5(c), cmt. 3.

3. Truthfulness in Statements to Others

a. No false statements of material fact or law

In representing a client, a lawyer must not knowingly make a false statement of material fact or law to a third person. MRPC 4.1(a). While a lawyer does not generally have a duty to inform an opposing party of relevant facts, the lawyer is not permitted to misrepresent facts.

b. Misrepresentation

A misrepresentation can occur if the lawyer incorporates or affirms a statement of another person that the lawyer knows is false. Misrepresentations can also occur by partially true but misleading statements or omissions that are the equivalent of affirmative false statements. MRPC 4.1, cmt. 1. In addition to professional discipline for misrepresentation, lawyers may be subject to criminal or tortious misrepresentation depending on the circumstances.

c. Statements of fact

Whether a statement is one "of fact" can depend on the circumstances. Under generally accepted conventions in negotiation, certain types of statements are not generally taken as statements of material fact (e.g., estimates of price or value placed on the subject of a transaction; a party's intentions as to an acceptable settlement of a claim; and the existence of an undisclosed principal, except when nondisclosure of the principal would constitute fraud). MRPC 4.1, cmt. 2.

d. Failure to disclose material fact when necessary to avoid assisting client's crime or fraud

1) In general

A lawyer must also not fail to disclose a material fact to a third person when disclosure is necessary to avoid assisting a criminal or fraudulent act by a client, unless disclosure is prohibited by Model Rule 1.6, regarding confidentiality. MRPC 4.1(b). See also MRPC 1.2(d) (prohibiting lawyers from counseling or assisting a client in conduct that the lawyer knows is criminal or fraudulent).

2) Withdrawal

Generally, a lawyer can avoid assisting a client's crime or fraud by withdrawing from the representation. If the duty of confidentiality prohibits the lawyer from disclosing the facts and the lawyer's continued representation would assist the client's crime or fraud, the lawyer is required to withdraw. MRPC 1.16(a)(1). The lawyer may notify the affected third person of the fact of the withdrawal. In some cases it may be necessary for the lawyer to disaffirm an opinion, document, or affirmation the lawyer made. In extreme cases, the lawyer may be required to disclose information relating to the representation to avoid being deemed to have assisted the client's crime or fraud. If the lawyer can avoid assisting a client's crime or fraud only by disclosing this information, then the lawyer is required to do so, unless the disclosure is prohibited by the ethics rules.

4. Communication With Persons Represented by Counsel

a. In general

In representing a client, a lawyer is not permitted to communicate about the subject of the representation with a person the lawyer **knows** to be represented by another lawyer in the matter, **unless** the lawyer has the **consent of the other lawyer** or is authorized to do so by law or a court order. MRPC 4.2.

b. Scope of rule

This prohibition applies to communications with any person who is **represented by counsel with regard to the matter to which the communication relates**. MRPC 4.2, cmt. 2. The rule applies even if the represented person initiates or consents to the communication. MRPC 4.2, cmt. 3.

A lawyer must immediately terminate communication with a person if, after commencing communication, the lawyer learns that the person is represented by counsel in a matter to which the communication relates.

Note that the rule does not apply to prohibit communication with a represented person, or an employee or agent of such person, with regard to any matter outside the representation. The rule also does not prohibit communication with a represented person who is seeking advice from a lawyer who is not otherwise representing a client in the matter. MRPC 4.2, cmt. 4.

A lawyer may not make a prohibited communication through the acts of another.

c. Parties

Parties to a matter may communicate directly with each other, and a lawyer is not prohibited from advising a client concerning a communication that the client is legally entitled to make. MRPC 4.2, cmt. 4.

Additionally, a lawyer having independent justification or legal authorization for communicating with a represented person is permitted to do so.

d. Knowledge

The prohibition on communications with a represented person only applies when the lawyer **knows** that the person is in fact represented in the matter to be discussed. This means that the lawyer has **actual knowledge** of the fact of the representation. Such actual knowledge, though, may be inferred from the circumstances. MRPC 4.2, cmt. 8.

e. Communications authorized by law or court order

Communications authorized by law may include communications by a lawyer on behalf of a client who is exercising a constitutional or other legal right to communicate with the government or investigative activities of lawyers representing governmental entities, directly or through investigative agents, prior to the commencement of criminal or civil enforcement proceedings. MRPC 4.2, cmt. 5. A lawyer who is uncertain whether a communication with a represented person is permissible may seek a court order. MRPC 4.2, cmt. 6.

f. Represented organization

1) In general

In the case of a represented organization, a lawyer is prohibited from communicating with a constituent (e.g., employee) of the organization who supervises, directs, or regularly consults with the organization's lawyer concerning the matter or has authority to obligate the organization with respect to the matter, or whose act or omission in connection with the matter may be imputed to the organization for purposes of civil or criminal liability. MRPC 4.2, cmt. 7.

2) Former constituent

Consent of the organization's lawyer is not required for communication with a former constituent. MRPC 4.2, cmt. 7.

3) Violating the legal rights of the organization

In communicating with a current or former constituent of an organization, a lawyer must not use methods of obtaining evidence that violate the legal rights of the organization (e.g., attorney-client privilege). MRPC 4.2, cmt. 7.

5. Dealing With Persons Unrepresented by Counsel

a. In general

In dealing on behalf of a client with a person who is not represented by counsel, a lawyer is not permitted to state or imply that the lawyer is disinterested. When the lawyer knows or reasonably should know that the unrepresented person misunderstands the lawyer's role in the matter, the lawyer must make reasonable efforts to correct the misunderstanding. The lawyer is not permitted to give legal advice to an unrepresented person, other than the advice to secure counsel, if the lawyer knows or reasonably should know that the interests of such person are or have a reasonable possibility of being in conflict with the interests of the lawyer's client. MRPC 4.3.

b. Lawyer may deal with unrepresented person

The Model Rules do not prohibit a lawyer from negotiating the terms of a transaction or settling a dispute with an unrepresented person. As long as the lawyer has explained that he represents an adverse party and is not representing the person, the lawyer may inform the unrepresented person of the terms on which the lawyer's client will enter into an agreement or settle a matter, prepare documents that require the person's signature, and explain the lawyer's own view of the meaning of the document or the lawyer's view of the underlying legal obligations. MRPC 4.3, cmt. 2.

6. **Respect for the Rights of Third Persons**

   a. **Improper means**

   In representing a client, a lawyer must not use means that have no substantial purpose other than to embarrass, delay, or burden a third person, or use methods of obtaining evidence that violate the legal rights of such a person. MRPC 4.4(a).

   b. **Receipt of inadvertently sent documents**

   A lawyer who receives a document or electronically-stored information relating to the representation of the lawyer's client and who **knows or reasonably should know** that the document or information was inadvertently sent must promptly notify the sender. MRPC 4.4(b). Documents and information are "inadvertently sent" when they are accidentally transmitted, such as when an email or letter is misaddressed or a document is accidentally included with information that was intentionally transmitted. Information covered by this rule includes e-mail, "metadata" (data embedded in electronic documents), and other forms of electronically-stored information that is subject to being read or put into readable form. MRPC 4.4, cmt. 2. The Model Rules do not address whether the document must be returned or whether any privileges attached to the document have been waived. These issues are generally addressed by local law. MRPC 4.4, cmt. 2.

7. **Trial Publicity**

   a. **General rule**

   A lawyer who is participating or has participated in the investigation or litigation of a matter is not permitted to make an extrajudicial statement that the lawyer **knows or reasonably should know** will be disseminated by means of public communication and **will have a substantial likelihood of materially prejudicing an adjudicative proceeding** in the matter. MRPC 3.6(a).

   b. **Exception**

   A lawyer may make a statement that a reasonable lawyer would believe is required to protect a client from the substantial undue prejudicial effect of recent publicity that was not initiated by the lawyer or the lawyer's client. Such a statement must be limited to such information as is necessary to mitigate the recent adverse publicity. MRPC 3.6(c).

   c. **Facts about the case may be discussed**

   The Model Rules permit a lawyer participating in the investigation or litigation of a matter to state:

   i) The claim, offense, or defense involved and, except when prohibited by law, the identity of the persons involved;

   ii) Information that is contained in a public record;

   iii) That an investigation of a matter is in progress;

   iv) The scheduling or result of any step in litigation;

   v) A request for assistance in obtaining evidence and information necessary to the case;

   vi) A warning of danger concerning the behavior of a person involved, when there is reason to believe that there exists the likelihood of substantial harm to an individual or to the public interest; and

vii) The identity, residence, occupation and family status of a criminal defendant, information necessary to aid in apprehending an accused person in a criminal case, the fact, time, and place of arrest; and the identity of investigating and arresting officers or agencies and the length of the investigation.

MRPC 3.6(b).

> **Example:** An attorney represents a famous actress in an action against a newspaper for libel. The case has attracted a lot of publicity, and a jury trial has been demanded. After one of the pretrial hearings, as the attorney left the courthouse, a television news reporter asked the attorney about the case on camera. In responding to the question, the attorney truthfully stated, "The judge has upheld our right to subpoena the reporter involved, identified in our motion as Paparazzi, and question him on his mental impressions when he prepared his article." The attorney is not subject to discipline for making the statement because it is a truthful statement relating to a matter of public record.

d. **Statements likely to be prohibited**

A key factor in determining prejudice can be the nature of the proceeding involved. A criminal jury trial will be most sensitive to extrajudicial speech, while a civil trial may be less sensitive. A non-jury hearing or arbitration proceedings may be even less sensitive. The Model Rules will still place limitations on prejudicial comments in these cases, but the likelihood of prejudice may be different depending on the type of proceeding. MRPC 3.6, cmt. 6. The comment to MRPC 3.6 sets forth several examples of topics that are more likely than not to have a material prejudicial effect on a proceeding, particularly when they refer to a civil matter triable to a jury, a criminal matter, or any other proceeding that could result in incarceration. These include:

i) The character, credibility, reputation, or criminal record of a party, suspect in a criminal investigation or witness, or the identity of a witness, or the expected testimony of a party or witness;

ii) In a criminal case or proceeding that could result in incarceration, the possibility of a plea of guilty to the offense or the existence or contents of any confession, admission, or statement given by a defendant or suspect or that person's refusal or failure to make a statement;

iii) The performance or results of any examination or test or the refusal or failure of a person to submit to an examination or test, or the identity or nature of physical evidence expected to be presented;

iv) Any opinion as to the guilt or innocence of a defendant or suspect in a criminal case or proceeding that could result in incarceration;

v) Information that the lawyer knows or reasonably should know is likely to be inadmissible as evidence in a trial and that would, if disclosed, create a substantial risk of prejudicing an impartial trial; and

vi) The fact that a defendant has been charged with a crime, unless there is included therein a statement explaining that the charge is merely an accusation and that the defendant is presumed innocent until and unless proven guilty.

MRPC 3.6, cmt. 5.

e. **Associated lawyers**

The rules with regard to trial publicity apply to any lawyer associated in a firm or government agency with a lawyer who is participating or has participated in the investigation or litigation of a matter. MRPC 3.6(d).

VIII. DIFFERENT ROLES OF THE LAWYER

In representing a client, a lawyer may perform various functions. Among those functions, a lawyer may act as an advocate, zealously asserting the client's position in the adversary system, and a negotiator, seeking an advantageous result for the client but subject to the requirements of fair dealings with others. In addition, a lawyer may act as an advisor to a client or as evaluator of the client's legal situation. In a non-representative capacity, a lawyer may act as third-party neutral. MRPC Preamble 2, 3.

A. LAWYER AS ADVISOR

1. Duty to Render Candid Advice

In representing a client, a lawyer is required to exercise independent professional judgment and render candid advice. In rendering advice, a lawyer may refer not only to law but to other considerations such as moral, economic, social, and political factors, which may be relevant to the client's situation. MRPC 2.1.

2. Offering Advice to the Client

In general, a lawyer is not expected to give advice until asked by the client. If, however, the lawyer knows that a client proposes a course of action that is likely to result in substantial adverse legal consequences to the client, the lawyer may have a duty to the client that requires that the lawyer offer advice if the client's course of action is related to the representation. MRPC 2.1, cmt. 5.

B. LAWYER AS EVALUATOR

1. Evaluation to Be Used by Third Persons

A lawyer may provide an evaluation of a matter affecting a client for the use of someone other than the client if the lawyer reasonably believes that making the evaluation is compatible with other aspects of the lawyer's relationship with the client. If the lawyer knows or reasonably should know that the evaluation is likely to affect the client's interests materially and adversely, the lawyer is not permitted to provide the evaluation unless the client gives informed consent. MRPC 2.3.

a. Examples of evaluation

Examples of evaluations that might be provided include: an opinion concerning the title of property rendered at the request of a seller for the information of a prospective buyer, or at the request of a borrower for the information of a prospective lender. In some situations, the evaluation may be required by a government agency, as for example, an opinion concerning the legality of securities registered for sale under the securities laws. In other instances, the evaluation may be required by a third person, such as a purchaser of a business. MRPC 2.3, cmt. 1.

b. Distinguished from investigation

A legal evaluation should be distinguished from an investigation of a person with whom the lawyer does not have a client-lawyer relationship. Thus, a lawyer retained by a buyer to analyze a seller's title to property does not have a client-lawyer relationship with the seller. If the lawyer is retained by the person whose affairs are being examined, then the requirements of MRPC 2.3 (as well as all other duties under the Model Rules) apply. MRPC 2.3, cmt. 2.

2.   Duty Owed to Third Person

If the evaluation is intended for the information or use of a third person, a legal duty to that person may or may not arise. When the evaluation does result in a legal obligation to a third person, the lawyer may be liable to that person for any negligence in rendering the evaluation. *See* VI.D. Civil Liability to Non-clients, *infra*. MRPC 2.3, cmt. 3.

3.   Access to and Disclosure of Information

If the terms of the evaluation are limited (e.g., when certain issues or sources have been categorically excluded, or the scope of a search has been limited by time constraints or the non-cooperation of persons having relevant information), such limitations that are material to the evaluation must be described in the lawyer's report. Under no circumstances is the lawyer permitted to knowingly make a false statement of material fact or law in providing an evaluation. MRPC 2.3, cmt. 4.

4.   Confidentiality

Except as disclosure is authorized in connection with a report of the evaluation, information relating to the evaluation is protected by the Model Rules regarding confidentiality. MRPC 2.3(c).

C.   LAWYER AS NEGOTIATOR

As noted above (*see* VII.E.3. Truthfulness in Statements to Others, *supra*) a lawyer is not permitted to make a false statement of material fact. *See* MRPC 4.1(a). Model Rule 8.4(c) overlaps with Model Rule 4.1(a), in providing that a lawyer may not engage in dishonesty, fraud, deceit, or misrepresentation." The Model Rules contain no exception for negotiations. A lawyer, though, has no specific duty to volunteer facts as part of a negotiation that might undermine a client's position. While a lawyer may not lie, a lawyer may make statements that constitute "puffing" as part of a negotiation. Puffing is an opinion or judgment that is not made as a representation of fact. Subjective statements, such as estimates of price or value or the relative merits of a case are not considered statements of material fact. MRPC 4.1, cmt. 2.

> **Example:** The attorney for a seller of real property is permitted to say as part of a sales negotiation that the seller expects a number of offers for the property in the million-dollar price range. The attorney is subject to discipline, however, if he tells a prospective buyer that the seller had a firm offer from an undisclosed buyer for a million dollars, when in fact there was no such offer.

D.   LAWYER AS ARBITRATOR, MEDIATOR, OR OTHER THIRD-PARTY NEUTRAL

1.   Service as a Third-Party Neutral

A lawyer serves as a third-party neutral when the lawyer assists two or more persons who are **not** clients of the lawyer to reach a resolution of a dispute or other matter that has arisen between them. Service as a third-party neutral may include service as an arbitrator, a mediator, or in such other capacity as will enable the lawyer to assist the parties to resolve the matter. MRPC 2.4(a). Note that a lawyer serving as a third-party neutral may also be subject to court rules or other law that apply either to third-party neutrals generally or to lawyers serving as third-party neutrals, as well as other ethical codes, such as the Code of Ethics for Arbitration in Commercial Disputes or the Model Standards of Conduct for Mediators. MRPC 2.4, cmt. 2.

2. Duty to Inform Unrepresented Parties

A lawyer who is serving as a third-party neutral is required to inform unrepresented parties that the lawyer is not representing them. If the lawyer knows or reasonably should know that a party does not understand the lawyer's role in the matter as a third-party neutral, the lawyer must explain the difference between his role as a third-party neutral and the role of a lawyer who represents a client. MRPC 2.4(b). The lawyer must specifically indicate that the attorney-client privilege does not apply in this context. MRPC 2.3, cmt. 3.

3. Conflicts of Interest

A lawyer who serves as a third-party neutral generally may not subsequently serve as a lawyer representing a client in the same matter, unless all parties give their informed consent, confirmed in writing. MRPC 1.12(a). *See* V.H. Conflicts based on lawyer's service as arbitrator, mediator, or judge, *supra*.

E. SPECIAL OBLIGATIONS OF A PROSECUTOR

A prosecutor is not just an advocate, but has the responsibility of a minister of justice. This responsibility includes the obligations to ensure that the defendant is accorded procedural justice, that guilt is decided upon the basis of sufficient evidence, and that special precautions are taken to prevent or rectify the conviction of innocent persons. MRPC 3.8, cmt. 1.

1. Avoiding Conflicts With Private Interests

A prosecutor must avoid representation of a private client that would result in a conflict with the prosecutor's obligation to seek justice on behalf of the public.

2. No Prosecution Without Probable Cause

A prosecutor must not prosecute a charge that the prosecutor knows is not supported by probable cause. MRPC 3.8(a).

3. Advising of Right to Counsel

A prosecutor must make reasonable efforts to assure defendants are advised of their right to and the procedure for obtaining counsel and have been given reasonable opportunity to obtain counsel. MRPC 3.8(b). The rule does not forbid the lawful questioning of an uncharged suspect who has knowingly waived the rights to counsel and silence. MRPC 3.8, cmt. 2.

4. Not Seeking Waiver of Pre-Trial Rights

A prosecutor must not attempt to obtain a waiver of important pre-trial rights from an unrepresented accused, such as the right to a preliminary hearing. MRPC 3.8(c). This rule does not apply to an accused appearing *pro se* with the approval of the tribunal. MRPC 3.8, cmt. 2.

5. Disclosure of Evidence That May Help Defendant

A prosecutor must make timely disclosure to the defense of all evidence or information known to the prosecutor that tends to negate the guilt of the accused or mitigates the offense. In connection with sentencing, the prosecutor must disclose to the defense and to the tribunal all unprivileged mitigating information known to the prosecutor, except when the prosecutor is relieved of this responsibility by a protective order of the tribunal. MRPC 3.8(d). This duty is broader than the *Brady v. Maryland* duty imposed on a prosecutor by the Due Process Clause of the Fourteenth Amendment, which only mandates the disclosure of evidence that is material (i.e., likely to lead to an acquittal). Moreover, a defendant's consent to a prosecutor's noncompliance with the disclosure requirement in exchange for favorable treatment does not relieve the prosecutor of this duty. ABA Formal Opinion 09-454 (2009).

6. Restrictions on Subpoenaing Lawyers

A prosecutor is not permitted to subpoena a lawyer in a grand jury or other criminal proceeding to present evidence about a past or present client unless the prosecutor reasonably believes that: (i) the information sought is **not protected** from disclosure by any applicable privilege; (ii) the evidence sought is **essential** to the successful completion of an ongoing investigation or prosecution; and (iii) there is **no other feasible alternative** to obtain the information. MRPC 3.8(e).

7. Public Statements About Pending Cases

Except for statements that are necessary to inform the public of the nature and extent of the prosecutor's action and that serve a legitimate law enforcement purpose, a prosecutor must refrain from making extrajudicial comments that have a substantial likelihood of heightening public condemnation of the accused. A prosecutor must also exercise reasonable care to prevent investigators, law enforcement personnel, employees or other persons assisting or associated with the prosecutor in a criminal case from making an extrajudicial statement that the prosecutor would be prohibited from making under the Model Rules. MRPC 3.8(f).

8. New Evidence After Conviction

a. Duty to disclose

The prosecutor has an obligation to disclose to the appropriate authority any new, credible evidence creating a reasonable likelihood that a convicted defendant did not commit the offense for which the defendant was convicted. MRPC 3.8(g)(1).

b. Within jurisdiction

If the conviction was obtained within the prosecutor's jurisdiction, the prosecutor must also: (i) promptly disclose the new evidence to the defendant (unless otherwise instructed by the court); and (ii) undertake further investigation to determine whether the defendant was wrongly convicted. MRPC 3.8(g)(2).

c. Clear and convincing

A prosecutor **must** seek to remedy a conviction of a defendant in the prosecutor's jurisdiction when the new exculpatory evidence is **clear and convincing**. MRPC 3.8(h).

d. Good faith judgment

As long as the prosecutor makes a good faith, independent judgment that the evidence does not require action, the prosecutor will not be subject to professional discipline. MRPC 3.8, cmt. 9.

9. Investigations

Prosecutors must be objective when investigating leads without regard to whether the leads favor the prosecutor's case.

F. APPEARANCES BEFORE LEGISLATIVE AND ADMINISTRATIVE BODIES

1. As Representative in Non-Adjudicative Proceeding

A lawyer who represents a client before a legislative body or administrative agency in a non-adjudicative proceeding must disclose that he is there in a representative capacity and must generally conform to the Model Rules with regard to candor toward the entity (*see* VII.C.3. Duty of Candor to the Tribunal, *supra*), fairness to the opposing party and counsel (*see* VII.C.4., Duty of Fairness to Opposing Party and Counsel *supra*), and impartiality and decorum of the tribunal (*see* VII.B. Impartiality, Civility, Courtesy, and Decorum, *supra*) as if the lawyer were before a tribunal. MRPC 3.9.

2. Scope of Rule

These duties only apply when a lawyer represents a client in connection with an official hearing or meeting of a governmental agency or a legislative body to which the lawyer or the lawyer's client is presenting evidence or argument. They do not apply to representation of a client in a negotiation or other bilateral transaction with a governmental agency or in connection with an application for a license or other privilege or the client's compliance with generally applicable reporting requirements, such as filing a tax return. MRPC 3.9, cmt. 3.

IX. SAFEKEEPING PROPERTY OF CLIENTS AND OTHERS

A lawyer owes a duty with respect to property in the lawyer's possession that belongs to another person to exercise the same care that is required of a professional fiduciary. MRPC 1.15, cmt. 1; Restatement (Third) of the Law Governing Lawyers § 44.

A. LAWYER'S PROTECTION OF CLIENT'S PROPERTY

During the course of a representation, a lawyer has a duty to protect a client's property that is in the lawyer's possession. MRPC 1.15.

1. Client's Funds—Trust Account

In general, a lawyer must not commingle a client's funds that are in the lawyer's possession in connection with a representation with the lawyer's own funds. A client's funds must be kept in a separate client trust account maintained in the state where the lawyer's office is situated, unless the client consents to another location. MRPC 1.15(a).

a. Interest On Lawyer's Trust Account (IOLTA)

Typically, the cost of creating and maintaining a separate trust account for each client during the period that the lawyer is in possession of the client's funds outweighs the economic benefit to the client of such an account (i.e., the interest that the account would earn). Consequently, by state law or rule, a lawyer who receives such client funds may be required to create a trust account into which all such funds are deposited. The interest on such an account is used for various public purposes, such as funding charitable legal aid services. Use of the interest in this manner does not violate the Fifth Amendment Takings Clause because, individually, the client did not have a compensable property interest. *Brown v. Legal Foundation of Washington*, 538 U.S. 216 (2003).

b. Other accounts

When, due to the amount of money or the length of time it would be in the lawyer's possession, the client would benefit from the creation of separate trust account, the lawyer typically must at least give the client the option of having the funds placed in a separate interest bearing account, with the interest payable to the client. Restatement (Third) of the Law Governing Lawyers § 44, cmt. d. Such a separate trust account may be warranted when the lawyer is administering estate monies or acting in a similar fiduciary capacity with regard to funds. MRPC 1.15, cmt. 1.

2. **Specific Property in Account**

   a. **Advance payment of fees**

   A lawyer is required to deposit into a client trust account legal fees and expenses that have been paid in advance by the client, to be withdrawn by the lawyer only as fees are earned or expenses incurred in the representation. MRPC 1.15(c).

   b. **Use of lawyer's own funds to pay bank service charge on account**

   As an exception to the commingling rule, a lawyer may deposit the lawyer's own funds in a client trust account for the sole purpose of paying bank service charges on the account, but only in an amount necessary for such purpose. MRPC 1.15(b).

3. **Recordkeeping**

   With regard to a client account, the lawyer must maintain on a current basis books and records in accordance with generally accepted accounting practice and comply with any recordkeeping rules established by law or court order. MRPC 1.15, cmt. 1. Accurate records must be kept that delineate the portion of the funds that is the lawyer's from the client's portion. MRPC 1.15, cmt. 2. The lawyer must keep complete records for at least five years after the termination of the representation. MRPC 1.15(a).

4. **Notice, Delivery, and Accounting**

   When a lawyer receives funds or other property in which a client has an interest, the lawyer must promptly notify the client. When required, the lawyer must promptly pay over the funds or deliver the other property to the client. Upon request by the client, the lawyer must promptly render a full accounting. MRPC 1.15(d).

   If a lawyer acquires possession of property belonging to a client or third party in connection with a representation, the lawyer must identify it as the other person's property and appropriately safeguard it separately from the lawyer's own property. MRPC 1.15(a). Securities should be kept in a safe deposit box, except when some other form of safekeeping is warranted by special circumstances. MRPC 1.15, cmt. 1.

B. **LAWYER'S PROTECTION OF THIRD PERSON'S PROPERTY**

In general, the same rules regarding a client's property in the possession of a lawyer apply to property of a third party received by a lawyer in connection with a representation. The prohibition on commingling as well as the account, recordkeeping, notice, delivery, and accounting requirements that apply to a client's property in the lawyer's possession apply to a third person's property being held by the lawyer. MRPC 1.15.

C. **DISPUTED CLAIMS**

If, as a part of the representation of a client, a lawyer is in possession of property in which two or more persons (one of whom may be the lawyer) claim interests, the property must be kept separate by the lawyer until the dispute is resolved. The lawyer is required to promptly distribute all portions of the property as to which the interests are not in dispute. MRPC 1.15(e).

1. **Dispute Over Lawyer's Fees**

   The lawyer is not required to remit to the client funds that the lawyer reasonably believes represent fees owed by the client to the lawyer. However, a lawyer may not hold funds to coerce a client into accepting the lawyer's contention. The disputed portion of the funds must be kept in a trust account and the lawyer should suggest means for prompt resolution of the dispute, such as arbitration. The undisputed portion of the funds must be promptly distributed. MRPC 1.15, cmt. 3.

Example: An attorney settles a contingent-fee malpractice suit on behalf of a plaintiff for $100,000. The defendant sends the attorney a check for that amount. The attorney deposits it in her client trust account and notifies the plaintiff of the receipt of the funds. The contingent fee agreement between the attorney and the plaintiff called for the attorney to receive 25% of the funds collected, or $25,000. The plaintiff notifies the attorney that he disputes her right to anything more than $10,000. The attorney must immediately pay the plaintiff $75,000, the amount the attorney admits is owed to the plaintiff. The attorney is immediately entitled to $10,000, the amount that the plaintiff admits is owed to the attorney, and must remove it from the trust account. The remaining $15,000 must stay in the trust account until the dispute over the fee is resolved.

2. Third-Party Claim to Property in Lawyer's Possession

A third party may also have a lawful claim to property in a lawyer's possession, such as a client's creditor who has lien on funds recovered in a personal injury action. Under state law, a lawyer may have a duty to protect such a claim against the client's wrongful interference. In such case, a lawyer must not turn over the property to client, despite the client's demand that the lawyer do so. The lawyer should not attempt to arbitrate the dispute between the client and the third party. If there are substantial grounds to dispute the person entitled to the property, the lawyer may file an interpleader action in order to have a court resolve the dispute. MRPC 1.15(e), cmt. 4.

X. COMMUNICATION ABOUT LEGAL SERVICES

Lawyers who advertise or solicit prospective clients are subject to restrictions on such activities. MRPC 7.1-7.3.

A. PUBLIC COMMUNICATIONS ABOUT SERVICES

1. Communications Concerning a Lawyer's Services

a. General rule

A lawyer must not make a false or misleading communication about the lawyer or the lawyer's services. A communication will be false or misleading if it contains a material misrepresentation of fact or law, or omits a fact necessary to make the statement considered as a whole not materially misleading. MRPC 7.1. This rule governs **all** communications about a lawyer's services, however transmitted. MRPC 7.1, cmt. 1. Thus, statements made in letters, e-mails, telephone calls, and other forms of communication, as well as in advertising permitted by the Model Rules, would be covered by the rule.

b. Statements that could lead to unjustified expectations

A communication that truthfully reports a lawyer's achievements on behalf of clients may be misleading if presented in a manner that may lead a reasonable person to form an unjustified expectation that the same results could be obtained for other clients in similar matters without reference to the specific factual and legal circumstances of each client's case. The inclusion of an appropriate disclaimer or qualifying language may preclude a finding that a statement is likely to create unjustified expectations or otherwise mislead the public. MRPC 7.1, cmt. 3.

c. Unsubstantiated comparisons

An unsubstantiated comparison of the lawyer's services or fees with the services or fees of other lawyers may be misleading if presented with such specificity as would lead a reasonable person to conclude that the comparison can be substantiated.

2. Advertising

Advertising refers to widely distributed public statements about the services available from a lawyer or law firm (such as phone book listings and newspaper or television ads).

a. General rule

A lawyer is generally permitted to communicate information regarding her services through written, recorded, or electronic communication, including public media, so long as the communications regarding such services are not false or misleading in violation of MRPC 7.1, or in violation of the rules against solicitation of clients under MRPC 7.3. MRPC 7.2(a).

This rule permits public dissemination of information concerning a lawyer's name or firm name, address, email address, website, and telephone number; the kinds of services the lawyer will undertake; the basis on which the lawyer's fees are determined, including prices for specific services and payment and credit arrangements; a lawyer's foreign language ability; names of references; and other information that might invite the attention of those seeking legal assistance. MRPC 7.2, cmt. 1.

b. Identification of advertiser

Any communication about a lawyer or law firm's services must include the name and contact information of at least one lawyer or law firm responsible for its content. MRPC 7.2(d). Contact information includes a website address, a telephone number, an email address or a physical office location. MRPC 7.2(d), cmt. 12.

c. Names of clients permissible only with their consent

The names of regularly-represented clients may be communicated in an advertisement only with their consent. MRPC 7.2, cmt. 1.

d. Limitations of practice and specialization

A lawyer is permitted to communicate the fact that the lawyer does or does not practice in particular fields of law. In doing so, the lawyer generally may state that he is a "specialist," practices a "specialty," or "specializes in" particular fields, but such communications must not violate the rule against false and misleading communications in MRPC Rule 7.1. MRPC 7.2, cmt. 9.

Note that there is a difference between stating that a lawyer is a specialist and that the lawyer is a "certified specialist."

However, a lawyer is not permitted to state or imply that she is certified as a specialist in a particular field of law, **unless**:

i) The lawyer has been certified as a specialist by an organization that has been approved by an appropriate state authority or that has been accredited by the American Bar Association; **and**

ii) The name of the certifying organization is clearly identified in the communication.

MRPC 7.2(c).

States may not impose blanket prohibitions on statements of certification. *Peel v. Illinois Attorney Registration and Disciplinary Commission*, 496 U.S. 91 (1990).

1) Patent lawyers

If a lawyer is admitted to practice before the United States Patent and Trademark Office, that lawyer may use the designation "Patent Attorney" or a substantially similar designation. MRPC 7.2(c), cmt. 9.

2) Proctors in admiralty

A lawyer engaged in Admiralty practice may use the designation "Admiralty," "Proctor in Admiralty," or a substantially similar designation. MRPC 7.2(c), cmt. 9.

3. Firm Names and Letterheads

> **EXAM NOTE:** Historically, this has been a frequently tested area on the MPRE.

Firm names, letterhead and professional designations are communications concerning a lawyer's services, and are therefore subject to MRPC 7.1.

A firm may be designated by (i) the names of all or some of its current members, (ii) the names of deceased members where there has been a succession in the firm's identity, or (iii) a trade name if it is not false or misleading. A lawyer or law firm also may be designated by a distinctive website address, social media username or comparable professional designation that is not misleading. MRPC 7.1, cmt. 5.

If a firm uses a trade name that includes a geographical name, an express statement explaining that it is not a public legal aid organization may be required to avoid a misleading implication. A law firm name or designation is also misleading if it implies a connection with:

i) A government agency;

ii) A deceased lawyer who was not a former member of the firm;

iii) A lawyer not associated with the firm or a predecessor firm;

iv) A nonlawyer; or

v) A public or charitable legal services organization.

MRPC 7.1, cmt. 5.

a. Firms with offices in more than one jurisdiction

Firms with offices in more than one jurisdiction may use the same name in each of the jurisdictions in which they operate. MRPC 7.1. cmt. 6.

b. Lawyers holding public office

The name of a lawyer holding a public office is not permitted to be used in the name of a law firm, or in communications on its behalf, during any substantial period in which the lawyer is not actively and regularly practicing with the firm. MRPC 7.1. cmt. 8.

c. No false claims of partnership

Lawyers may not imply or hold themselves out as practicing together in one firm when they are not a firm. MRPC 7.1, cmt. 7.

> **Example:** Two lawyers, Jane Smith and Sam Jones, share office space, but are not in fact associated with each other in a law firm. They decide to denominate

themselves as "Smith and Jones." This designation is misleading and is impermissible because such a title suggests that they are practicing law together in a firm when they really are not.

B. RESTRICTIONS ON PAYMENT FOR RECOMMENDING A LAWYER

1. No Payment for Recommending a Lawyer

A lawyer is not generally permitted to give anything of value to a person for recommending the lawyer's services. MRPC 7.2(b). A communication contains a recommendation if it endorses or vouches for a lawyer's credentials, abilities, competence, character, or other professional qualities. Directory listings and group advertisements that list lawyers by practice area, without more, do not constitute impermissible recommendations. MRPC 7.2, cmt. 2.

a. Payment for advertising is allowed

The rule against payment for recommending a lawyer's services does not prevent a lawyer from paying the reasonable costs of advertisements or other communications permitted by the Model Rules. MRPC 7.2(b)(1). This would include the costs of print directory listings, online directory listings, newspaper ads, television and radio airtime, domain name registrations, sponsorship fees, Internet-based advertisements, and group advertising. A lawyer may compensate employees, agents, and vendors who are engaged to provide marketing or client development services, such as publicists, public relations personnel, business development staff, television and radio station employees or spokespersons and website designers. MRPC 7.2, cmt. 3. A lawyer may also pay others for generating client leads, such as Internet-based client leads, as long as the lead generator does not recommend the lawyer, any payment to the lead generator is consistent with Rules 1.5(e) (division of fees) and 5.4 (professional independence of the lawyer), and the lead generator's communications are consistent with Rule 7.1 (communications concerning a lawyer's services). MRPC 7.2, cmt. 5.

b. Receipt of payment in sale of law practice permitted

The rule against payment for recommending a lawyer's services does not prevent a lawyer from accepting payment in the sale of a law practice in accordance with the Model Rules. MRPC 7.2(b)(3).

2. Payment for Certain Referrals Is Permitted

In limited circumstances, payment for referrals is permitted.

a. Payment of usual charges of legal service plan or not-for-profit or qualified lawyer referral service

The rule against payment for recommending a lawyer's services does not prevent a lawyer from paying the usual charges of a legal service plan or a not-for-profit or qualified lawyer referral service. Qualified referral services are consumer-oriented organizations that provide unbiased referrals to lawyers with appropriate experience in the subject matter of the representation and afford other client protections, such as complaint procedures or malpractice insurance requirements. MRPC 7.2(b)(2).

A legal service plan is a pre-paid or group legal service plan or a similar delivery system that assists people who seek to secure legal representation. A lawyer referral service, on the other hand, is any organization that holds itself out to the public as a lawyer referral service. A qualified lawyer referral service is one that is approved by an appropriate regulatory authority as affording adequate protections for the public. MRPC 7.2, cmt. 6.

b. Reciprocal referral agreements

Under certain circumstances, a lawyer may agree to refer clients to another lawyer or a non-lawyer professional, in return for the undertaking of that person to refer clients or customers to the lawyer. This is known as a reciprocal referral agreement.

1) Requirements

The reciprocal referral agreement must not be exclusive, and the client must be informed of the existence and nature of the agreement. MRPC 7.2(b)(4). In addition, such an agreement must not interfere with the lawyer's professional judgment as to making referrals or providing substantive legal services. MRPC 7.2, cmt. 8.

2) Duration

A reciprocal referral agreement should not be of indefinite duration and should be reviewed periodically to determine whether it is in compliance with the Model Rules. MRPC 7.2, cmt. 8.

3) Lawyers within firms comprised of multiple entities

This rule does not restrict referrals or division of revenues or net income among lawyers within firms that are comprised of multiple entities. MRPC 7.2, cmt. 8.

C. GROUP LEGAL SERVICES

1. Requirements for Participation

Under certain circumstances, a lawyer may provide legal services through a prepaid or group legal service plan that uses in-person, telephone, or real time electronic contact to solicit memberships or subscriptions for the plan. The plan must not be operated by an organization that is owned or directed by the lawyer. In addition, the plan may not solicit persons who are known to need legal services in a particular matter, but can inform potential plan members that the plan represents a means of securing affordable legal services. Also, a lawyer who provides legal services through the plan may not engage in solicitation of potential members on behalf of the plan, but may contact representatives of groups or organizations who are interested in establishing such a plan concerning the terms under which the lawyer is willing to participate in such a plan. MRPC 7.3(e), cmts. 6, 8.

2. Lawyer's Responsibilities to Assure

A lawyer who participates in such a legal service plan must act reasonably to assure that the plan sponsors are in compliance with the Model Rules with respect to advertising, communications, and solicitation and the lawyer's professional obligations in general. MRPC 7.2, cmt. 7; 7.3, cmt. 8. Thus, advertising must not be false or misleading, as would be the case if the communications of a group legal services plan misled the public to think that the plan was a lawyer referral service sponsored by a state agency or bar association. MRPC 7.2, cmt. 7.

D. SOLICITATION OF CLIENTS

A solicitation is a targeted communication initiated by the lawyer that is directed to a specific person and that offers to provide, or can reasonably be understood as offering to provide, legal services (such as letters sent to accident victims, in-person solicitation of employment, or real-time electronic contact). MRPC 7.3(a).

In contrast, a lawyer's communication typically does not constitute a solicitation if it is directed to the general public, such as through a billboard, an Internet banner advertisement, a website or a television commercial, or if it is in response to a request for information or is automatically generated in response to Internet searches. MRPC 7.3(a), cmt. 1.

1. **Live Person-to-Person Contact**

    Solicitation of professional employment by live person-to-person contact is prohibited when a significant motive for the lawyer's doing so is the lawyer's or law firm's pecuniary gain, **unless** the person contacted is:

    i) A lawyer;

    ii) A person who has a family, close personal, or prior business or professional relationship with the soliciting lawyer or law firm; or

    iii) A person who routinely uses for business purposes the type of legal services offered by the lawyer.

    MRPC 7.3(a).

    a. **Live person-to-person contact defined**

        "Live person-to-person contact" means in-person, face-to-face, live telephone and other real-time visual or auditory person-to-person communications where the person is subject to a direct personal encounter without time for reflection. Such person-to-person contact does not include chat rooms, text messages or other written communications that recipients may easily disregard. MRPC 7.3(a), cmt. 2.

    b. **Reasoning**

        A person known to need legal services, who may already feel overwhelmed by the circumstances giving rise to the need for legal services, may find it difficult to fully evaluate all available alternatives with reasoned judgment and appropriate self-interest in the face of the lawyer's presence and insistence upon an immediate response. As solicitation via live person-to-person contact raises strong possibilities of undue influence, intimidation, and over-reaching, the Model Rules prohibit such solicitation. MRPC 7.3, cmt. 2.

    c. **Allowed if not for pecuniary gain**

        This prohibition only applies if a significant motive of the lawyer's solicitation of the client is for the lawyer's own pecuniary gain. If the lawyer is volunteering to work for the client *pro bono*, the prohibition on solicitation will not apply.

2. **Duress, Coercion, or Harassment of Prospective Clients**

    A lawyer is not permitted to solicit professional employment, even when not otherwise prohibited by the Model Rules, if: (i) the target of the solicitation has made known to the lawyer a desire not to be solicited by the lawyer; or (ii) the solicitation involves coercion, duress, or harassment. MRPC 7.3(c).

3. **Exempt Communications**

    Model Rule 7.3 does not prohibit communications authorized by law or ordered by a court or other tribunal. MRPC 7.3(d).

XI. LAWYERS AND THE LEGAL SYSTEM

A. LAWYER ACTIVITY IN IMPROVING THE LEGAL SYSTEM

1. *Pro Bono Publico*

a. Voluntary responsibility

The Model Rules set forth a *voluntary* professional responsibility for a lawyer to accept representation of clients who are unable to pay, suggesting that lawyers should offer at least fifty hours of *pro bono* legal services per year. MRPC 6.1. The responsibility is not intended to be enforced through disciplinary process. MRPC 6.1, cmt. 12.

b. Work for persons of limited means

The Model Rules indicate that a lawyer should provide a substantial majority of the fifty hours of legal services without fee or expectation of fee to persons of limited means or charitable, religious, civic, community, governmental, and educational organizations in matters that are designed primarily to address the needs of persons of limited means. MRPC 6.1(a).

2. Membership in a Legal Services Organization

a. In general

A lawyer may serve as a director, officer, or member of a legal services organization, apart from the law firm in which the lawyer practices, even if the organization serves persons having interests that are adverse to a client of the lawyer. MRPC 6.3.

b. Lawyer must avoid conflicts

The lawyer, however, is not permitted to knowingly participate in a decision or action of the organization if such participation would be incompatible with the lawyer's obligations to a client under the Model Rules concerning conflicts of interest, or when the decision or action could have a material adverse effect on the representation of a client of the organization whose interests are adverse to a client of the lawyer. MRPC 6.3.

3. Law Reform Activities Affecting Client Interests

a. General rule

A lawyer may serve as a director, officer, or member of an organization involved in reform of the law or its administration, even if such reform may affect the interests of a client of the lawyer. MRPC 6.4.

b. Must avoid conflict of interest

In determining the nature and scope of participation in such activities, the lawyer must be careful to avoid any conflict of interest or other violation of the Model Rules. MRPC 6.4, cmt. 1.

c. Client may be materially benefitted

When the lawyer knows that the interests of a client may be materially benefitted by a decision in which the lawyer participates, **the lawyer must disclose that fact but need not identify the client**. MRPC 6.4.

4. **Non-Profit and Court-Annexed Limited Legal Services Programs**

   a. **In general**

   Legal services organizations, courts, and certain nonprofit organizations have established programs (e.g., legal-advice hotlines, advice-only clinics, or *pro se* counseling programs) in which lawyers provide short-term limited legal services, such as advice or the completion of legal forms, to help persons to address their legal problems without further representation by a lawyer. A client-lawyer relationship is established in these programs, but there is no expectation that the lawyer's representation of the client will continue beyond the limited consultation. Such programs normally operate under circumstances in which it is not feasible for a lawyer to systematically screen for conflicts of interest as is generally required before undertaking a representation. MRPC 6.5, cmt. 1.

   b. **Must secure client's consent to limited relationship**

   A lawyer who provides such short-term limited legal services must secure the client's informed consent to the limited scope of the representation. MRPC 6.5, cmt. 2; see also MRPC 1.2(c). If a short-term limited representation would not be reasonable under the circumstances, the lawyer may offer advice to the client but must also advise the client of the need for further assistance of counsel. MRPC 6.5, cmt. 2.

   c. **Special rule regarding conflicts of interest**

      1) **For the lawyer**

      Under the Model Rules, a lawyer who, under the auspices of a program sponsored by a non-profit organization or court, provides short-term limited legal services to a client without expectation by either the lawyer or the client that the lawyer will provide continuing representation in the matter, is only subject to the Model Rules regarding conflicts of interest if the lawyer knows that the representation of the client involves a conflict of interest for the lawyer or for another lawyer associated with the lawyer in a law firm.

      2) **For the lawyer's firm**

      A lawyer's participation in a short-term limited legal services program will not prohibit the lawyer's firm from undertaking or continuing the representation of a client with interests that are adverse to a client being represented under the program. MRPC 6.5(b), cmt. 4.

      3) **Lawyer subsequently undertakes ongoing representation**

      If, after the lawyer has begun a short-term limited representation under a non-profit or court-annexed limited legal service, the lawyer undertakes to represent the client in the matter on an ongoing basis, all of the regular conflict of interest rules (MRPC 1.7, 1.9(a), and 1.10) become applicable.

B. **IMPROPRIETY INCIDENT TO PUBLIC SERVICE**

   1. **Political Contributions to Obtain Government Legal Engagements or Appointments by Judges**

      a. **General rule**

      A lawyer or law firm (or any political action committee or other entity owned or controlled by a lawyer or law firm) is not permitted to accept a government legal engagement or an appointment by a judge if the lawyer or law firm makes a political contribution or solicits political contributions **for the purpose of** obtaining or being considered for that type of legal engagement or appointment. MRPC 7.6, cmt. 4. A political contribution is for the purpose of obtaining or being considered for a government legal engagement or appointment by a judge if, but for the desire to be considered for the legal engagement or appointment, the lawyer or law firm would not have made or solicited the contributions. MRPC 7.6, cmt. 5.

b. "Political contribution"

The term "political contribution" means any gift, subscription, loan, advance, or deposit of anything of value made directly or indirectly to a candidate, incumbent, political party or campaign committee to influence or provide financial support for election to or retention in judicial or other government office. Political contributions in initiative and referendum elections are not included. The Model Rules exclude uncompensated services from the definition of "political contribution." MRPC 7.6, cmt. 2.

c. "Government legal engagement"

The term "government legal engagement" means any engagement to provide legal services that a public official has the direct or indirect power to award. The term does not, however, include: substantially uncompensated services; engagements or appointments made on the basis of experience, expertise, professional qualifications and cost following a request for proposal or other process that is free from influence based upon political contributions; and engagements or appointments made on a rotational basis from a list compiled without regard to political contributions. MRPC 7.6, cmt. 3.

d. "Appointment by a judge"

The term "appointment by a judge" denotes an appointment to a position such as referee, commissioner, special master, receiver, guardian, or other similar position that is made by a judge. The term does not, include: substantially uncompensated services; engagements or appointments made on the basis of experience, expertise, professional qualifications and cost following a request for proposal or other process that is free from influence based upon political contributions; and engagements or appointments made on a rotational basis from a list compiled without regard to political contributions. MRPC 7.6, cmt. 3.

2. Judicial and Legal Officials

a. Statements concerning qualifications or integrity

A lawyer must not make a statement that the lawyer knows to be false or with reckless disregard as to its truth or falsity concerning the qualifications or integrity of a judge, adjudicatory officer, or public legal officer, or of a candidate for election or appointment to judicial or legal office. MRPC 8.2(a).

b. Obligations of lawyers as candidates for judicial office

A lawyer who is a candidate for judicial office is required to comply with the applicable provisions of the ABA Model Code of Judicial Conduct (*see* XII.E. Political and Campaign Activity of Judges, *infra*). MRPC 8.2(b).

XII. JUDICIAL ETHICS

Judges are bound by the general rules of professional conduct for all lawyers, but special rules of professional conduct for judges also exist. The ABA Model Code of Judicial Conduct (CJC) was adopted in 1972 and was revised most recently in 2007.

The CJC encompasses the precepts that judges must respect, honor, and uphold the judicial office as a public trust and must strive to maintain and enhance confidence in the legal system. It consists of four Canons, numbered Rules under each Canon, and Comments that explain each Rule. The Canons state overarching principles of judicial ethics that all judges must observe. Although a judge may be disciplined only for violating a Rule, the Canons provide guidance in interpreting the Rules.

The provisions of the CJC apply to all full-time judges. A judge, within the meaning of the CJC, is anyone who is authorized to perform judicial functions, including an officer such as a justice of the peace, magistrate, court commissioner, special master, referee, or member of the administrative law judiciary. Part-time judges (including periodic, *pro tempore*, and retired judges who are subject to recall) are subject to a variety of exemptions to the CJC. Canon 4 of the CJC applies to judicial candidates. A retired judge who is not subject to recall is not subject to the provisions of the CJC. CJC, Application.

> **EXAM NOTE:** When answering questions related to a judge's behavior, remember that most judges are also lawyers, and are thus **also** bound by the professional ethics rules that apply to lawyers.

A. DUTY TO UPHOLD THE INTEGRITY AND INDEPENDENCE OF THE JUDICIARY

A judge must uphold and promote the independence, integrity, and impartiality of the judiciary, and must avoid impropriety and the appearance of impropriety. CJC Canon 1.

1. Compliance With the Law

A judge is required to comply with the law, including the CJC. CJC Rule 1.1. A conviction is not required for a judge to be considered to have violated this rule if a judge refuses to follow precedent or other mandatory authority. See, e.g., *In re Hauge*, 315 N.W.2d 524 (Mich. 1982).

2. Promoting Confidence in the Judiciary

A judge is required to act at all times in a manner that promotes public confidence in the independence, integrity, and impartiality of the judiciary. CJC Rule 1.2. The CJC indicates that judges should participate in activities that promote ethical conduct among judges and lawyers, support professionalism within the judiciary and the legal profession, and promote access to justice for all. CJC Rule 1.2, cmt. 4. It also provides that a judge should initiate and participate in community outreach activities for the purpose of promoting public understanding of and confidence in the administration of justice. In conducting such activities, a judge is required to act in a manner consistent with the CJC. CJC Rule 1.2, cmt. 6.

B. DUTY TO AVOID IMPROPRIETY AND THE APPEARANCE OF IMPROPRIETY

1. General Rule

A judge is required to avoid both impropriety and the appearance of impropriety. CJC Rule 1.2.

2. Appearance of Impropriety

The test for appearance of impropriety is whether the conduct would create in reasonable minds a perception that the judge violated the CJC or engaged in other conduct that reflects adversely on the judge's honesty, impartiality, temperament, or fitness to serve as a judge. CJC Rule 1.2, cmt. 5.

3. Avoiding Abuse of the Prestige of Judicial Office

A judge must not abuse the prestige of judicial office to advance the personal or economic interests of the judge or others, or allow others to do so. CJC Rule 1.3. It is improper for a judge to use or attempt to use her position in order to gain personal advantage or deferential treatment of any kind. CJC Rule 1.3, cmt. 1.

> **Example:** It would be improper for a judge to allude to her judicial status in order to attempt to gain favorable treatment in encounters with traffic officials.

a. References

A judge is permitted to provide a reference or recommendation for an individual based upon the judge's personal knowledge. While a judge must not use judicial letterhead to gain an advantage in conducting his personal business, the judge may use official letterhead for a reference for someone else if the judge indicates that the reference is personal and if there is no likelihood that the use of the letterhead would reasonably be perceived as an attempt to use the judge's official position to exert pressure. CJC Rule 1.3, cmt. 2.

b. Writing for publications of for-profit entities

If a judge writes or contributes to a publication of a for-profit entity, whether or not related to the law, the judge should not permit anyone associated with the publication to exploit the judge's office in a manner that violates the CJC or other applicable law. A judge should retain sufficient control over advertising in any contract for publication of a judges writing to avoid such exploitation. CJC Rule 1.3, cmt. 4.

C. DUTIES OF IMPARTIALITY, COMPETENCE, AND DILIGENCE

A judge is required to perform the duties of judicial office impartially, competently, and diligently. CJC Canon 2.

1. Giving Precedence to the Duties of Judicial Office

The duties of judicial office, as prescribed by law, are required to take precedence over all of a judge's personal and extrajudicial activities. CJC Rule 2.1.

2. Impartiality and Fairness

a. General rule

A judge is required to uphold and apply the law, and to perform all duties of judicial office fairly and impartially. CJC Rule 2.2.

b. Upholding the law despite personal views

A judge must interpret and apply the law without regard to whether the judge approves or disapproves of the law in question. CJC Rule 2.2, cmt. 2.

c. Good faith errors

If a judge makes a good-faith error of fact or law when applying and interpreting the law, such error is not a violation of the rule requiring a judge to uphold and apply the law. CJC Rule 2.2, cmt. 3.

d. Reasonable accommodations to *pro se* litigants

It is not a violation of the rule requiring fairness and impartiality for a judge to make reasonable accommodations to ensure *pro se* litigants the opportunity to have their matters fairly heard. CJC Rule 2.2, cmt. 4.

3. **Bias, Prejudice, and Harassment**

   a. **Judge's duty with regard to self**

   A judge is required to perform the duties of judicial office, including administrative duties, without bias or prejudice. CJC Rule 2.3(A). In performing judicial duties, a judge must not by words or conduct manifest bias or prejudice, or engage in harassment, including but not limited to bias, prejudice, or harassment based on race, sex, gender, religion, national origin, ethnicity, disability, age, sexual orientation, marital status, socio-economic status, or political affiliation. CJC Rule 2.3(B). A judge must avoid any conduct that may reasonably be perceived as prejudiced or biased. CJC Rule 2.3, cmt. 2.

   b. **Judge's duty with regard to staff**

   A judge must not permit court staff, court officials, or others subject to the judge's direction and control to engage in conduct that manifests bias or prejudice or to engage in harassment based on race, sex, gender, religion, national origin, ethnicity, disability, age, sexual orientation, marital status, socio-economic status, or political affiliation. CJC Rule 2.3(B).

   c. **Judge's duty with regard to lawyers in proceedings before the court**

   A judge must require lawyers appearing in proceedings before the court to refrain from manifesting bias or prejudice or engaging in harassment based on attributes including, but not limited to, race, sex, gender, religion, national origin, ethnicity, disability, age, sexual orientation, marital status, socio-economic status, or political affiliation, against parties, witnesses, lawyers, or others. CJC Rule 2.3(C).

   d. **Manifestations of bias or prejudice**

   Examples of manifestations of bias or prejudice include, but are not limited to: epithets; slurs; demeaning nicknames; negative stereotyping; attempted humor based upon stereotypes; threatening, intimidating, or hostile acts; suggestions of connections between race, ethnicity, or nationality and crime; and irrelevant references to personal characteristics. Facial expressions and body language may also convey an appearance of bias or prejudice. CJC Rule 2.3, cmt. 2.

   e. **Legitimate advocacy not precluded**

   The requirements of the CJC do not preclude judges or lawyers from making legitimate reference to race, sex, gender, religion, national origin, ethnicity, disability, age, sexual orientation, marital status, socio-economic status, or political affiliation, or similar factors, when they are relevant to an issue in a proceeding. CJC Rule 2.3(D).

4. **External Influences on Judicial Conduct**

   A judge must not be swayed by public clamor or fear of criticism. CJC Rule 2.4(A). Judges must not permit family, social, political, financial, or other interests or relationships to influence their judicial conduct or judgment. CJC Rule 2.4(B). In addition, they must not convey or permit others to convey the impression that any person or organization is in a position to influence them. CJC Rule 2.4(C).

5. **Competence and Diligence**

   a. **In general**

   A judge is required to perform judicial and administrative duties competently and diligently. CJC Rule 2.5(A).

b. Competence

Competence in performing judicial duties requires the legal knowledge, skill, thoroughness, and preparation reasonably necessary to perform a judge's responsibilities. CJC Rule 2.5, cmt. 1.

c. Diligence

Prompt disposition of court business requires a judge to devote adequate time to judicial duties, to be punctual in attending court and expeditious in determining matters under submission, and to take reasonable measures to ensure that court officials, litigants, and their lawyers cooperate with the judge. CJC Rule 2.5, cmt. 2. In disposing of matters promptly and efficiently, a judge must show due regard for the rights of parties to be heard and try to have issues resolved without unnecessary cost or delay. A judge should monitor and supervise cases in ways that reduce or eliminate dilatory practices, avoidable delays, and unnecessary costs. CJC Rule 2.5, cmt. 4.

6. Administrative Cooperation

A judge must cooperate with other judges and court officials in the administration of court business. CJC Rule 2.5(B).

7. Ensuring the Right to Be Heard

Judges must accord all those with legal interests in a proceeding or their lawyers a right to be heard according to law. Judges may encourage parties and their lawyers to settle disputes, but must do so without using coercion. CJC Rule 2.6. If there are instances when information obtained during settlement discussions could influence a judge's decision making during trial, the judge should consider whether disqualification may be appropriate. CJC Rule 2.6, cmt. 3; see also CJC Rule 2.11(A)(1).

8. Responsibility to Decide

A judge must hear and decide matters assigned to the judge, except when disqualification is required by the CJC or other law. CJC Rule 2.7. A judge should not use disqualification to avoid cases that present difficult, controversial, or unpopular issues. CJC Rule 2.7, cmt. 1.

9. Decorum and Demeanor

A judge must require order and decorum in proceedings before the court. CJC Rule 2.8(A). The CJC requires judges to be patient, dignified, and courteous to litigants, jurors, witnesses, lawyers, court staff, court officials, and others with whom the judge deals in an official capacity. Judges are required to ensure similar conduct from lawyers, court staff, court officials, and others subject to the judge's direction and control. CJC Rule 2.8(B).

10. Communication With Jurors

A judge is not permitted to commend or criticize jurors for their verdict other than in a court order or opinion in a proceeding. CJC Rule 2.8(C). Commending or criticizing jurors for a verdict may imply a judicial expectation in future cases and may impair a juror's ability to be fair and impartial in a subsequent case. CJC Rule 2.8, cmt. 2. Unless otherwise prohibited by law, a judge may meet with jurors who choose to remain after trial, but should be careful not to discuss the merits of the case. CJC Rule 2.8, cmt. 3.

11. Ex Parte Communications

a. General rule

In general, a judge must not initiate, permit, or consider ex parte communications, or consider other communications made to the judge outside the presence of the parties or their lawyers, with regard to a pending or impending matter. A judge is required to make reasonable efforts, including providing appropriate supervision, to ensure that this rule is not violated by court staff, court officials, and others subject to the judge's direction and control. CJC Rule 2.9(D).

Note that even innocently intended ex parte communications are generally prohibited.

b. Exceptions

1) Scheduling, administrative, or emergency reasons

If circumstances require it, ex parte communication is permissible for scheduling, administrative, or emergency purposes, which do not address substantive matters, but only if: (i) the judge reasonably believes that no party will gain a procedural, substantive, or tactical advantage as a result of the ex parte communication; and (ii) the judge makes provision promptly to notify all other parties of the substance of the ex parte communication, and gives the parties an opportunity to respond. CJC Rule 2.9(A)(1).

2) Disinterested legal expert

A judge is permitted to obtain the written advice of a disinterested expert on the law applicable to a proceeding before the judge, if the judge gives advance notice to the parties of the person to be consulted and the subject matter of the advice to be solicited, and gives them a reasonable opportunity to object and respond to the notice and to the advice received. CJC Rule 2.9(A)(2).

3) Consulting with court staff

A judge may consult with court staff and court officials whose functions are to aid the judge in carrying out her adjudicative responsibilities, or with other judges, provided that the judge makes reasonable efforts to avoid receiving factual information that is not part of the record and does not abrogate the judge's personal responsibility to decide the matter. CJC Rule 2.9(A)(3). A judge must avoid ex parte discussions of a case with judges who have previously been disqualified from hearing the matter and with judges who have appellate jurisdiction over the matter. CJC Rule 2.9, cmt. 5.

4) Settlement efforts

A judge may, with the consent of the parties, confer separately with the parties and their lawyers in an effort to settle matters pending before the judge. CJC Rule 2.9(A)(4).

5) When expressly authorized by law

A judge may initiate, permit, or consider any ex parte communication when expressly authorized by law to do so, such as when serving on a therapeutic or problem-solving court, a mental health court, or a drug court. CJC Rule 2.9(A)(5), cmt. 4. A judge may consult ethics advisory committees, outside counsel, or legal experts concerning the judge's compliance with the Code of Judicial Conduct. CJC Rule 2.9, cmt. 7.

c. Inadvertent receipt

If a judge inadvertently receives an unauthorized ex parte communication that bears on the substance of a matter, the judge is required to promptly notify the parties of the substance of the communication and provide the parties with an opportunity to respond. CJC Rule 2.9(B).

d. Prohibition on independent investigation of facts

A judge is not permitted to investigate facts in a matter independently, and must only consider the evidence presented and any facts that may properly be judicially noticed. CJC Rule 2.9(C). The prohibition against a judge investigating the facts in a matter extends to information available in all media, including electronic. CJC Rule 2.9, cmt. 6.

12. Judicial Statements on Pending and Impending Cases

a. Public comment

A judge is not permitted to make any public statement that might reasonably be expected to affect the outcome or impair the fairness of a matter pending or impending **in any court**, or make any nonpublic statement that might substantially interfere with a fair trial or hearing. CJC Rule 2.10(A).

b. Permissible statements

1) Official duties

A judge is permitted to make public statements in the course of official duties and may explain court procedures. CJC Rule 2.10(D).

2) Judge as litigant

A judge may comment on any proceeding in which the judge is a litigant in a **personal** (as opposed to official) capacity. CJC Rule 2.10(D). A judge may also comment on proceedings in which the judge represents a client as permitted by the Code of Judicial Conduct. CJC Rule 2.10, cmt. 2.

c. Use of third party

When a judge may permissibly comment under the rules, the judge may do so personally or through a third party. CJC Rule 2.10(E).

d. No pledges

A judge must not make promises, pledges, or commitments that put the judge's impartiality or integrity in question. CJC Rule 2.10(B).

e. Court staff

A judge must require court staff, court officials, and others subject to the judge's direction and control to refrain from making statements that the judge would be prohibited from making about a case.

13. Disqualification of a Judge

A judge must disqualify (i.e., recuse) herself from a proceeding in which the judge's **"impartiality may reasonably be questioned."** CJC Rule 2.11. Disqualification is required even if a party has not sought to disqualify the judge. CJC Rule 2.11, cmt. 2.

Although the basic standard for judicial disqualification is objective, the judge must also be subjectively unbiased.

However, in most situations, a judge may ask the parties to consider waiving the disqualification (*see* d. Waiver, *below*).

a. Rule of necessity

The rule of necessity may override the rule of disqualification. Thus, if the judge is the only judge available in a matter requiring immediate judicial action, such as a hearing on probable cause or a temporary restraining order, the judge may rule on the matter. The judge must disclose on the record the basis for possible disqualification and make reasonable efforts to transfer the matter to another judge as soon as practicable. CJC Rule 2.11, cmt. 3.

b. Grounds for disqualification

Even if none of the specific grounds for disqualification enumerated below are met, a judge is still required to disqualify herself if the judge's "impartiality may reasonably be questioned." CJC Rule 2.11. In determining when a judge's "impartiality may reasonably be questioned" apart from the enumerated grounds, a judge who has expressed a general opinion or formulated policy prior to becoming a judge that runs counter to a party's position in the current proceeding is not required to disqualify herself. A judge is presumed to be able put aside general preferences and be impartial with regard to the case over which the judge is presiding. *See*, e.g., *Laird v. Tatum*, 409 U.S. 824 (1972) (Justice Rehnquist's public statements, including testimony before Congress, regarding the constitutionality of governmental surveillance methods did not constitute grounds for his disqualification in hearing a case in which the constitutionality of those methods were challenged).

1) General bias

A judge must disqualify herself in any proceeding if there is reasonable ground to believe that the judge has a personal bias or prejudice concerning a party or a party's lawyer, or personal knowledge of facts that are in dispute in the proceeding. CJC Rule 2.11(A)(1).

2) Relationship to party, witness, or lawyer

A judge must disqualify herself in a matter in which the judge knows that she or her spouse or domestic partner shares a third degree relationship or closer to a party, lawyer, material witness, or person who has more than a de minimis interest that could be affected by the proceedings. Disqualification is also required when the spouse or domestic partner of the related person is a party, lawyer, material witness, or interested party in the matter. CJC Rule 2.11(A)(2). A "third degree of relationship" includes a: great-grandparent, grandparent, parent, uncle, aunt, brother, sister, child, grandchild, great-grandchild, nephew, and niece. CJC, Terminology.

The fact that a lawyer in a proceeding is affiliated with a law firm with which a relative of the judge is affiliated does not itself disqualify the judge. If the judge's impartiality might reasonably be questioned, or the relative is known by the judge to have an interest in the law firm that could be substantially affected by the proceeding under paragraph, the judge must be disqualified.

3) Economic interest

A judge is disqualified when the judge knows that he, individually or as a fiduciary, or the judge's spouse, domestic partner, parent, or child, or any other member of the judge's family residing in the judge's household, has an economic interest in the subject matter in controversy or in a party to the proceeding. CJC Rule 2.11(A)(3), cmt. 6.

a) Definition of "economic interest"

"Economic interest" means ownership of more than a de minimis legal or equitable interest. Unless the judge participates in the management of such a legal or equitable interest, or the interest could be substantially affected by the outcome of a proceeding before a judge, it does **not** include: (i) an interest in the individual holdings within a mutual fund; (ii) an interest in securities held by an educational, religious, charitable, fraternal, or civic organization in which the judge or the judge's spouse, domestic partner, parent, or child serves as a director, an officer, an advisor, or other participant; (iii) a deposit in a financial institution or deposits or proprietary interests the judge may maintain as a member of a mutual savings association or credit union, or similar interests; or (iv) an interest in the issuer of government securities held by the judge. CJC, Terminology.

4) Contributors to judge's campaign

A judge is disqualified when he knows or learns by means of a timely motion that a party, a party's lawyer, or the law firm of a party's lawyer has within recent years made total contributions to the judge's campaign in an amount that is greater than an amount set by the local jurisdiction in its ethics code. CJC Rule 2.11(A)(4).

5) Judge has made public statements committing the judge to rule in a particular way

A judge is disqualified if she, while a judge or a judicial candidate, has made a public statement, other than in a court proceeding, judicial decision, or opinion, **that commits or appears to commit** the judge to reach a particular result or rule in a particular way in the proceeding or controversy. CJC Rule 2.11(A)(5).

6) Prior relationship to matter

A judge is disqualified if she: (i) formerly served as a lawyer in the matter in controversy, or was associated with a lawyer who participated substantially as a lawyer in the matter during such association; (ii) served in governmental employment and participated personally and substantially as a lawyer or public official concerning the proceeding, or publicly expressed an opinion concerning the merits of the particular matter in controversy; (iii) was a material witness concerning the matter; or (iv) previously presided as a judge over the matter in another court. CJC Rule 2.11(A)(6).

> **Example:** A judge has been assigned to try a criminal prosecution against a defendant. Twelve years earlier, the judge, while serving as a local prosecutor, initiated a criminal investigation of the same defendant. The investigation did not establish any basis for prosecution and none of the matters previously investigated are involved in or affect the present prosecution. Although the matters are different, the judge **may not** properly try the current case if her "impartiality may reasonably be questioned" with regard to the defendant because of the prior investigation.

c. Disclosure by the judge

A judge should disclose on the record information that he believes the parties or their lawyers might reasonably consider relevant to a possible disqualification motion, even when the judge believes that there is no basis for disqualification. CJC Rule 2.11, cmt. 5.

d. Waiver

A judge who is subject to disqualification under the CJC, other than for bias or prejudice (*see* b.1) General bias, *above*), may disclose on the record the basis of the judge's disqualification and may ask the parties and their lawyers to consider, outside the presence of the judge and court personnel, whether to waive disqualification. If, after such disclosure, the parties and lawyers agree, without participation by the judge or court personnel, that the judge should not be disqualified, the judge may participate in the proceeding. The agreement must be incorporated into the record of the proceeding. CJC Rule 2.11(C).

e. Personal and fiduciary economic interests

A judge is required to keep informed about the judge's personal and fiduciary economic interests, and make a reasonable effort to keep informed about the personal economic interests of the judge's spouse or domestic partner and minor children residing in the judge's household. CJC Rule 2.11(B).

14. Supervisory Duties

A judge must require court staff, court officials, and others subject to the judge's direction and control to act in a manner consistent with the judge's obligations under the CJC. A judge with supervisory authority for the performance of other judges must take reasonable measures to ensure that those judges properly discharge their judicial responsibilities, including the prompt disposition of matters before them. CJC Rule 2.12.

15. Administrative Appointments

a. In general

Judges sometimes make administrative appointments, such as assigned counsel, referees, commissioners, special masters, receivers, and guardians, and hire personnel such as clerks, secretaries, and bailiffs. In making such administrative appointments, a judge is required to exercise the power of appointment impartially and on the basis of merit; and must avoid nepotism, favoritism, and unnecessary appointments. CJC Rule 2.13(A). In addition, when a judge makes an appointment, she must not approve compensation of the appointed person beyond the fair value of services rendered. CJC Rule 2.13(C).

b. Restrictions on appointing lawyers who were campaign contributors

In general, a judge is not permitted to appoint a lawyer to a position if the judge either knows that the lawyer, or the lawyer's spouse or domestic partner, has contributed more than the local jurisdiction's designated amount within a recent period of years to the judge's election campaign, or learns of such a contribution by means of a timely motion by a party or other person properly interested in the matter. A judge may appoint such a lawyer to a position if: (i) the position is substantially uncompensated; (ii) the lawyer has been selected in rotation from a list of qualified and available lawyers compiled without regard to their having made political contributions; or (iii) the judge or another presiding or administrative judge specifically finds that no other lawyer is willing, competent, and able to accept the position. CJC Rule 2.13(B).

16. Disability and Impairment of Lawyers or Other Judges

a. In general

A judge who has a reasonable belief that the performance of a lawyer or another judge is impaired by drugs or alcohol, or by a mental, emotional, or physical condition, is required to take appropriate action. CJC Rule 2.14.

b. "Appropriate action"

"Appropriate action" means action intended and reasonably likely to help the judge or lawyer in question address the problem and prevent harm to the justice system. Depending upon the circumstances, appropriate action may include but is not limited to, speaking directly to the impaired person, notifying an individual with supervisory responsibility over the impaired person, or making a referral to an assistance program. CJC Rule 2.14, cmt. 1. Depending on the seriousness of the conduct that has come to the judge's attention, however, the judge may be required to take other action, such as reporting the impaired judge or lawyer to the appropriate authority, agency, or body. CJC Rule 2.14, cmt. 2.

17. Responding to Judicial and Lawyer Misconduct

a. Judicial misconduct

1) Knowledge

A judge who has knowledge that another judge has committed a violation of the CJC that raises a substantial question regarding the judge's honesty, trustworthiness, or fitness as a judge in other respects is required to inform the authority having responsibility for initiation of the disciplinary process in connection with the violation to be reported. CJC Rule 2.15(A).

2) Substantial likelihood

A judge who receives information indicating a substantial likelihood that another judge has committed a violation of the CJC is required to take appropriate action. CJC Rule 2.15(C). Appropriate action can vary depending on the seriousness of the issue and may include: conferring with the judge, communicating with a supervising judge, or reporting the suspected violation to the appropriate authority or other agency or body. CJC Rule 2.15, cmt. 2.

b. Lawyer misconduct

1) Knowledge

A judge who has knowledge that a lawyer has committed a violation of the Model Rules that raises a substantial question regarding the lawyer's honesty, trustworthiness, or fitness as a lawyer in other respects is required to inform the authority having responsibility for initiation of the disciplinary process in connection with the violation to be reported. CJC Rule 2.15(B).

2) Substantial likelihood

A judge who receives information indicating a substantial likelihood that a lawyer has committed a violation of the Model Rules is required to take appropriate action. CJC Rule 2.15(D). Appropriate action can vary depending on the seriousness of the issue and may include conferring with the lawyer or reporting the suspected violation to the appropriate authority or other agency or body. CJC Rule 2.15, cmt. 2.

18. **Cooperation With Disciplinary Authorities**

A judge must cooperate and be candid and honest with judicial and lawyer disciplinary agencies. CJC Rule 2.16(A). A judge must not retaliate, directly or indirectly, against a person known or suspected to have assisted or cooperated with an investigation of a judge or a lawyer. CJC Rule 2.16(B).

D. **EXTRAJUDICIAL ACTIVITIES**

A judge must conduct the judge's personal and extrajudicial activities to minimize the risk of conflict with the obligations of judicial office. CJC Canon 3.

1. **Extrajudicial Activities in General**

A judge is permitted to engage in extrajudicial activities, except as prohibited by law or the CJC. When engaging in extrajudicial activities, a judge is not allowed to:

i) Participate in activities that will interfere with the proper performance of the judge's judicial duties;

ii) Participate in activities that will lead to frequent disqualification of the judge;

iii) Participate in activities that would appear to a reasonable person to undermine the judge's independence, integrity, or impartiality;

iv) Engage in conduct that would appear to a reasonable person to be coercive; or

v) Make use of court premises, staff, stationery, equipment, or other resources, except for incidental use for activities that concern the law, the legal system, or the administration of justice, or unless such additional use is permitted by law.

CJC Rule 3.1.

2. **Appearances Before Governmental Bodies and Consultation With Government Officials**

A judge must not appear voluntarily at a public hearing before, or otherwise consult with, an executive or a legislative body or official, **except**:

i) In connection with matters concerning the law, the legal system, or the administration of justice;

ii) In connection with matters about which the judge acquired knowledge or expertise in the course of the judge's judicial duties; or

iii) When the judge is acting *pro se* in a matter involving the judge's legal or economic interests, or when the judge is acting in a fiduciary capacity.

CJC Rule 3.2.

3. **Testifying as a Character Witness**

A judge must not testify as a character witness in a judicial, administrative, or other adjudicatory proceeding or otherwise vouch for the character of a person in a legal proceeding, **except** when duly summoned. The concern is that a judge who, without being subpoenaed, testifies as a character witness is abusing the prestige of judicial office to advance the interests of another. Except in unusual circumstances when the demands of justice require, a judge should discourage a party from requiring the judge to testify as a character witness. CJC Rule 3.3, cmt. 1.

4. Appointments to Governmental Positions

A judge is not permitted to accept appointment to a governmental committee, board, commission, or other governmental position, **unless** it concerns the law, the legal system, or the administration of justice. CJC Rule 3.4. A judge may represent his country, state, or locality on ceremonial occasions or in connection with historical, educational, or cultural activities. Such representation does not constitute acceptance of a government position. CJC Rule 3.4, cmt. 2.

5. Use of Nonpublic Information

A judge must not intentionally disclose or use nonpublic information acquired in a judicial capacity for any purpose unrelated to the judge's judicial duties. CJC Rule 3.5. This rule is not intended, however, to affect a judge's ability to act on information as necessary to protect the health or safety of the judge or a member of a judge's family, court personnel, or other judicial officers if consistent with other provisions of the CJC. CJC Rule 3.5, cmt. 2.

6. Affiliation With Discriminatory Organizations

The CJC prohibits a judge from holding membership in any organization that practices invidious discrimination on the basis of race, sex, gender, religion, national origin, ethnicity, or sexual orientation. CJC Rule 3.6(A). A judge's membership in a religious organization as a lawful exercise of the freedom of religion is not a violation of the rule. CJC Rule 3.6, cmt. 4. If a judge learns that an organization to which the judge belongs engages in invidious discrimination, the judge must resign immediately from the organization. CJC Rule 3.6, cmt. 3. A judge must also not use the benefits or facilities of an organization if the judge knows or should know that the organization practices invidious discrimination on one or more such bases. CJC Rule 3.6(B). A judge's attendance at an event in a facility of an organization that the judge is not permitted to join is not a violation of the CJC when the judge's attendance is an isolated event that could not reasonably be perceived as an endorsement of the organization's practices. CJC Rule 3.6(C).

7. Participation in Organizations and Activities

As long a judge meets the general requirements of the CJC with regard to extrajudicial activities (see CJC Rule 3.1), he may participate in activities sponsored by organizations or governmental entities concerned with the law, the legal system, or the administration of justice, and those sponsored by or on behalf of educational, religious, charitable, fraternal, or civic organizations not conducted for profit. CJC Rule 3.7(A). Such activities include (but are not limited to):

i) Assistance in planning related to fundraising, and participating in the management and investment of the organization's or entity's funds;

ii) Solicitation of contributions for such an organization or entity, but only from members of the judge's family, or from judges over whom the judge does not exercise supervisory or appellate authority;

iii) Solicitation of membership for such an organization or entity, even though the membership dues or fees generated may be used to support the objectives of the organization or entity, but only if the organization or entity is concerned with the law, the legal system, or the administration of justice;

iv) Appearing or speaking at, receiving an award or other recognition at, being featured on the program of, and permitting his title to be used in connection with an event of such an organization or entity, but if the event serves a fundraising purpose, the judge may participate only if the event concerns the law, the legal system, or the administration of justice;

v) Making recommendations to such a public or private fund-granting organization or entity in connection with its programs and activities, but only if the organization or entity is concerned with the law, the legal system, or the administration of justice; and

vi) Serving as an officer, director, trustee, or non-legal advisor of such an organization or entity, unless it is likely that the organization or entity will be engaged in proceedings that would ordinarily come before the judge; or will frequently be engaged in adversary proceedings in the court of which the judge is a member, or in any court subject to the appellate jurisdiction of the court of which the judge is a member.

CJC Rule 3.7(A).

8. **Encouragement of *Pro Bono Publico* Legal Service**

A judge may encourage lawyers to provide *pro bono publico* legal services. CJC Rule 3.7(B).

9. **Appointments to Fiduciary Positions**

    a. **In general**

    A judge is not permitted to accept appointment to serve in a fiduciary position, such as executor, administrator, trustee, guardian, attorney in fact, or other personal representative, except for the estate, trust, or person of a member of the judge's family, and then only if such service will not interfere with the proper performance of judicial duties. CJC Rule 3.8(A). A judge may not serve in a fiduciary position if the judge as fiduciary will likely be engaged in proceedings that would ordinarily come before the judge, or if the estate, trust, or ward becomes involved in adversary proceedings in the court on which the judge serves, or one under its appellate jurisdiction. CJC Rule 3.8(B). A member of the judge's family includes a spouse, domestic partner, child, parent, grandparent, or other relative or person with whom the judge maintains a close familial relationship. CJC, Terminology.

    b. **Restrictions on judge's activities as a fiduciary**

    A judge acting in a fiduciary capacity is subject to the same restrictions on engaging in financial activities that apply to a judge personally.

    c. **Person who becomes judge**

    If a person who is currently serving in a fiduciary position becomes a judge, she must comply with CJC Rule 3.8 as soon as reasonably practicable, but in no event later than one year after becoming a judge. CJC Rule 3.8(D).

10. **Service as Arbitrator or Mediator**

A judge is not permitted to act as an arbitrator or a mediator or perform other judicial functions apart from the judge's official duties unless expressly authorized by law. CJC Rule 3.9. This rule does not prohibit a judge from participating in arbitration, mediation, or settlement conferences performed as part of assigned judicial duties. CJC Rule 3.9, cmt. 1.

11. **Practice of Law**

A full-time judge is generally not permitted to practice law. Such a judge may act *pro se* in any legal matter or, for family members, give legal advice or draft or review documents without charge, but cannot serve as the family member's lawyer. A judge must not use the prestige of the judge's position to advance family interests. CJC Rule 3.10, cmt. 1.

12. **Financial, Business, or Remunerative Activities**

a. **In general**

In general, a judge is permitted to hold and manage investments of the judge and members of the judge's family. CJC Rule 3.11(A). A judge is not permitted to serve as an officer, director, manager, general partner, advisor, or employee of any business entity except that a judge may manage or participate in: (i) a business closely held by the judge or members of the judge's family; or (ii) a business entity primarily engaged in investment of the financial resources of the judge or members of the judge's family. CJC Rule 3.11(B).

b. **Restrictions**

A judge may not engage in any of these activities, however, if they will interfere with the proper performance of judicial duties; lead to frequent disqualification of the judge; involve the judge in frequent transactions or continuing business relationships with lawyers or other persons likely to come before the court on which the judge serves; or result in violation of other provisions of the CJC.

c. **When divestment is required**

As soon as practicable without serious financial detriment, the judge must divest himself or herself of investments and other financial interests that might require frequent disqualification or otherwise violate the CJC. CJC Rule 3.11, cmt. 2.

13. **Compensation for Extrajudicial Activities**

A judge may receive compensation for extrajudicial activities, but such outside income must be reasonable and commensurate with the task performed, and must not create the appearance of impartiality or compromise the judge's independence or integrity. CJC Rule 3.12. Compensation derived from extrajudicial activities is subject to public reporting.

14. **Acceptance and Reporting of Things of Value**

a. **General rule**

A judge is not permitted to accept any gifts, loans, bequests, benefits, or other things of value, if acceptance is prohibited by law or would appear to a reasonable person to undermine the judge's independence, integrity, or impartiality. CJC Rule 3.13(A).

b. **Acceptable gifts that do not require public reporting**

Unless otherwise prohibited by law, or under the general rule stated above, a judge may accept the following **without publicly reporting** such acceptance:

   i)   Items with little intrinsic value, such as plaques, certificates, trophies, and greeting cards;

   ii) Gifts, loans, bequests, benefits, or other things of value from friends, relatives, or other persons, including lawyers, whose appearance or interest in a proceeding pending or impending before the judge would in any event require disqualification of the judge;

iii) Ordinary social hospitality;

iv) Commercial or financial opportunities and benefits, including special pricing and discounts, and loans from lending institutions in their regular course of business, if the same opportunities and benefits or loans are made available on the same terms to similarly situated persons who are not judges;

v) Rewards and prizes given to competitors or participants in random drawings, contests, or other events that are open to persons who are not judges;

vi) Scholarships, fellowships, and similar benefits or awards, if they are available to similarly-situated persons who are not judges, based on the same terms and criteria;

vii) Books, magazines, journals, audiovisual materials, and other resource materials supplied by publishers on a complimentary basis for official use; or

viii) Gifts, awards, or benefits associated with the business, profession, or other separate activity of a spouse, a domestic partner, or other family member of a judge residing in the judge's household, but that incidentally benefit the judge.

CJC Rule 3.13(B).

c. **Acceptable gifts that require public reporting**

Unless otherwise prohibited by law or under the general rule stated above, a judge may accept the following items, but must generally report such acceptance:

i) Gifts incident to a public testimonial;

ii) Invitations to the judge and the judge's spouse, domestic partner, or guest to attend without charge an event associated with a bar-related function or other activity relating to the law, or an event associated with any of the judge's permitted extrajudicial activities, if the same invitation is offered to non-judges who are engaged in similar ways in the activity as is the judge; and

iii) Gifts, loans, bequests, benefits, or other things of value, if the source is a party or other person, including a lawyer, who has come or is likely to come before the judge, or whose interests have come or are likely to come before the judge.

CJC Rule 3.13(C).

15. **Reimbursement of Expenses and Waivers of Fees or Charges**

a. **In general**

Unless otherwise prohibited by law or by the CJC, a judge may accept reimbursement of necessary and reasonable expenses for travel, food, lodging, or other incidental expenses, or a waiver or partial waiver of fees or charges for registration, tuition, and similar items, from sources other than the judge's employing entity, if the expenses or charges are associated with the judge's participation in extrajudicial activities permitted by the CJC. CJC Rule 3.14(A). Reimbursement of expenses for necessary travel, food, lodging, or other incidental expenses must be limited to the actual costs reasonably incurred by the judge and, when appropriate to the occasion, by the judge's spouse, domestic partner, or guest. CJC Rule 3.14(B). A judge who accepts reimbursement of expenses or waivers must publicly report such acceptance. CJC Rule 3.14(C).

b. Factors a judge must consider prior to acceptance

A judge must assure himself or herself that acceptance of reimbursement or fee waivers would not appear to a reasonable person to undermine the judge's independence, integrity, or impartiality. The factors that a judge should consider when deciding whether to accept reimbursement or a fee waiver for attendance at a particular activity include:

i) Whether the sponsor is an accredited educational institution or bar association rather than a trade association or a for-profit entity;

ii) Whether the funding comes largely from numerous contributors rather than from a single entity and is earmarked for programs with specific content;

iii) Whether the content is related or unrelated to the subject matter of litigation pending or impending before the judge, or to matters that are likely to come before the judge;

iv) Whether the activity is primarily educational rather than recreational, and whether the costs of the event are reasonable and comparable to those associated with similar events sponsored by the judiciary, bar associations, or similar groups;

v) Whether information concerning the activity and its funding sources is available upon inquiry;

vi) Whether the sponsor or source of funding is generally associated with particular parties or interests currently appearing or likely to appear in the judge's court, thus possibly requiring disqualification of the judge;

vii) Whether differing viewpoints are presented; and

viii) Whether a broad range of judicial and non-judicial participants are invited, whether a large number of participants are invited, and whether the program is designed specifically for judges.

CJC Rule 3.14, cmt. 3.

16. Reporting Requirements

a. In general

A judge is required to **publicly** report the amount or value of:

i) Compensation received for permitted extrajudicial activities;

ii) Permitted gifts and other things of value, unless the value of such items, alone or in the aggregate with other items received from the same source in the same calendar year, does not exceed a designated amount determined by local law; and

iii) Reimbursement of permitted expenses and waiver of fees or charges, unless the amount of reimbursement or waiver, alone or in the aggregate with other reimbursements or waivers received from the same source in the same calendar year, does not exceed a designated amount determined by local law.

CJC Rule 3.15(A).

b. Contents of report

If public reporting is required, a judge must report the date, place, and nature of the activity for which the judge received any compensation; the description of any gift, loan, bequest, benefit, or other thing of value accepted; and the source of reimbursement of expenses or waiver or partial waiver of fees or charges. CJC Rule 3.15(B).

c. Timing

A required public report must be made at least annually, except that for reimbursement of expenses and waiver or partial waiver of fees or charges, the report must be made within 30 days following the conclusion of the event or program. CJC Rule 3.15(C).

d. Location of filing

A required report must be filed as a public document in the office of the clerk of the court on which the judge serves or other office designated by law, and, when technically feasible, posted by the court or office personnel on the court's website. CJC Rule 3.15(D).

E. POLITICAL AND CAMPAIGN ACTIVITY OF JUDGES

A judge or a candidate for judicial office must not engage in political activity that is inconsistent with the independence, integrity, or impartiality of the judiciary. CJC Canon 4. The following rules also apply to a candidate for judicial office who is not a judge.

1. Prohibited Political Activity in General

Except as permitted by law or by other CJC rules, a judge must not:

i) Serve as a leader or officer of a political organization;

ii) Publicly endorse or oppose a candidate for any political office;

iii) Make speeches on behalf of political organizations;

iv) Solicit funds for or make contributions to such organizations or to a candidate for public office;

v) Attend or purchase tickets for dinners or other events sponsored by a political organization or candidate;

vi) Publicly identify himself or herself as a candidate of a political organization;

vii) Seek, accept, or use endorsements from a political organization;

viii) Personally solicit or accept campaign contributions other than through a campaign committee authorized by CJC Rule 4.4;

ix) Use or permit the use of campaign contributions for the private benefit of the judge, the candidate, or others;

x) Use court staff, facilities, or other court resources in a campaign for judicial office;

xi) Knowingly, or with reckless disregard for the truth, make any false or misleading statement;

xii) Make any statement that would reasonably be expected to affect the outcome or impair the fairness of a matter pending or impending in any court; or

xiii) In connection with cases, controversies, or issues that are likely to come before the court, make pledges, promises, or commitments that are inconsistent with the impartial performance of the adjudicative duties of judicial office.

CJC Rule 4.1.

This rule does not prohibit candidates from campaigning on their own behalf, or from endorsing or opposing candidates for the same judicial office for which they are running. CJC Rule 4.1, cmt. 4.

2. Actions by Other Persons

A judge or judicial candidate must take reasonable measures to ensure that other persons do not undertake any of these prohibited activities on behalf of the judge or judicial candidate. CJC Rule 4.1(B).

3. Family Members

Note that while members of the families of judges and judicial candidates are free to engage in their own political activity, including running for public office, there is no "family exception" to the prohibition against a judge or candidate publicly endorsing candidates for public office. A judge or judicial candidate must not become involved in, or publicly associated with, a family member's political activity or campaign for public office. To avoid public misunderstanding, judges and judicial candidates should take, and should urge members of their families to take, reasonable steps to avoid any implication that they endorse any family member's candidacy or other political activity. CJC Rule 4.1, cmt. 5.

4. Voting and Caucus Elections

Judges are entitled to engage in the political process as voters. Judges in jurisdictions that have caucus procedures to select candidates may participate in those caucuses. CJC Rule 4.1, cmt. 6.

5. Response to False, Misleading, or Unfair Allegations

If a judicial candidate is the subject of false, misleading, or unfair allegations made by an opposing candidate, third party, or the media, the candidate may respond, so long as the candidate does not: make any false or misleading statement; make a statement that would reasonably be expected to affect the outcome or impair the fairness of a pending or impending matter in court; or for issues that are likely to come before the court, make pledges, promises, or commitments that are inconsistent with the duty of impartiality. A judicial candidate may respond directly to false, misleading, or unfair allegations, but it is preferable for someone else to respond if the allegations relate to a pending case. CJC Rule 4.1, cmt. 8.

6. Pledges, Promises, or Commitments

The making of a pledge, promise, or commitment prohibited by CJC Rule 4.1 is not dependent upon, or limited to, the use of any specific words or phrases. Instead, the totality of the statement must be examined to determine if a reasonable person would believe that the candidate for judicial office has specifically undertaken to reach a particular result. Pledges, promises, or commitments must be contrasted with statements or announcements of personal views on legal, political, or other issues, which are not prohibited. CJC Rule 4.1, cmt. 13. A judicial candidate is permitted to make campaign promises related to judicial organization, administration, and court management, such as a promise to dispose of a backlog of cases, start court sessions on time, or avoid favoritism in appointments and hiring. A candidate may also pledge to take action outside the courtroom, such as working toward an improved jury selection system, or advocating for more funds to improve the physical plant and amenities of the courthouse. CJC Rule 4.1, cmt. 14.

7. **Political and Campaign Activities of Judicial Candidates in Public Elections**

   a. **General requirements**

   Judges who are candidates for judicial office in a partisan, nonpartisan, or retention public election must:

   i)   Act at all times in a manner consistent with the independence, integrity, and impartiality of the judiciary;

   ii) Comply with all applicable election, election campaign, and election campaign fundraising laws and regulations of their jurisdiction;

   iii) Review and approve the content of all campaign statements and materials produced by the candidate or her campaign committee, before their distribution; and

   iv) Take reasonable measures to ensure that other persons do not undertake, on behalf of the candidate, activities that the candidate is prohibited from doing.

   CJC Rule 4.2(A).

   b. **Permissible activities**

   A candidate for elective judicial office may, unless prohibited by law, and not earlier than the time set by local law before the first applicable primary election, caucus, or general or retention election:

   i)   Establish a campaign committee pursuant to the CJC;

   ii) Speak on behalf of his candidacy through any medium, including but not limited to advertisements, websites, or other campaign literature;

   iii) Publicly endorse or oppose candidates for the same judicial office for which the candidate is running;

   iv) Attend or purchase tickets for dinners or other events sponsored by a political organization or a candidate for public office;

   v)   Seek, accept, or use endorsements from any person or organization other than a partisan political organization; and

   vi) Contribute to a political organization or candidate for public office, but not more than the amount that the law permits to any one organization or candidate.

   CJC Rule 4.2(B).

   c. **Additional permissible activities in a partisan political election**

   A judicial candidate in a **partisan** public election **may**, unless prohibited by law, and not earlier than the time set by the local jurisdiction before the first applicable primary election, caucus, or general election: (i) identify himself or herself as a candidate of a political organization; and (ii) seek, accept, and use endorsements of a political organization. CJC Rule 4.2(C).

8. **Activities of Candidates for Appointive Judicial Office**

   A candidate for **appointment** to judicial office is permitted to communicate with the appointing or confirming authority, including any selection, screening, or nominating commission or similar agency. CJC Rule 4.3(A). The candidate may also seek endorsements for the appointment from any person or organization **other than** a partisan political organization. CJC Rule 4.3(B).

> **Example:** A person is nominated to be a federal appellate judge. The nominee, who must be confirmed by the Senate, may communicate with the committee reviewing his confirmation, and may seek the endorsement of the American Bar Association for his nomination. The nominee must not make any pledges, promises, or commitments that are inconsistent with the impartial performance of the adjudicative duties of the office. The nominee is also prohibited from seeking the endorsement of a political party for his nomination.

9. Judges Who Become Candidates for Non-Judicial Office

Unless permitted by law, a judge who becomes a candidate for an **elective** non-judicial office is required to resign. Conversely, a judge who becomes a candidate for an **appointed** non-judicial office is not required to resign, so long as the judge complies with the other provisions of the CJC. CJC Rule 4.5.

10. Campaign Committees

a. In general

A judicial candidate who is subject to public election is permitted to establish a campaign committee to manage and conduct a campaign for the candidate, subject to the provisions of the CJC. The candidate is responsible for ensuring that his campaign committee complies with the CJC and other applicable law. CJC Rule 4.4(A).

Except as may be permitted by law, a judicial candidate is not permitted to personally solicit or accept campaign contributions other than through such a campaign committee. CJC Rule 4.1.

> **Example:** An attorney, a member of the state bar, is a candidate for judicial office in an election. The candidate personally asked several of her friends to contribute $100 each to start off her campaign. After the candidate's friends made the contributions, the candidate formed a committee to collect more contributions. The candidate then turned over the contributions to the committee and began campaigning for the office in earnest. Unless the law otherwise allows such solicitation, the candidate is subject to discipline because she personally solicited funds.

b. Limitations on committee's activities

1) Limitations on the amount of campaign contributions

A judicial candidate subject to public election must direct the candidate's campaign committee to only solicit and accept campaign contributions that are **reasonable** and do not exceed, in the aggregate, the amounts set by law from any individual or from any entity or organization. CJC Rule 4.4(B)(1).

2) Time limits on solicitation of contributions

A judicial candidate subject to public election must direct the candidate's campaign committee not to solicit or accept contributions for a candidate's current campaign more than a set time designated by law before the applicable primary election, caucus, or general or retention election, nor more than a set number of days after the last election in which the candidate participated, as designated by law. CJC Rule 4.4(B)(2).

3) Disclosure and divestiture requirements

A judicial candidate subject to public election must direct the candidate's campaign committee to comply with all applicable statutory requirements for disclosure and divestiture of campaign contributions, and to file with the appropriate regulatory authorities a report stating the name, address, occupation, and employer of each person who has made campaign contributions to the committee in an aggregate value exceeding an amount set by law. The report must be filed within a time period set by law following an election.

Themis
Bar Review

Themis
Bar Review

MULTISTATE PROFESSIONAL RESPONSIBILITY EXAM (MPRE)
PROFESSOR ZACHARY KRAMER
ARIZONA STATE UNIVERSITY - SANDRA DAY O'CONNOR COLLEGE OF LAW

CHAPTER 1:   THE TEST, THE RULES, KEY TERMINOLOGY

A. **The Test**

1. **Why must you?** Because _____

2. **What is tested?**

    a. **Sources of law**

        ▪ ABA Model Rules of Professional Conduct (MRPC)

            ● The MPRE only tests on law that is at least one year old.

        ▪ ABA Model Code of Judicial Conduct (MCJC)

    b. **Other authorities**

        ▪ Rules of Evidence (such as attorney-client privilege)
        ▪ Constitutional Law
        ▪ Criminal Law

    c. **Breadth of exam**—breakdown by subject:

6–12%:	Regulation of the Legal Profession	2–8%:	Transactions with Non-Clients
10–16%:	Client-Lawyer Relationship	4–10%:	Differing Roles of a Lawyer
6–12%:	Client Confidentiality	2–8%:	Safekeeping Client Funds
12–18%:	Conflict of Interest	4–10%:	Communications about Legal Services
6–12%:	Competence & Malpractice	2–4%:	Duty to the Public
10–16%:	Litigation	2–8%:	Judicial Conduct

3. **How is it tested?**

    ▪ 60 multiple-choice questions
    ▪ 10 "test" questions

    a. **Structure of questions**

        ▪ Answer format: Yes, Yes, No, No

- No "none of the above" or "A and B only"

4. **Exam day**—three things to remember:
   - Bring a _____.
   - Bring a _____.
   - Answer _____ question.

B. The ABA Model Rules of Professional Conduct

1. **Rules and Comments**
   - The Rules are _____.
   - The Comments are _____.

2. **Mandatory v. aspirational**
   - Mandatory rules ("_____ rules")
     - Say what a lawyer must or must not do
     - Violation of these rules can lead to _____.
   - Aspirational rules ("_____ rules")
     - Tell lawyers what they _____ do
   - "Must" rules vs. "should" rules: The MPRE tends to test
     "_____" rules.

C. What's What?

1. **Two primary forms of discipline of an attorney**—_____ or
   _____
   - **Censure**: Getting _____
     - Privately—by the disciplinary authority
     - Publicly—by the Supreme Court
   - **Disbarment**: _____ of license to practice law
     - Long-term suspension (more common)

2. **The word "may"**—the lawyer has a _____; it is
   _____.
   - *In other words,* the lawyer has _____.

3. **Non-disciplinary sanctions**
   - _____: Thrown out of representing a particular client
   - _____: Usually, malpractice
   - _____

4. **Tribunal**—usually a court, but not always

   ○ Key: Binding _____

> ***Example 1:*** *Larry Lawyer is representing a client in a hearing before the EEOC.*
> *Do the Model Rules apply? _____. The Rules*
> *apply to certain administrative agencies, too.*

5. **Law firm**—all forms of legal groups

   ○ Includes: _____ law offices, insurance company law
   offices, _____ office, public defender office, etc.

   ○ Facts and circumstances:

     ▪ No factor is dispositive: Office sharing, sharing fees, etc.

     ▪ Only authorized _____ entities can practice law

6. **Writings** (also informed consent/confirmed in writing)

   ○ Writing can be _____.

   ○ Informed consent; requires:

     ▪ _____ (i.e., communication), and

     ▪ _____

     ▪ Confirmed in writing

       • Consent may sometimes be oral.

7. **Mental states**—knowledge/belief/reason to know

   ○ "Knowingly" (or "known," or "knows"): Actual subjective knowledge
   ○ "Belief" (or "believes"): Actual subjective belief
   ○ "Reasonable" (or "reasonably"): What a reasonably prudent and competent lawyer would
   know/believe/do; an objective standard

> **Editor's Note 1:** Professor Kramer slightly misstates the mental state of
> "belief" by combining it with subjective reasonableness. The rules are correct
> as provided here and in your outline.

CHAPTER 2:   REGULATION OF THE LEGAL PROFESSION (PART 1)

A. **Who Regulates Attorneys?**

1. **State supreme courts**

2. **Federal district courts**

   ○ ABA Model Rules are just a _____.

   ○ Very few states have adopted ABA Model Rules in their entirety.

B. **Regulation before Admission**

1. **Education**—graduation from ABA-accredited law school

2. **Character and fitness test**

   o Principally concerned with the _____ history of the candidate
   o **But**, not all crimes are disqualifying.

   > *Example 2:* Lorraine Law Student was an unruly young adult, earning two
   > disorderly conduct charges in college. She has since straightened her ways.
   > Will this disqualify her from admission? Probably not, so long as she
   > _____ what happened.

   o Disqualifying crimes involve _____.

   > *Example 3:* Before law school, Larry Lawyer worked at a bank, from which he
   > stole money. Disqualifying? _____.

   - Increased concern with crimes associated with drug and alcohol addiction

   o **Keep in mind**—the failure to disclose even non-disqualifying crimes can result in
     disqualification. Err on the side of _____.
   o Bar examiners are increasingly concerned with debt.

   - The existence of debt is not disqualifying.
   - The main concern is making reasonable efforts to pay debts as they come due.

3. **Residency**—no residency requirement for admission (a constitutional issue)

4. **Truthfulness**—no lying on the application for bar admission or law school admission

5. **Exam**—requires a passing score

   > **Editor's Note 2:** Each state sets its own passing score. The number of
   > questions you correctly answer out of the 50 scored questions is your raw
   > score. The NCBE uses a statistical process to convert your raw score into a
   > scaled score between 50 and 150, with an average score that is typically close
   > to 100. The scaling factor used to convert a raw score into a scaled score varies
   > with each administration of the exam, so it is impossible to predict exactly how
   > many questions must be correctly answered to achieve a given scaled score.

6. **How do these issues come up?**

   o Admissions issues will present in one of two ways:

   - Permission to _____; and
   - Permission to _____.

   o **Permission to sit** cases arise when an issue is discovered
     _____ the exam.
   o **Permission to enter** cases arise _____ the exam.

- Both are treated the same way.
  - Penalty—usually _____

C. Regulation after Admission

Various ways in which an admitted attorney can be subject to discipline:

1. **Violation of the** _____

2. _____ **act that touches on attorney's honesty or fitness to** _____

   > *Example 4:* Lorraine Lawyer has a lead foot, racking up speeding tickets galore. Will this lead to discipline? _____, as it doesn't speak to her honesty or fitness to practice.

   > *Example 5:* Larry Lawyer was caught lying on a mortgage application. Could this lead to discipline? _____, as it calls his honesty into question.

3. _____ **or** _____ **, even if not criminal**

   - Fraud upon the court ("procedural fraud")—_____ to the court
   - Common law fraud ("conventional fraud")—elements:
     - Making a _____;
     - Knowing it is _____;
     - _____ to deceive;
     - Causing reasonable reliance; and
     - Resulting in _____.
   - For disciplinary purposes under the MRPC, it is not necessary that anyone relied upon or suffered damages from the misrepresentation.

D. Vicarious Liability of Attorneys

1. **Partners within firms** (or similar managers)

   a. **Firms**

      - "Law firm" is broad—includes D.A.'s office, corporate staff, public defender's office
      - Partners must make reasonable efforts to ensure that the _____ and _____ employees comply with the Rules.

   b. **Compliance**

      - Must have a _____ in place to ensure compliance

> *Example 6:* *Lorraine Lawyer's new firm has been up and running for a year.*
> *The firm does not, however, have a conflict check system in place. Is the firm in*
> *compliance with the Rules? _____.* *It is a*
> *violation for a firm not to have conflict-check procedures in place, even if there*
> *is no conflict.*

> *Example 7:* *The same is true if Lorraine's firm does not have a system in place*
> *to preserve confidentiality of client records.*

    c. Non-professional employees

- Applies to any non-lawyer who works with the law firm (employee, independent contractor, IT staff, etc.)

2. Supervisory attorneys

- Liable for Rules violations of supervised attorneys and non-professionals if they:

    1) _____;

    2) _____; or

    3) After learning of a violation, fail to take _____.

> *Example 8:* *Larry Lawyer tells Junior Associate to file a frivolous complaint.*

> *Example 9:* *Lorraine Lawyer congratulates Junior Associate after finding out*
> *she filed a frivolous complaint.*

> *Example 10:* *After learning that Junior Associate filed a frivolous complaint,*
> *Larry Lawyer does nothing, moving on to the next case.*

- Responsibility for the conduct of non-professional employees is exactly the same as it is for lawyers.

3. No Nuremburg defense

- A subordinate lawyer or staff person _____ defend by saying, "I was only following orders."
- Only a _____ order by a supervisor is a defense.

> *Example 11:* *Lorraine Lawyer's boss tells her to file a complaint. If the*
> *complaint ends up being frivolous, Lorraine's only defense will be if there was,*
> *in fact, a good reason to file it.*

CHAPTER 3: REGULATION OF THE LEGAL PROFESSION (PART 2)

A. Out-of-State Conduct

- Out-of-state conduct can expose you to discipline at home.

    Example 12: *Larry Lawyer is licensed in Arizona. He commits perjury in a matter in Maine. The perjury can lead to discipline in*

    _____.

- Conflict of Laws—which law applies (other than the home state)?

    ○ Lawyer's belief—the conduct must conform to the rules of the jurisdiction in which the lawyer reasonably believes his conduct will have a _____ effect.

B. "Snitch" Rule

- A lawyer is required to _____ violations to disciplinary authorities.

    ○ The reporting lawyer has

    _____ of

    _____.

    ○ The violation goes to lawyer's substantial _____,

    _____, and _____

    to practice law.

    Example 13: *Lorraine Lawyer brings a successful suit against Larry Lawyer for stealing funds from his client. Lorraine doesn't notify the authorities about Larry's conduct. Is Lorraine subject to discipline?*

    _____. *Lorraine has to snitch.*

- Same obligation for bad _____ conduct

C. Out-of-State Lawyers

An out-of-state lawyer may practice in a jurisdiction on a temporary basis.

1. Pro hac vice admission

- There must be a "_____" (dispute).

    Note 1: Also applies to mediation and arbitration

2. Association with _____ counsel

- Local counsel must _____ participate; she can't be a mere silent partner

3. Working for a client from _____

- The attorney must have home-state qualification.

D. **Unauthorized Practice of Law**

1. **What is the practice of law?**

   o The Rules do not define the practice of law...

   o Any activity which develops facts or law

      Example 14: Jurisdictions differ. Real estate brokers, insurance agents, etc.

2. **What is the result?**

   o Non-lawyers—_____ (e.g., "Stop doing that.")

   o Lawyers—_____ (e.g., the lawyer is not qualified or licensed)

3. **Aiding and abetting**

   o A lawyer is prohibited from aiding and abetting the unauthorized practice of law by failing to supervise non-professionals.

      Example 15: Divorce mills, bankruptcy mills

      Example 16: Larry Lawyer hires Peggy Paralegal. Peggy meets with clients, fills out papers, sends the bill, and collects fees. Client never meets Larry. Is this a violation? _____. Even if Peggy represents client soundly? _____, it's still a violation.

   o To avoid this, the lawyer:

      ▪ Must have _____; and

      ▪ Must _____ and _____ for the work of the non-professional

4. **Pro se litigants**

   o Ghostwriting—a lawyer can give limited aid and assistance.

   o Pro se litigants cannot be entities.

E. **Fee-Division with Non-Lawyers**

1. **A lawyer CANNOT divide legal fees with non-lawyers**

   o **Exceptions:** Estates of decedent lawyer, retirement plans, etc.

   o Legal fees are for _____.

      Example 17: Lorraine hires a private detective to work on a current divorce case. Rather than pay him directly, she offers the detective a percentage of the fees? Is this permitted under the Rules? _____.

2. **Real firms may split fees**—the entity must be a professional corporation.

3. No non-lawyer can be _____ of a lawyer's judgment.

   o No control by a _____ payor

      Example 18: *Insurance company is generally not the client.*

4. **Lawyer-owned related services** (e.g., document retention or delivery services)

   o Clients must know they are _____ with a lawyer.

F. Sale of Practice

1. **The sale of a practice to other lawyers is permitted.**

   o The Lawyer:

      ▪ Must _____ practice;
      ▪ Give _____ to the client; **and**
      ▪ Sell the practice to a _____.

   o May sell the whole practice or only one area
   o Cannot increase the _____ associated with the sale

2. **Can the lawyer return to practice?** Yes, if:

   o _____ counsel;
   o _____
   o _____ area of law;
   o _____ (e.g., illness, financial difficulty).

G. Restrictions on Practice

- No covenants _____ with other lawyers
- **Exception**—sale of practice

   Note 2: Covenants are not allowed in settlements, either.

CHAPTER 4:   THE CLIENT-LAWYER RELATIONSHIP

A. No Duty to Represent Clients

- Generally, a lawyer has no duty to represent a client.

   o **Exception**—court appointments; however, they may be declined for cause.
   o **Sufficient causes**—not being paid, violation of rule of professional responsibility, commission of a crime

B. Duty to Reject a Client

- Duty is _____ with the Rules for mandatory withdrawal.

C. Attorney-Client Relationship

Triggering event—the formation of an attorney-client relationship triggers civil and ethical responsibilities.

> ***Example 19:*** *A victim of an accident consults with Lorraine Lawyer, who determines that the victim does not have a case. This was a consult. There was no agreement, and the victim did not pay any fees. Has an attorney-client relationship been formed? Think about the elements…*

1. **Requirements**—no need for fee or agreement to create the relationship

2. **Type of test**
   o The test is not contractual.
   o The test is like a _____ test.

3. **Formation test**
   o Would a _____ determine that an attorney-client relationship has been formed?

4. **Prevention of attorney-client relationship**
   o Just say, "_____."
   o Make clear to the prospective client that you _____ in an attorney-client relationship.

D. Scope, Objective, and Means of Representation

1. **Limitation on scope**
   o Lawyers and clients may limit the scope of representation.

   > ***Example 20:*** *Larry Lawyer will only handle tax matters.*

   o The scope cannot be so limited as to create ineffective representation.

   > ***Example 21:*** *An individual who caused an automobile accident while driving drunk goes to Lorraine Lawyer. The client is charged with the drunk driving, but also vehicular homicide. Lorraine Lawyer wants to limit representation. "I don't do homicide," she says. Is this permissible?* _____.

2. **Communication with client**
   o The lawyer must tell the client everything the client needs to know to make an _____ decision about the case.
   o Settlement offers must be communicated to the client.
   o **Exception**—a prior agreement with client concerning a limitation

Example 22: *Client will not accept less than $1,000,000. If an offer is less than $1,000,000, does Lorraine Lawyer need not convey lower offer to client?* _____.

3. Criminal prosecution

Only the client can make the following decisions:

- ○ Whether to _____;
- ○ Whether to exercise the right to trial by _____; and
- ○ _____ must be communicated to the client.

4. Client under a disability

a. **Minority** (underage)

b. _____ (mental disability, drug addiction)

c. **Lawyer Duties:**

- ▪ Maintain an _____ relationship;
- ▪ Seek appointment of a _____, if necessary; and
- ▪ Permitted to _____ information as necessary to _____ the client.

- • You are allowed to take protective action.

5. Counseling on crime and fraud

- ○ *Yes*, as to legal _____.
- ○ *No*, as to _____ commit a crime.

E. Withdrawal and Termination of Representation

1. Mandatory withdrawal—coextensive with the attorney-client relationship

a. **Violation of Rules of Professional Conduct**

Example 23: *Lorraine Lawyer's new client wants to bring a claim against another of Lorraine's clients. Can Lorraine represent the new client?* _____.

b. **Attorney impairment**

Example 24: *Larry Lawyer is struggling with a drug dependence, which is interfering with his responsibilities. Can he continue to represent his client?* _____.

c. **Discharge of attorney** (i.e., you get fired)

- ▪ A client has an _____ to fire an attorney.

- Cannot be modified by contract
- Cannot have a penalty provision such as liquidated damages or elevated fees
  - Client still owes _____ to the discharged attorney (unless discharged for cause).

d. **Withdrawal after court processes begun**

- Must get _____ to withdraw, even when withdrawal is _____

2. **Permissive withdrawal** (*may*)

   a. **Harmless withdrawal**

   - May withdraw even if the client objects, so long as there is no harm to the client

     Example 25: *Shortly after being hired, before the case started in earnest, Larry Lawyer fires his old client for a new and better client. This is permissible.*

   b. **Harmful withdrawal** (*may*)

   - " _____ " the client is pursuing crime or fraud and the lawyer's _____ were used in the client's crime or fraud

     Example 26: *Lorraine Lawyer drafted a standard form lease for her client, a landlord. The landlord is using the lease to rent apartments he doesn't actually own. Can Lorraine withdraw? _____.*

   - Client's action is _____ to the attorney

     Example 27: *Larry Lawyer learns that his client is a Neo-Nazi. Can he withdraw? _____.*

   - _____ financial burden

     - Usually arises in the case of a court appointment
     - **Caution:** A bad deal is not enough.

   - Client _____ an obligation to the lawyer

     - What Obligation? _____.

   - _____ (e.g., illness or family emergency)

     Exam Tip 1: **REMEMBER:** When in the court process, an attorney must **always** obtain court permission to withdraw.

3. **After withdrawal or termination**

   o Return the client's _____ and

   _____

- If the client still owes a fee, the lawyer can have a _____ on the client's property.

  - Should not harm the client
  - *Passive lien*—cannot sell the property; operates like collateral

a. Disbursement of funds (third-party dispute)

> *Example 28:* Larry Lawyer wins suit for Client, placing the proceeds of the judgment in the client's trust account. The client's medical insurer asserts a claim on those funds. What should Larry do with those funds? _____.

- An attorney must _____ disputed funds until the third-party's dispute is _____.

CHAPTER 5: FEES, FEES, FEES!

> **Note 3:** You deserve to be paid.

A. Fees must be Reasonable

> *Example 29:* Bank USA hires Lorraine Lawyer to seek recovery on a $100,000 note. Lorraine knows that this will require the same amount of work to recover on a $1,000 note. Can she charge more? Let's go to the test!

"Lodestar Test"—four factors to determine the reasonableness of rates

> **Note 4:** The reasonableness trumps any contract.
>
> **Note 5:** Fees applicable to FRCP 11 sanctions are subject to _____.
>
> Court review also applies to other fees.

> *Example 30:* Larry Lawyer is administering the estate of a client. The estate was rather large, containing loads of property and an extensive portfolio of investments. Who will review the reasonableness of Larry's fees? The probate court, of course.

1. Factors

a. _____—explain the fee up front, it cannot be changed afterward.

> *Example 31:* Lorraine agreed to an hourly rate of $250. The work ended up being harder than she expected. Can she change the rate to $400? _____. The rate is set. No premium afterward.

     b. _____—two types:

- Is the issue **new to you?** If education is required, it may not be reasonable to charge as much.
- Is the issue **new to everyone?** It might be reasonable to charge a little more.

     c. _____

- More _____ = more _____

     d. Precluding _____

- E.g., paying a lawyer to conflict out a superstar lawyer

  Example 32: Now you know the factors. Go back to Lorraine and the $100,000 note. Can she charge more? _____.

2. Form

- A fee agreement _____ have to be in writing.

  - Under ABA rules, fees just need to be _____.

- Exception—_____ agreements must be in writing.

  - Often means a percentage of the amount of recovery
  - Cannot be used in _____ or _____ cases
  - Always must be signed by the _____
  - Must have a _____ methodology for fees and expenses (i.e., explain how the fees will be determined.)

B. Retainers

- **Main question**—whose money is it?
- **Basic rule**—the lawyer must keep the client's money separate.

  - All unearned legal fees must be placed in an _____ or _____ account and unearned fees must be _____.

    Note 6: REMEMBER: It's still the client's money.

  - All _____ advanced to the lawyer must also be placed in escrow.
  - Accounts of the lawyer and clients must be kept _____.

C. Interests in client as a fee

- The lawyer takes something from the client instead of a fee.

Example 33: *Rather than taking a cash payment, Larry Lawyer takes stock from his corporate client.*

Example 34: *To secure payment of a cash fee, Lorraine Lawyer takes a mortgage on the client's property.*

- Interest in a client can create a _____ of interest.
- Business transactions with clients AND acquisitions of an ownership or security interest in client's property trigger certain requirements:

  o Terms must be in _____

  o Terms must be _____ and
  _____

  o Attorney must advise the client, _____, of the prudence of hiring *independent* counsel to review the agreement

  o _____, in writing, signed by the client

D. Fee Sharing

1. **With other lawyers**—the referring attorney may receive a portion of the fee, so long as:

   o The overall fee is _____ to the client;

   o The fee-sharing arrangement is _____ to the client; and

   o The referring lawyer provides actual _____ or joint representation.

   Example 35: *Larry refers a super wealthy and very litigious client to Lorraine. In appreciation, Lorraine kicks back a portion of her fee to Larry. Is this allowed? _____. Larry didn't provide legal services. Referral is not enough.*

2. **With non-lawyers**—legal fees can be shared only among _____.

   o What about investigators? _____.

   o What about forensic accountants? _____.

   o What about Earl, the sandwich delivery guy? _____.

CHAPTER 6:   CONFIDENTIALITY & PRIVILEGE

A. Duty of Confidentiality

- **Baseline rule**—_____ALL_____ information learned relating to the representation must be kept in confidence.

  o What if it's public information? ___Still Confidential___.

  o What about my client's identity? ___Still Confidential___.

  o Lawyer's observations? ___Still Confidential___

- **Important!** The duty of confidentiality is ___*broader*___ than the attorney-client privilege.

  ○ *Why does this matter?* You need to follow the contours of the attorney-client privilege.

  ○ Certain things may not be privileged yet still protected by the duty of confidentiality.

B. Attorney-Client Privilege

1. **Attorney-client privilege**—more ___*narrow / limited*___ than the duty of confidentially.

   ○ The privilege ___*shields*___ information from the court.

   ○ Limited application; applies to:

     ▪ ___*testimonial communication*___ (i.e., words);

     ▪ Information ___*given confidentially*___ to attorney; and

     ▪ Information actually ___*kept*___ confidential.

   ○ Presence of third party may destroy privilege

   ○ Applies to speech, not objects

> **Example 36:** *Conrad Client comes to Lorraine Lawyer in a tizzy. He says, "I hacked the government with this," and he slams down a laptop on Lorraine's desk.*
>
> *Is the statement "I hacked the government" privileged?*
> ___*yes*___, *the statement was given confidentially.*
>
> *Is the laptop privileged?* ___*No*___, *privilege is about words, not things.*
>
> *Does Lorraine have an obligation to turn the laptop over to the authorities?*
> ___*yes*___.
>
> *Can Lorraine Lawyer publicly reveal information about the laptop?*
> ___*No*___, *she has a duty to keep it confidential.*

   a. **Inadvertent disclosure and waiver**

     ▪ **Rule**—no waiver of privilege if:

       • Attorney took _____ to *prevent* disclosure; **and**

       • Attorney took _____ *after* the disclosure.

     ▪ What do these cases look like?

Example 37: Responding to a discovery request, Larry Lawyer discloses a massive amount of documents. Included in the document dump is a privileged document.

Example 38: Lorraine disclosed documents to Larry. Lorraine did not, however, scrub the metadata hidden in one of the documents, which contained critical information that should have been privileged.

2. Exceptions to attorney-client privilege

- ○ _____—an attorney cannot participate in ongoing crime.
- ○ _____ with the attorney

   Example 39: Conrad is suing Larry for malpractice. Conrad _____ prevent the disclosure of privileged information that is relevant to the malpractice issue.

   Example 40: Cassandra has brought a claim against Lorraine for violating their fee agreement. Information that would normally be privilege _____ be disclosed.

C. Work-Product Doctrine

- • Protects documents prepared for use in connection with a client's case, (e.g., strategy memo, observations about client, reports on witnesses, etc.)
- • **Basic Rule**—work product _____ subject to discovery.
- • **Exceptions**—an attorney compelled to reveal work product when:

   - ○ There is a _____ for the information; and
   - ○ No other means to gather the information without undue hardship.

      Example 41: Larry interviewed a witness in Conrad's criminal case. Shortly after the interview, the witness died of a heart attack. Lorraine did not get a chance to interview the witness before he died. Might Larry's notes from the interview be disclosed later? _____.

      Editor's Note 3: To clarify the parties in the above example, **Lorraine** may ask that Larry's interview notes be disclosed because Lorraine did not have a chance to interview the witness before he died.

D. Court Compulsion

- • A court *cannot* order a lawyer to reveal information protected by

   _____.

- • A court *may* order revelation of material protected under the ethical duty of

   _____.

   - ○ You must assert every non-frivolous claim you have to prevent disclosure.

E. **Permissive Disclosures of Confidential Information** (*May*)

1. **Client** _____

   > *Example 42:* Conrad says to Larry Lawyer, "Advocate for me publicly. Talk to the media."

2. **Implied by the** _____

   > *Example 43:* Conrad says to Lorraine, "Take them to court." This will require revealing the client's identity, as well as other confidential material within Lorraine's firm.

3. **To prevent** _____ **or**
   _____

   > *Example 44:* Cassandra has been in a drawn-out dispute with her now ex-partner, Bruce. She says of Bruce, "I can't take it anymore. He's gonna bleed."

4. **Financial injury** (the "Enron" case)

   o **To prevent:**

      ▪ The client's _____ criminal act or fraud;
      ▪ The lawyer must believe it is necessary to *prevent* substantial
        _____ ;
      ▪ For which the lawyer's _____ are used.

   o **Or, to prevent, mitigate, or rectify:**

      ▪ Substantial financial harm;
      ▪ Caused by a client's completed criminal act or fraud;
      ▪ In which the lawyer's _____ were used.

      > *Example 45:* Larry helped Conrad develop a system to pay his company's creditors. Later, Larry learns that Conrad used this system to skim a tiny amount from each transaction and dump them into an off-shore account in his own name.

5. **Review: Physical and financial harm**

   o Disclosing to prevent:

      ▪ **Physical harm**—the lawyer's services _____ required.
      ▪ **Financial harm**—the lawyer's services _____ required.

   o Must disclose if failure to do so would assist the client's crime

6. **Controversies with lawyers or disciplinary proceedings**

   > *Example 46:* Fee dispute with client; disciplinary matter

7. _____ ordered disclosure

8. **Necessary to discover conflicts**

F. **Duration**

- The duty lasts _____; it survives the death of the client and of the lawyer.

G. **Education** ("The Law Professor Exception")

- May disclose for educational purposes, so long as the client's identity is not revealed, and the listener cannot determine who the client is

H. **Prospective Clients**

- Entity representation (e.g., corporation)

  o The entity is the client, but must communicate with a representative

    Editor's Note 4: A lawyer representing an entity represents the entity acting through its duly authorized constituents. The lawyer owes the duties of loyalty and confidentiality to the entity.

  o Control group—representatives (managers, board of directors, etc.)

- Communications from prospective clients

  o Information must be held in confidence if the lawyer _____ communication.

  o Screening is available.

I. **Electronically Stored Information** ("The Cloud")

- A lawyer is obligated to secure information to comply with the Rules.
- Factors:

  o Sensitivity;
  o Cost; and
  o Client consent.

CHAPTER 7:   CONFLICTS OF INTEREST

A. **Purposes of the Conflicts Rules**

- Maintain duty of loyalty and independent professional judgment; and
- Preserve confidentiality.

B. **Enforcement of Conflict Rules**

- Conflicts of interest may result in both:

  o Litigation sanctions (e.g., disqualification from representation); and

      ○   _____ sanctions.

    • *Who enforces?* The _____.

C. Basic Types of Conflicts

1. _____ **adversity with concurrent client**

> ***Example 47:*** *Lorraine is representing the landlord and tenant in an eviction dispute.*

> ***Example 48:*** *Larry represents two clients who are in litigation unrelated to your case.*

> **Note 7:** Usually not waivable.

2. _____ **on lawyer's ability to represent client**

      ○   Can be a limitation caused by another client, former client, third party, or the lawyer's own interests

> **Editor's Note 5:** To clarify the above rule, a lawyer's ability to represent a client may be materially limited by the interests of another client, former, client, third party, or the **lawyer's** own interests.

D. Waivable Conflicts

    • Requirements for waiver:

      ○   Client's informed consent, in _____;

      ○   The lawyer must have a _____ that the representation will not adversely affect representation of another client; **and**

      ○   _____ clients *must* waive.

> ***Example 49:*** *Larry is representing the driver and passenger, who were injured when their car was struck by another car. In most cases, this _____ a conflict.*

> *Say that facts emerge indicating that the driver may have actually been at fault, and the passenger may want to sue the driver herself. Can Larry still represent the passenger and client? _____, if all clients properly waive.*

E. Former Clients

1. **Basic idea**

If a lawyer previously represented a client in a matter, the lawyer cannot represent another person in the _____ matter or a _____ matter.

2. **What does "substantially related" mean?**

   o It is an _____ test:

      ▪ What was the _____ of the prior representation?

      ▪ Could the lawyer have learned information?

      ▪ Would that information be _____ in the current litigation?

   > **Note 8:** This is objective. No testimony about what the lawyer really knew because such disclosure would breach duty of confidentiality.

F. Personal Interest of Lawyer

1. **Business dealings or acquisition of an interest in client or client's property**

2. **Draft a _____ or gift in which lawyer is the heir or donee** (*unless* for a family member)

3. **No _____ lawyers on the other side**

   > ***Example 50:*** *Lorraine and Larry are happily married. Lorraine is prosecuting Conrad for manslaughter and Larry intends to defend him. This is a conflict.*

4. **No acquisition of _____ until the representation of client concludes**

   > ***Example 51:*** *Lorraine represents Cassandra, who has been charged with murder in a case that is receiving substantial media attention. Cassandra asks Lorraine to negotiate with FlixNet to produce a miniseries about her life. Lorraine _____ do this until the criminal matter is over.*

   > **Editor's Note 6:** The above arrangement would be permissible as long as Lorraine did not make or negotiate an agreement that gave her (Lorraine) literary or media rights to a portrayal or account based in substantial part on information relating to the representation of Cassandra in the murder case. *See* ch. 12, Question 2.

5. **Proprietary interest in litigation** (champerty)

   o Do not _____ to clients.

   o No advances to clients *except* for _____.

      ▪ Client still ultimately responsible

      ▪ Lawyer can pay court costs of _____ client

      ▪ Lawyer can advance court costs to *any* client; repayment can be contingent on outcome.

   > ***Example 52:*** *Lorraine represents Conrad in a domestic relations matter. Conrad is very sick and needs treatment immediately, but he can't afford the*

care. Can Lorraine pay for Conrad's treatment?
_____.

> *Example 53: Larry represents Cassandra in a property dispute with her*
> *neighbor. Larry hires a surveyor to be an expert at trial about the neighbor's*
> *trespass. Can Larry pay for the expert in advance of the trial?*
> _____. *The expert witness is a court cost, and*
> *court costs can be advanced by the lawyer.*

6. **No** _____ **with clients**

    o **Exception**—pre-existing relationship
    o This is a _____ disqualification; it is not contagious to the firm.

G. Lawyer as Witness

*   A lawyer cannot take representation where the lawyer may be a witness.
*   Exceptions:

    o _____ issues
    o _____ in this case

    > *Example 54: Say the matter is a fee-shifting case under FRCP Rule 11, Lorraine*
    > *can testify as to the value of her services in her case.*

H. Imputed Disqualification

1. Contagious conflicts

    o If a lawyer is in conflict with representation of a client, _____ lawyer in the firm may represent the client. The lawyer is contagious.

2. Exceptions

    o Client _____, informed, and confirmed in writing
    o The conflict is based upon the lawyer's _____ interest. (e.g., sex with clients).

    > **Note 9:** There is no appearance of impropriety standard for lawyers. It does
    > not matter if it *looks* bad, it must *actually be* bad.

3. Incoming Lawyer—(ripe for testing!)

Arises when a new lawyer is contagious with a conflict

a. Application

*   ▪ This rule only applies to the _____ lawyer.

- The incoming lawyer will not give the law firm a conflict as long as there is _____ and the incoming lawyer receives no part of the _____.

    b. **Screening**

    - No information is passed between the incoming lawyer and the firm;
    - The lawyer is apportioned _____ part of the fee; **and**
    - The affected client must be afforded _____, but consent is *not* required.

4. **Non-lawyers**

    o Nonprofessional employees (paralegals, secretaries, etc.) can also create conflicts.
    o The same rules apply.

I. **Government Lawyers**

1. **Conflict of interest**

    o A former government lawyer who becomes associated with a firm _____ create a conflict.

2. **Requirements to deal with conflict:**

    o The lawyer is screened on the matter.
    o The affected client must be notified.

        - Gives the client opportunity to monitor the screening

3. **Job search**

    o Government lawyers, agency lawyers, arbitrators, mediators, and third-party neutrals cannot negotiate for _____ with a party if that party is involved in a matter in which the lawyer participates.
    o **Exception**—_____ can seek employment with parties before the court, provided they tell the judge.

J. **Prospective Clients**

- Information learned from a prospective client can create a conflict.

    Example 55: *Husband approaches Larry to discuss getting a divorce from Wife. Husband reveals lots of information about the marriage. Husband then informs Larry that he will not retain his services. Can Larry represent Wife in the divorce? _____.*

- **Is it contagious?** Can be avoided immediate screening of the lawyer who dealt with the prospective client

- Conflict exists if the attorney _____ information from a prospective client
  - An unsolicited communication from a prospective client does not trigger this conflict.

K. Third-Party Interference

- The client is the client the third-party payor (e.g., insurance agency) is not the client.
- Three forms of impermissible interference with the attorney's independent representation of a client:
  - _____ control (e.g., task approval system);
  - Information control (e.g., demand to see all case-related information);
  - _____ control (e.g., regulation of the nature and amount of settlement).
- A client can consent to these forms of improper influence.
- An agreement to eliminate or limit malpractice _____ valid.

L. Organization as a Client

"Organization" includes corporations and other entities.

1. Who is the client?

  - The lawyer represents _____, not its constituents.
  - Joint representation of organization and its constituents _____ permissible.

2. Control group

  - The principal managers of organization
  - May have joint representation of this group

3. Bad behavior of organization

  - If a lawyer _____ (*actual knowledge*) of a violation of law that may be imputed to the organization and likely to result in _____ to the organization, the lawyer should take measures including referring the matter to the highest organizational authority.

    - Board control—the lawyer may have to go to the board.

  - If the organization does not correct the matter, the lawyer may _____.

    - "_____ withdrawal" is allowed.

CHAPTER 8: COMPETENCE, LEGAL MALPRACTICE, & OTHER CIVIL LIABILITY

A. Professional Competence

1. **Basic rule**—lawyers must be _____.

2. **Malpractice v. ethics violation**

   - Malpractice requires _____.
   - Discipline _____ require damage.

     Example 56: *The law firm of Larry and Lorraine does not have a conflict-check system in place. This is a violation under the Model Rules. It will not, by itself, subject the firm to malpractice liability.*

   a. **Malpractice = legal liability**

      - Conventional malpractice is coextensive with _____.

        - Basic tort test—duty, breach, causation, damage
        - The duty arises out of the attorney-client relationship.

      - Breach of fiduciary relationship (e.g., a conflict)
      - Breach of contract for failure of performance

        - Damages are usually limited to recovering _____.

   b. **Burden of proof**

      - Malpractice, fiduciary, and contracts—

        _____ evidence

      - Ethics violation—

        _____ evidence

   c. **Violations of the MRPC do not set up a cause of action for malpractice**

      - Violation of the MRPC may be _____ of a breach of duty.

3. **Duty to decline or withdraw**

   - Arises if the lawyer is not _____ or cannot become competent without unreasonable delay

4. **Limits on Recovery**

   - A lawyer cannot contractually limit recovery.
   - Can enter an agreement limiting the lawyer's malpractice liability _____ the client is represented by _____ counsel

5. **Settlement with unrepresented clients**

   - A lawyer _____ tell the client when the lawyer has made an error.

B. Duties to Non-Clients

1. Third-party beneficiaries

Example 57: Larry wrote a will for Daryl, the dead guy. The will accidentally cut out Daryl's nephew Michael, who was very close to Daryl. Can Michael bring a claim against Larry? _____, even though he didn't have a lawyer-client relationship.

2. Unauthorized acts

Example 58: Lorraine represents Cassandra. Without permission, Lorraine enters into a contract to sell Cassandra's prized stamp collection to an antique stamp dealer. Cassandra is not happy. Is Lorraine on the hook with the stamp dealer? _____.

C. Referrals/Outsourcing to Other Lawyers Outside Your Firm

- Must _____ the other lawyer will contribute

D. Other Tort Defenses for Attorneys

- Defamation defense—privilege when the publication is related to a proceeding in which the lawyer is counsel
- Malicious prosecution defense—_____ for the action brought by the attorney

E. Crimes

- Advice about crime is not criminal if the lawyer attempts to _____ the client.

CHAPTER 9:   FAIRNESS & LITIGATION

A. Diligence

- **Basic rule**—lawyers must be diligent.
- If you cannot be diligent, you must _____.

    Example 59: Lorraine is suffocating under her existing caseload, with barely enough time to eat, let alone do more work. Conrad comes to her with a potentially interesting case that would help her extend into a brand-new practice area. If she takes the case, her other work will suffer. Should she take it? _____. Lorraine is too busy.

    Example 60: Larry's drinking is getting in the way of his defense of Cassandra, who faces a long prison sentence if she is found guilty. What should Larry do? _____.

- Cannot delay for the sake of delay.

B. **"Zealous" Advocacy**

1. **Frivolous claims**

    ○ A lawyer may not _____ or

    _____ a claim that is frivolous absent a *good-faith* argument

    to extend the law.

      Example 61: *Civil rights cases are great examples.* Take Brown v. Board *or the*
      recent marriage equality litigation.

    ○ **Important**—"frivolous" is subject to interpretation.

    ○ Reliance on a client's factual assertion *may* be permissible under ethical rules.

      ▪ FRCP 11 and its state cognates require "_____

      investigation" into the client's facts.

    ○ _____ may make an action frivolous later.

      Example 62: *Conrad told Lorraine that he was injured in a high-profile train*
      accident. Lorraine later determines that Conrad wasn't even in the same state
      as the train accident. Is this a frivolous claim?

      _____ .

      What should Lorraine do? _____ .

2. **Don't delay!**

    ○ Can ask for/consent to a _____ extension

C. **Candor to the Tribunal**

    • "Tribunal" includes _____ as well as courts.

    • A lawyer may not "knowingly" (actual knowledge):

    ○ Make _____ statements as to

    _____ or _____ ;

    ○ Fail to disclose _____ on the other side; **or**

    ○ Offer evidence the lawyer "_____" to be false.

    • A lawyer _____ refuse to offer evidence the lawyer

    "_____" is false.

      Example 63: *Larry represents Cassandra in a case against her insurance*
      company. After the insurance company filed its reply brief, the state Supreme
      Court issued an opinion that weakens Cassandra's case. Does Larry have to
      disclose it to the court? _____ .

D. Remedial Measures

- When a lawyer "knows" evidence submitted was false or, typically, when perjury has been committed or is about to be committed:

  o Lawyer must _____ with the witness (i.e., attempt to dissuade) to correct the falsity;

  o Lawyer may take the matter to the court and seek to _____;

  o When withdrawal is denied (and it usually will be), the lawyer can present "trial by narrative"

    - Trial by narrative—the witness testifies without lawyer's participation (i.e., no questions or objections).

      Example 64: Prepping Conrad to take the stand in his assault case, Lorraine gets the feeling that Conrad is going to lie about where he was when the incident occurred. Is she required to tell the court? _____. She does not have actual knowledge.

      What should Lorraine do? _____, in the hope of dissuading him from committing perjury.

- A lawyer has a duty to correct errors (false testimony, etc.).

  o *Does it last forever?* It ends when the _____.

E. Tampering

- A lawyer cannot tamper with _____ or _____.

  Example 65: Cassandra hands Larry a laptop and says, "I used this to steal thousands for my company." Can Larry destroy the laptop? _____.

  Can Larry wipe the hard drive? _____, that's not any better.

  Can Larry store the laptop in his office indefinitely? _____, still bad.

  What should Larry do? _____.

  Can the police say they got it from Larry? _____.

- No destruction of evidence (including moving)
- No payment of witness except for the cost of coming to the proceedings

  o **Exception—**_____ can be paid.

  o **But**—no contingency fees for experts.

F. **"Ex Parte" Communications**

- Generally, no "ex parte" communications by the lawyer

    o Applies to pending and impending litigation

- Persons with whom lawyer cannot communicate ex parte: Judges, jurors, the prospective venire (potential jurors)

    o Might be permitted to speak to jurors after the trial (survey)

        ▪ Regulated by local court rules
        ▪ Typically requires judicial permission
        ▪ Cannot talk to the juror about inadmissible evidence

G. **Communications with Represented Persons**

1. **General rule**

    o A lawyer (or the lawyer's agent) may not communicate with represented people.
    o A lawyer must have _____ of representation.
    o Once a lawyer knows a person is represented, the lawyer must deal with the

    _____ .

2. **Entities**

    o Presume that members of the control group of an entity are represented by the lawyer for the entity.

3. **Admissions**

    o A lawyer _____ talk to a person who could make a statement that would be used as an admission.
    o Former employees are no longer represented by the entity's attorney.

H. **Communications with Unrepresented Persons**

1. **Generally**

    o A lawyer cannot _____ the unrepresented person.

        Example 66: *Suggesting you are not interested in the case.*

        Example 67: *Concealing the fact that you are a lawyer in the case.*

    o Special rule—undercover attorneys

        ▪ Use of an undercover agent is permitted, particularly in criminal cases and in civil litigation, where information cannot be obtained by other means.

2. **Inadvertent communication**

> *Example 68:* *Larry receives an email concerning his client. After a quick glance, it's clear that the email was sent in error.*

- o Larry must _____.
- o Can he read it? _____. There's no prohibition on the recipient reading or using the inadvertent communication.

I. **Media Contact Rule**

- • **Prejudice**—lawyers cannot make statements to media that have a substantial likelihood of _____ the proceeding.
- • Exceptions:
  - o To protect from other publicity
  - o General facts of the case and procedure (e.g., how litigation will proceed, scheduling, or warning to public)
- • Specific prohibited circumstance—bad comments about _____
- • A lawyer *may* respond in the media to protect client from publicity _____ by the client or lawyer ("He started it.")

> *Example 69:* *Lorraine is defending Conrad in a high-profile murder case. McCoy Jack, the District Attorney, gave a long press conference condemning Conrad. Can Lorraine speak to the media in response?*
> _____, *because McCoy Jack started it.*

CHAPTER 10:   DIFFERENT ROLES OF THE LAWYER

A. **Candid Advisor/Third-Party Evaluation**

1. **Overview**

- o Client asks an attorney to evaluate something;
- o The attorney's evaluation will be given to the third party.

> *Example 70:* *Cassandra is trying to sell a piece of property. The potential buyer wants a report on the title, which Cassandra asks Lorraine to prepare. The sale is in Cassandra's best interests.*

2. **Basic rule**

- o An attorney must give _____ to a third party.

> *Example 71:* *Say that Lorraine learns that a neighbor has a significant right-of-way easement on Cassandra's property, which may render title unmarketable.*

- o An attorney must tell the client before communicating unfavorable information.

B. Neutrals (Mediator, Arbitrator, etc.)

- Neutral as to third parties, not _____.

> ***Example 72:*** *In addition to his practice, Larry also serves as a mediator in water disputes. In this capacity, Larry must remain neutral.*

C. Prosecutors

- Prosecutors are subject to a set of constitutionally mandated rules:
    - Must have ____probable cause____ to bring a criminal action;
    - Cannot take advantage of ____Unrepresented____ persons;
    - Must disclose ____exculpatory____ information;
    - No subpoena of a lawyer in order to destroy ____attorney - client privilege____;
    - Like other lawyers, restrictions against talking to ____media____; and
    - Required to seek a ____remedy____ if new evidence is clear and convincing.

D. Safekeeping Property

- General rule—a lawyer must keep her own property ____Separate____ from the client's property.
    - no comingling

E. Advertising

- ____All____ forms of communications are considered advertising.

> ***Example 73:*** *Shameless about getting his name out there, Larry always has business cards at the ready to hand out to prospective clients. The business cards are advertising—as is a website, a mailing, letterhead, etc.*

1. Restrictions on advertising

a. May not be ____false____ **or** ____Misleading____.

> ***Example 74:*** *Lorraine advertises on Headbook, a social media site. Her advertisement says, "I'm not capable of losing." Could this lead to discipline?*
>
> Yes

b. Unverifiable self-promotion

> ***Example 75:*** *Larry's current commercial says, "There can be no doubt. When it comes to trusts and estates, I am the greatest lawyer ever." Is this a problem?*
>
> Yes

c. Expertise and fields of practice

- A lawyer ____Can____ state her fields of practice.

Example 76: Lorraine's billboard says, "I want to be <u>your</u> tax lawyer." Is this permissible? __yes__ . It states her field of practice.

- A lawyer can call herself a <u>specialist.</u>

    Example 77: Larry's website says he "specializes in DUI defense." Is this permissible? __yes__ .

- A lawyer cannot call herself a "certified specialist" **unless:**

    - She has been certified as a specialist by an organization approved by 1) an appropriate statue authority or 2) that has been accredited by the ABA, **and**
    - The name of the certifying organization is clearly identified.

    Example 78: Lorraine's leaflet says "I'm a certified child custody expert," but the leaflet doesn't identify the certifying organization. Is this permissible? __no__ .

- **Patent:** If a lawyer is <u>admitted to practice before the US Patent and Trademark Office,</u> the lawyer can call herself a <u>"Patent Attorney."</u>

- **Admiralty:** If a lawyer is <u>engaged in admiralty practice,</u> the lawyer can call herself <u>"Proctor in Admiralty,"</u> or designate her practice <u>"Admiralty"</u>

d. **Disclosure of location of offices**

e. **Names of Client**

    o Advertisement can include the name of regularly represented client, provided lawyer has the client's __consent__ .

f. **Identification of Advertiser**

    o Any communication about a lawyer or firm must include the *name* and *contact information* of at least one attorney or law firm responsible for its content.

g. **No implication of a __partnership__ unless one really exists**

    Example 79: Lorraine and Larry share office space and an assistant, but they practice independently. The door on their office says "Smith and Johnson." Is this permissible? __no__ , it implies a partnership.

2. **Firm Names and Letterhead**

    a. **Firm names and letterhead, as well as website and social media, are all subject to rule, *i.e.* they can't be false or misleading**

        o Firm may be designated by names of all or some of its members, including __deceased__ members.

- If a firm uses a trade name that includes a geographic name—"The Phoenix Legal Group" ("We'll rise from the ashes defending you!")—the communication must include a statement that it is not a public legal aid organization.

b. **Firm name cannot imply a connection with:**

- Government agency
- A deceased lawyer who was not a former member of the firm
- A lawyer not associated with the firm
- A nonlawyer, or
- A Public or charitable legal services organization.

c. **Firm cannot use the name of a lawyer holding public office**

d. **Firms with offices in more than one jurisdiction may use the same name in each.**

3. **Real-time Direct Contact**

a. **Real-time, direct contact to solicit business is prohibited.**

- This includes in-person, on the telephone, and synchronous electronic communication.
  - **But:** Does not include chat rooms, text messages, other communications that recipients may easily disregard.
- **Exceptions:**
  i) Another lawyer
  ii) Family, close personal, or prior business relationship
  iii) Person who routinely uses the lawyer's type of legal services
- The prohibition is on the lawyer seeking pecuniary gain.

b. **Mail and non real-time electronic communications**

- These are okay.

  But: communication cannot involve coercion, duress, or harassment and cannot be to someone who has said they don't want to be solicited

  Example 80: *A USA Air flight crashed, killing 75 people. After researching their stories, Larry sent a mailing to the relatives of the victims. Is this gross?* _Yes_ . *Is it permissible?* _probably, depends on content (yes)_

c. **Constitutional issues**

- General mail should not be restricted

- *Florida Bar v. Went For It*

    - Florida enacted a 30-day restriction on contact with accident victims.

    - The restriction was upheld as a reasonable restriction on advertising rights.

- New York courts ruled that an outright ban on pop-up ads was unconstitutional.

F. Referrals/Endorsement

- Referral services are permitted.

    o Watch for Internet-based client generators: E.g., "divorce.com"

- No payments for percentage of fees, **but**, ad rates are okay

G. Pro Bono

- Aspirational rule (i.e., not mandatory)—_____ *50* _____ hours of service per year

- Conflicts may arise between your pro bono and legal services work and your regular work.

    o Special conflicts rules apply:

        - Conflicts rules do not apply unless the lawyer is ____ *aware* ____ of the conflict.

        - "Special Material Benefit Disclosure" rule—this is the situation where a decision in the pro bono matter will benefit one of lawyer's other clients.

            - A lawyer must disclose the existence of a conflict, **but...**

            - The duty of confidentiality prevents disclosure of the client's identity.

        Example 81: *Lorraine successfully represented a client in a pro bono immigration matter. She must disclose that she has a client with an interest in this pro bono activity, but she need not say who the client is.*

H. Limited Legal Services

Hotlines OK!

- Potential tension between providing public with legal services and the lawyer's possible liability for such services

- These services are nevertheless allowed.

    Example 82: *Larry volunteers for a criminal defense legal hotline. This is permissible behavior.*

I. Politics

1. Campaign contributions

    o Solicitation of campaign contributions and participation in political work is permitted.

- ○ No _**bribery**_, because of course not
- ○ Cannot make contributions in exchange for an appointment or for favor in a lawsuit
- ○ Applies to all political offices, not just judicial offices

2. **Comments on candidate's qualifications**

   - ○ Not permitted to _**lie**_ about candidate's fitness for office
   - ○ *NY Times v. Sullivan*—the First Amendment protects speech against public figures.
     - ▪ Not defamation unless the speaker made the comment with _**actual Malice**_
     - ▪ "Actual Malice"—knowing falsity or reckless disregard for truth

3. **Running for judge**

   - ○ Permitted, subject to legal ethics as well as judicial ethics

CHAPTER 11: JUDICIAL ETHICS

A. Number of Questions

- • About 6% (3 or 4 questions), on average, of the MPRE is devoted to judicial ethics.

B. Interplay with Lawyer's Ethics

- • A lawyer may not induce a judge in the violation of judicial ethics.

  > **Example 83:** In the hope of currying favor, Larry offered Judge Williams tickets to the hit Broadway musical Burr, in exchange for a few conversations about his upcoming trial before the judge. Is this permissible?
  > _**No**_, it's ex parte communication.

C. Model Code of Judicial Conduct (CJC)

- • Structure

  - ○ Canons = _**general principles**_
  - ○ Rules = _**specific rules**_
  - ○ Comments = _**Suggestions**_

D. Judicial Integrity

1. **Judges must comply with the law.**

   - ○ Unlike a lawyer, a judge must avoid the _**appearance of inappropriety**_

2. **No abuse of office for gain**

   > **Example 84:** Judge Williams is a self-described foodie. When he couldn't get a reservation at Crouton, the city's hottest new restaurant, he called the owner and said, "I'm a federal judge. I get a table tomorrow night."

Example 85: Judge Williams calls Lorraine to recommend one of his clerks for an open associate position at Lorraine's firm. Is this permissible? ___yes___.

E. Impartiality and Diligence

- Judges must be diligent and impartial (i.e., no ___favoritism___).
- Justice must be ___blind___.

F. Ex Parte Communications

1. **Generally prohibited**

   o The prohibition applies to judges as well as lawyers.

   o **Staff control**—the judge is responsible for controlling her ___staff___, particularly in the area of ex parte communications

2. **Permitted ex parte contacts**—scheduling, consultation with experts, communication with staff, settlement discussions (only with parties' consent), etc.

3. **Judge as detective**—a judge may not conduct an independent factual ___investigation___ of any matter before the court

G. Public Comment

- Judges should not make public comments on ___pending___ or ___impending___ cases.
- Applies to cases before any court if it might affect the outcome or fairness

   Example 86: After the Court's term is over, Justice Bornstein gives a speech at a law school outlining his view of the decisions handed down that term. Is this a violation? ___No, cases were already handed down___

H. Recusal

1. **Judge: "I will not hear this case."**

   o Arises when the judge's ___impartiality___ is questioned

   o Look for:

   - Money—some interest in the outcome
   - Relatives
   - Anger
   - Bias

   o **Exception**—rule of ___necessity___

   - If no judge can hear the case, someone has to do it.

2. **Mandatory recusal**

   o Personal ___bias___ toward a party or lawyer;

BRAM [handwritten circled note]

- Personal knowledge of _____*facts*_____ in the case;
- Judge and spouse's relationship;
- _____*Money*_____ for the judge or the judge's family;
- Political contributions by one party generally _____*are* *NOT*_____ grounds for recusal;
  - **Exception**—contribution in _____*EXCESS*_____ of what is legal
- Judicial conflict—judge has previously served as a:
  - A lawyer in the matter;
  - _____*Prior* *official*_____ ; or
  - Prior judge in the matter before the court.

3. **Disclosure**

- Must disclose to the litigants all _____*information*_____ that is useful to judge whether recusal is appropriate

4. **Waiver**

- Recusal may be _____*waived*_____ by the parties, even in cases of mandatory recusal.
- **Exceptions**—recusal based on personal bias and personal knowledge may not be waived.

I. **Squealing by Judges**

- Judges are obligated to report _____*Known*_____ violations of the rules by another lawyer that implicates the lawyer's honesty, trustworthiness, or fitness as a lawyer.
- Impairment—if the judge has a _____*rsnbl belief*_____ that a lawyer is impaired, the judge must take appropriate action.

> **Note 10:** The Rules treat knowledge and reasonable belief the same. A judge must disclose.

differs from (L) rules

J. **Extra-Judicial Activities**

1. **Overall theme**

- Judges cannot engage in activities that _____*Undermine*_____ of the judge or of the court.

> **Example 87:** The local paper reveals that Judge Williams has been hosting an illegal gambling ring in the basement of his townhouse.

2. **Character witness**

- A judge cannot be a _____*Voluntary*_____ character witness.
- A judge can be a character witness if _____*Summoned*_____ to testify.

3. **Fiduciary**

   o No _____fiduciary_____ appointments (e.g., trustee, executor)

   o **Exception**—_____family_____ matters

4. **Practice of law**

   o A judge may not _____practice_____ law.

   o **Exception**—_____pro se_____ practice

5. **Outside business**

   o No _____outside_____ business

   o **Exception**—_____family_____ business, so long as it does not interfere with judicial work.

   > **Example 88:** Judge Williams' family has long owned a lucrative soda bottling business, from which Judge Williams earns a hefty profit. Is this permissible?
   > _____yes_____.
   >
   > Can he hear a case in which an ex-employee is suing his family's company?
   > _____No_____, that would be easy grounds for recusal.

K. Gifts to Judges

1. **Non-reportable gifts**

   o Gifts to judges are permitted _____w/ out reporting_____, if in the ordinary course.

   > **Example 89:** East legal publisher sends Judge Williams—as well as every judge on the court—a complimentary copy of its updated Professional Responsibility desk book, for use in official matters.

2. **Reportable gifts**

   o Large gifts are subject to reporting rules.

   o Conventions—reimbursement for judge's attendance at a convention

      ▪ Recreation—the judge must _____report_____.

      ▪ Education—the judge need not _____report_____.

L. Politics for Judges

1. **Easy rule**

   o A judge must _____stay out_____ of politics—including endorsement of political candidates, even family members

2. **Impartiality**—no pledges, promises, or commitments

   o No commitments

- Candidate for judicial office (issues v. parties)
  - General comments about **issues**— _allowed_

    Example 90: *In a speech to high school students, Judge Williams says "I am a firm believer in strict campaign finance regulations."*

  - Specific comments about **parties**—not allowed

    Example 91: *Asked by a reporter about the campaign finance case before the Supreme Court, Judge Williams says "The defendants have no chance in that one."*

- **Keep in mind!** Judge comments might be the basis for recusal.

3. **Judge running for judicial post in an election**
   - A judge can have a campaign committee.
   - A judge can endorse candidates for the same office.

4. **Judge running for elective office other than judgeship** (e.g., legislature)
   - A judge must _quit_ the judgeship.

5. **Judge seeking appointment to non-elective office** (e.g., federal court judge)
   - A judge _does NOT_ have to quit job.

CHAPTER 12: MPRE PRACTICE PROBLEMS

Question 1

An attorney was retained to represent a client charged with assault. The attorney interviewed several of the client's friends and colleagues in a search of character witnesses. In one such interview, the client's secretary revealed that the client, who was a banker, often skirted legal and ethical lines. After the client was acquitted, the attorney's friend called to congratulate him. The attorney mentioned that it might not be long before the client found himself in legal trouble again, and he told his friend about the conversation with the client's secretary.

Was the attorney's action in revealing what he learned from the client's secretary proper?

A.   No, because the attorney was bound by the duty of confidentiality.

B.   No, because the conversation with the secretary was protected by attorney-client privilege.

C.   Yes, because the attorney's representation of the client had concluded.

D.   Yes, because the conversation was not protected by the attorney-client privilege.

NOTES:

_____
_____
_____
_____
_____
_____
_____
_____
_____
_____
_____

Question 2

A well-known defense attorney met with a criminal defendant regarding representation of the defendant in a highly publicized case. During the meeting, the attorney told the defendant, who was indigent, that she would represent him if he agreed to grant her movie rights regarding the representation. The client agreed to these terms, and the attorney provided him with a written consent form setting forth the terms of the representation and advising him to seek independent counsel. The attorney met with the defendant several days later, at which time he returned a signed copy of the written consent form. He told her that he had not consulted with another attorney. The attorney succeeded in obtaining an acquittal at trial and began shopping a movie based on the case to television studios shortly thereafter.

Were the attorney's actions in securing the movie rights based on the case proper?

A.   No, because the attorney negotiated for movie rights prior to the conclusion of the representation.

B.   No, because the defendant did not obtain independent legal counsel before signing the consent form.

C.   Yes, because the defendant signed a written consent form after being advised of his right to seek independent counsel.

D.   Yes, because the attorney negotiated for movie rights as a replacement for fees.

NOTES:

_____
_____
_____
_____
_____
_____
_____
_____
_____
_____
_____

Question 3

An attorney represented a criminal defendant in a murder case. The attorney's client told the attorney that he wanted to testify in his own defense. The attorney tried to dissuade his client from testifying, in part because although he had no evidence to support it, he suspected that the client's version of the events was fabricated. The attorney also believed that the jury would not believe his client. The client insisted, however, that he testify. The attorney told his client that he would call the client to the stand but reminded him that he was under oath and that it was imperative that he answer all questions truthfully. At trial, the client testified in his own defense, and the prosecution subsequently impeached the defendant's testimony.

Was the attorney's action in allowing his client to testify proper?

A.   No, because the attorney reasonably believed that his client's testimony would be false.

B.   No, because the attorney was required to take remedial measures.

C.   Yes, because the attorney did not know that the client's testimony would be false.

D.   Yes, because an attorney is required to respect a criminal defendant's decision to testify.

NOTES:

_____
_____
_____
_____
_____
_____
_____
_____
_____
_____
_____

Question 4

An attorney filed a motion for summary judgment on behalf of his client despite knowledge of directly adverse case law from the highest court in the state. Since the issuance of that decision, however, courts in other states had reached the opposite conclusion. In the motion, the attorney cited the decisions from other states but did not mention the decision from the state's highest court. The opposing attorney filed a brief in opposition to the motion for summary judgment that did not cite the decision from the state's highest court. The court did not hold oral argument but granted summary judgment based on the briefs.

Were the attorney's actions in not disclosing the decision of the state's highest court proper?

A.   No, because the attorney was required to disclose the decision in his initial brief supporting the motion for summary judgment.

B.   No, because the attorney was required to disclose the decision after the opposing counsel failed to disclose it.

C.   Yes, because an attorney does not have a duty to disclose cases that are adverse to his client's position.

D.   Yes, because disclosure of the case would violate the attorney's duty to zealously advocate his client's position.

NOTES:

_____
_____
_____
_____
_____
_____
_____
_____
_____
_____

Question 5

An attorney opened a trust account at a local bank into which she deposited a check from a client that constituted an advance payment for future services to be rendered by the attorney. Subsequently, the attorney received an engagement fee from another client, which the attorney also deposited into the account. The engagement fee represented payment to the attorney for accepting the case, being available to handle the case, and agreeing not to represent another party in the case. The fee did not require the attorney to perform specific legal services. The attorney maintained records related to all account transactions in accordance with the state rules of professional conduct, which were identical to the ABA Model Rules of Professional Conduct, but she did not pay bank service charges on the account from her own funds.

Is the attorney subject to discipline with regard to her actions concerning the trust fund account?

A.   No, because the attorney properly maintained the records related to the account.

B.   No, because the attorney maintained a trust fund account to keep her property separate from her client's property.

C.   Yes, because the attorney failed to pay the bank service charges on the account from her own funds.

D.   Yes, because the attorney did not keep her client's property separate from her own property.

NOTES:

_____
_____
_____
_____
_____
_____
_____
_____
_____
_____

A. **Summary**

1. Start with the call of the question.

2. Make notes while reading the facts.

3. Try to come up with an answer on your own.

4. Check your work by reading all the answer choices.

5. Always choose an answer!

B. **Final Advice**

1. Study! Put in the time.

2. Study your way. What has worked for you in the past should work for you on the MPRE.

3. Be nice to the people around you. They will still be there after the exam!

GOOD LUCK ON THE MPRE!

[END OF HANDOUT]

Themis
Bar Review

MPRE
Final Review Outline and
Legal Terminology List

FINAL REVIEW OUTLINE: MULTISTATE PROFESSIONAL RESPONSIBILITY EXAM (MPRE)

I. Regulation of the Legal Profession

A. Inherent powers of courts to regulate lawyer

1. **State courts**—regulate all aspects of the practice of law within their jurisdiction, each state with its own rules of professional conduct often based on the ABA Model Rules

2. **Federal courts**—each court has its own bar to which a lawyer must be admitted in order to practice before the court

B. Admission to the profession

1. **Requirements for admission**

   - **Education**—most states require graduation from an ABA-accredited law school

   - **Knowledge**—most states require applicants to pass a bar examination

   - **Character**—past conduct may be considered when assessing an applicant's good character and general fitness to practice law; false statements to the bar examiners may result in a denial of admission

   - **Residency**—no residency requirements

2. **Application process**—restrictions on applicant

   - Prohibited from knowingly making a false statement of material fact regarding bar admission, failing to disclose a material fact, or knowingly failing to respond to lawful demand by an admissions authority regarding application

   - Can invoke the Fifth Amendment privilege; must do so openly, not simply omit information

   - Violations of the Model Rules (MR) may prevent admission

C. Regulation after admission

1. **Grounds of misconduct**

   - Violate or attempt to violate MR, or knowingly assist or induce another to do so

   - Commit a criminal act that adversely reflects on the lawyer's honesty, trustworthiness, or fitness as lawyer

   - Engage in conduct involving dishonesty, fraud, deceit, or misrepresentation

   - Engage in conduct prejudicial to administration of justice

   - State or imply an ability to influence improperly government agency or official

   - Knowingly assist a judge or judicial officer in a violation of judicial conduct rules or other law

   - Engage in conduct that the lawyer knows or reasonably should know is harassment or discrimination

2. **Misconduct committed by others in law firm**

   - Misconduct of another lawyer or non-lawyer, ordered or ratified by a lawyer

- **Manager's responsibility for firm's preventive measures**—must make reasonable efforts to ensure the firm has measures in place that give reasonable assurance that the conduct of all lawyers and non-lawyers conforms to the MR
- **Direct supervisor's responsibility for supervised person's conduct**—must make reasonable efforts to ensure that the supervised person's conduct conforms to the MR
- **Failure to remediate known misconduct**—when a lawyer with managerial authority knows that the consequences of misconduct can be avoided or mitigated but fails to take reasonable remedial action
- **Duties of subordinate lawyer**—must conform to the MR even if acting under the direction of a supervising lawyer; not liable for violation of the MR if the subordinate acts in accordance with the supervising lawyer's reasonable resolution of an arguable question of professional duty

3. **Misconduct outside of the jurisdiction** (JX)—a lawyer is subject to discipline for misconduct in any JX where the lawyer is admitted to practice, even if the misconduct occurred outside of that JX; also subject to discipline by the JX where misconduct occurred

4. **Sanctions for misconduct**—set by each state; ranges from public/private censure to disbarment

D. **Peer responsibility**—duty to report another lawyer's misconduct to the appropriate authority

1. The matter must raise a **substantial question** about the lawyer's honesty, trustworthiness or professional fitness

2. There is **no requirement** to disclose **confidential information** protected by the MR

3. The lawyer must have **actual knowledge** of the misconduct (may be inferred)

4. Similar duty to report **judicial misconduct**

5. **Failure to report** misconduct may subject the lawyer to discipline

6. The report is **privileged from a defamation** claim by the other lawyer

E. **Unauthorized practice of law**

1. **Not admitted to practice in a jurisdiction**—unless pro hac vice appearance, in association with a local lawyer, or other temporary practice of law

2. **Exceptions permitting permanent practice**
   - Provision of legal services only to the lawyer's employer or its organizational affiliates, if the forum does not require pro hac vice admission
   - Services rendered are permitted by federal or local law

3. **Assisting non-lawyers in the unauthorized practice of law**—subject to civil/criminal penalties as well as disciplinary proceedings; can provide professional guidance to non-lawyers whose employment requires legal knowledge

F. **Fee division with non-lawyers**—not permitted unless paid as a death benefit, a lawyer purchases the practice of a deceased/disabled lawyer, part of a compensation/retirement plan, or shared court-awarded fees with a non-profit organization that employed or retained the lawyer

G. **Law firm and other forms of practice**

1. **"Law firm"**—a lawyer or lawyers in a partnership, professional corporation, sole proprietorship, or other association authorized to practice law, or lawyers employed in a

legal services organization/legal department of organization; can include public holding out as firm

- Sharing of fees with lawyers in the same law firm is permitted

2. **Limitations on associations with non-lawyers**

- **Partnership**—no partnership with a non-lawyer if any of the partnership's activities consist of the practice of law

- **Professional corporation**—no practice of law for profit in or with an entity in which a non-lawyer (i) owns an interest, (ii) is a corporate director, or (iii) has the right to direct or control a lawyer's professional judgment

3. **Third party refers client or pays fee**—a lawyer may accept compensation from a third party so long as there is no interference with the lawyer's independent professional judgment and the client gives informed consent

4. **Law-related services**

- Services reasonably related to legal services, but not prohibited as unauthorized practice of law when provided by non-lawyer—subject to MR if services are not distinct from lawyer's provision of legal services to clients (e.g., accounting, tax prep)

- Lawyer who fails to take reasonable measures to assure that person obtaining law-related services knows that protections of client-lawyer relationship do not exist—subject to the MR

5. **Sale of law practice** (including goodwill)—compensation for the reasonable value of a law practice may be paid and received

- **Requirements:**

  o Seller ceases to practice all areas of law or an area of law

    ▪ Cessation may be everywhere or only within certain geographic area

  o Written notice to clients about the proposed sale; the client has the right to seek other counsel, but consent is presumed after 90 days

  o Entire practice or area of practice sold to one or more lawyers or law firms

    ▪ Seller must in good faith offer the entire practice or area of practice: clients need not remain clients of the buyer

  o Client fees not increased due to sale

- **Situations in which seller may still practice or return to practice:**

  o Seller may work for a public agency, legal services to poor, or in-house counsel to a business

  o Sale is only of an area of practice

  o Return to private practice due to unanticipated circumstances

- **Obligations of purchaser**—undertake all client matters in the practice or practice area, subject to client consent and conflict of interest constraints

6. **Contractual restrictions on practice**

- A lawyer cannot agree to restrict the lawyer's right to practice after termination of a partnership, shareholder, or employment agreement (except for retirement benefits)

- A lawyer cannot agree to restrict the lawyer's right to practice as part of the settlement of a client controversy

II. Client-Lawyer Relationship

A. Acceptance or rejection of clients

1. **No general duty to accept representation of any client** (exception: court appointments—appointed lawyer has same duties to client as retained lawyer)

2. **Undertaking representation**—a lawyer is both a fiduciary and agent of the client

   - **Creation of relationship**—when the client reasonably believes the relationship exists; no formal writing or agreement is needed

   - **Duty to reject**—violation of rule of ethics/law or material impairment of the lawyer's ability to represent the client due to the lawyer's physical or mental condition

B. Scope, objectives and means of the representation

1. **Decisions made by lawyer**—means of achieving the client's objectives, after reasonably consulting with the client

   - May make most decisions relating to strategy and methods for achieving client's goals

   - Must reasonably consult with client about client's objectives and keep him reasonably informed

   - May limit the scope of representation if the limitation is reasonable under the circumstances and the client provides informed consent

2. **Decisions made by client**—objectives and goals of representation (can be negotiated)

   - **Civil case**—acceptance of a settlement offer

   - **Criminal case**—whether the client will testify, waive the right to a jury trial, and enter a guilty plea

3. **Client with diminished capacity**—the lawyer must maintain an ordinary lawyer-client relationship to the extent possible

   - May take reasonably necessary protective action (e.g., the appointment of a guardian or conservator)

   - In an emergency when the client is threatened with imminent and irreparable harm, may take legal action to the extent necessary to avoid harm

4. **Prohibition on counseling crimes or fraud**—if a lawyer does so, she is subject to civil/criminal liability as well as discipline

   - A lawyer can discuss the legal consequences of a proposed course of conduct with the client and make a good-faith effort to determine the validity, scope, and application of the law

5. **Apparent authority**—a lawyer's act is the client's act in proceedings before a tribunal or in dealings with a third person if either reasonably assumes that the lawyer is authorized to do the act on the basis of the client's manifestations of such authorization

6. **Knowledge and notice**—information imparted to the lawyer by the client is attributed to the client for purposes of determining the client's rights and liabilities

   - **Exceptions**—transactions not within the scope of the representation, other lawyers in the same firm who are unaware that information is relevant to the firm's representation, or the lawyer's knowledge regarding the client's criminal liability

C. Withdrawal or termination of representation

1. Mandatory withdrawal

- Failure to withdraw would violate the MRPC or law (when the client **demands** such conduct)

- Lawyer's physical or mental condition materially impairs his ability to represent the client

- Lawyer is discharged by the client, unless ordered by the court to continue representation

2. Permissive withdrawal

- For any reason, if there is no material harm to the client

- Even with harm to the client, when:

  o Client persists in a course of action involving the lawyer's services that the lawyer reasonably believes is criminal or fraudulent

  o Lawyer learns that previous services have been used by the client to perpetrate a crime or fraud

  o Client insists on a course of action the lawyer finds repugnant or fundamentally disagrees with

  o Client deliberately disregards agreement/obligation to lawyer as to expenses or fees

  o Representation will result in unreasonable financial burden on the lawyer

  o Client has made representation unreasonably difficult

  o Other good cause exists

- Court permission must be obtained when required before withdrawing

3. Duties on termination—duty to take reasonable measures to protect the client's interests and minimize the harm done to the client (even if the lawyer is unfairly discharged)

- Reasonable notice to the client and allowance of time to employ other counsel

- Return client's papers and property, including unearned fees

D. Fees

1. No unreasonable fees

- **Reasonableness factors**—include: difficulty of case, preclusion of other employment, type of fee, nature of lawyer-client relationship, fee arrangement, expertise of lawyer, amount at issue and results obtained, customary fee charged locally

2. Contingent fees—must be in writing and reasonable

- **Prohibited**—criminal and domestic relations cases (may be charged in domestic relations cases to recover post-judgment balances due for support)

- **Writing requirement**

  o Signature of client

  o Calculation methodology of the fee, and

  o Details of the calculation for deductions for expenses, including whether such expenses are to be deducted before or after the contingency fee is calculated

3. **Terms of payment**
   - **Payment in advance**—permitted if any unearned portion is returned when the representation is terminated
   - **Property as payment**—permitted as long as it is not a proprietary interest in the cause of action or subject matter of the litigation
   - No agreement with terms which might induce the lawyer to curtail services or cause the lawyer to perform duties contrary to the client's interest; it is proper to define the extent of services based on the client's ability to pay

4. **Reasonable expenses**—expenses charged to the client cannot be unreasonable

5. **Fee splitting**
   - Permitted among members of the same law firm, including retired members
   - Among members of different firms, permitted if:
     o Fee is in proportion to the services rendered by each lawyer or all lawyers assume joint responsibility for the representation
     o Client agrees in writing to the fee splitting arrangement, and
     o The total fee is reasonable
   - **Referral fees**—not permitted; however, the referring lawyer is entitled to a fee for work done before making the referral

6. **Modification of fee agreement**—must be reasonable at the time of the modification

7. **Communication with client**—the lawyer must generally communicate about the basis and rate of fee within a reasonable time after the representation begins; written communication about fees is advised but is not required except for a contingency fee

8. **Fee disputes**
   - **Arbitration/mediation procedures**—a lawyer must comply if mandatory (e.g., established by the bar); a lawyer should conscientiously consider complying if voluntary
   - **Retention of disputed funds in trust account pending dispute resolution**—a lawyer must promptly distribute all undisputed funds to the client

III. **Privilege and Confidentiality**

A. **Duty vs. privilege in general**

1. **Duty of confidentiality**—applies to all information gained from any source relating to the representation of the client

2. **Lawyer-client privilege**—an evidentiary rule protecting information communicated in confidence by the client to the attorney from disclosure

B. **Attorney-client privilege**—the client may prevent a confidential communication made to the lawyer from disclosure by the lawyer at a judicial or other governmental proceeding

1. **Elements**
   - **Confidential**—communication must be intended to be confidential
     o Waiver and disclosure (federal proceedings)

- Client may waive the privilege directly or by disclosure of the information communicated; inadvertent disclosure does not waive the privilege if reasonable steps are promptly taken to prevent disclosure and rectify error
- Intentional disclosure of privileged material waives the privilege
  - **Communication**—must be for the purpose of obtaining or providing legal advice or representation
  - **Client holds the privilege**
  - **Indefinite duration**—the privilege survives the termination of the representation and the death of the client
2. **Exceptions**—the following confidential communications are not protected by the privilege:
   - Future crime or fraud
   - Dispute between client and lawyer
   - Dispute between former co-clients who are now adverse to each other
   - Dispute between parties who claim through the same deceased client
3. **Work product doctrine**
   - Documents prepared by a lawyer for his own use in connection with the client's case are not subject to discovery unless there is a substantial need and no other means to get the information without undue hardship
   - Mental impressions, conclusions, and trial tactics are always protected

C. **Professional obligation of confidentiality**
1. **Duty of confidentiality to prospective client**—a lawyer is generally not permitted to use or reveal information learned in a consultation (even if no lawyer-client relationship is formed)
   - **Unilateral communication**—if there is no reasonable expectation that the lawyer is willing to discuss the possibility of forming a lawyer-client relationship, then the person is not a prospective client
2. **Duty of confidentiality to former client**—a lawyer must not reveal information relating to representation except when permitted or required by MR
3. **Acting to preserve confidentiality**—a lawyer must take reasonable precautions to safeguard against disclosures by others participating in the representation or subject to the lawyer's supervision

D. **Client-authorized disclosure**
1. **Informed consent by client**—the lawyer may reveal confidential information
2. **Implied authority**—the lawyer may disclose information relating to the representation of the client if disclosure is impliedly authorized to carry out the representation (lawyers in a firm may disclose information to each other unless the client instructs otherwise)

E. **Exceptions to confidentiality**—permissible disclosures
1. **Reasonably certain death or substantial bodily harm**—no more than necessary to prevent the harm; source of harm need not be client; harm/death need not be imminent
2. **Substantial financial harm to another**—to the extent that the lawyer reasonably believes necessary to prevent the client or another person from committing a crime, and to

mitigate substantial injury to financial interests or property of another in furtherance of which the client used or is using the lawyer's services

3. **Securing legal advice about lawyer's compliance with MR**—permitted

4. **Controversy between lawyer and client**—to the extent that the lawyer reasonably believes necessary to establish a claim or defense on behalf of the lawyer, to establish a defense to a criminal charge or civil claim against the lawyer based on conduct in which the client was involved, or to respond to allegations in any proceeding concerning the lawyer's representation of the client

5. **Compliance with other law or court order**—to the extent reasonably necessary

6. **Detecting/resolving conflicts of interest**—arising from a change of employment (but not if it will compromise the lawyer-client privilege or prejudice the client)

IV. Conflicts of Interest

A. **As affected by lawyer's personal interest**—a lawyer must not represent a client if the representation may be materially limited by the lawyer's personal interest

1. **Exception**
   - Lawyer reasonably believes that she can provide competent and diligent representation to the affected client
   - Representation is not prohibited by law, and
   - Client gives informed consent, confirmed in writing

2. **Opposing lawyers related** (e.g., parent, child, sibling, or spouse)—can be waived by informed consent of each client; not imputed to members of related lawyers' firms

3. **Sexual relations with client**
   - Prohibited unless a consensual sexual relationship predated the commencement of the lawyer-client relationship
   - Cannot be waived by informed consent

B. **Lawyer as witness**—a lawyer may not represent a client if the lawyer is likely to be a necessary witness

1. **Exceptions**
   - Testimony relates to an uncontested issue
   - Testimony relates to the nature and value of the legal services rendered in the case, or
   - Disqualification of the lawyer would work a substantial hardship on the client

2. **Other lawyers in firm**—may act as an advocate in a trial if another lawyer in firm is likely to be called as a witness, unless the conflict rules prevent the lawyer from doing so

C. **Acquiring an interest in litigation**

1. **Proprietary interest in cause of action**—prohibited
   - **Exceptions:** lien to secure payment of fee; permissible contingent fee

2. **Financial assistance to client**—prohibited
   - **Exceptions:** lawyer may advance litigation costs to a client, even if repayment is made contingent on the outcome; for indigent clients, repayment need not be required

D. **Entering into business transactions with client**

1. **Business transactions with client**—a lawyer must not enter into a business transaction with a client or knowingly acquire any interest adverse to a client

   • **Exceptions**

     ○ Terms are fair and reasonable to client, the client is advised in writing of the desirability of seeking independent counsel and given an opportunity to do so, and the client consents in writing after full written disclosure of terms and lawyer's role

     ○ Standard commercial transactions for products or services the client generally markets to others

2. **Literary or media rights**—a lawyer is prohibited from negotiating for such rights prior to the conclusion of the representation

3. **Soliciting gifts**—a lawyer is prohibited from soliciting a gift or preparing an instrument that gives a substantial gift to the lawyer or a person related to the lawyer

   • **Exception:** the lawyer is related to the client, or an unsolicited simple gift

   • Lawyer may accept an unsolicited gift, but the gift may be voidable if undue influence

4. **Prospectively limiting malpractice recovery**—prohibited unless the client is represented by another independent lawyer

E. **Conflicting interests between clients**

1. **Current clients**

   • **Directly adverse**—a lawyer cannot represent a client if doing so would be directly adverse to the interests of another current client (opposing parties in the same lawsuit)

     ○ An unnamed member of class action is not treated as a client of lawyer who represents class

   • **Material limitation**—a lawyer cannot represent a client if there is a significant risk that the representation will be materially limited by the lawyer's responsibilities to a current client

     ○ **Exception:** The lawyer reasonably believes that she can provide competent and diligent representation to each affected client, the representation is not prohibited by law, and each client gives informed consent, confirmed in writing

   • **Aggregate settlement for co-parties**—need informed consent by each client in a signed writing after full consultation and disclosure by the lawyer

2. **Conflicts between current and former clients**

   • **General rule**—a lawyer who has previously represented a client in a matter must not subsequently represent another person in the same or a substantially related matter in which that person's interests are materially adverse to the former client's interests

     ○ Former client may waive conflict by giving informed consent, confirmed in writing

   • **Use of information**—a lawyer (including the lawyer's present and former firm) who has formerly represented a client in a matter must not use information relating to the representation to the former client's disadvantage

     ○ **Exceptions:** MR allow; info generally known; waiver by client

- **Lawyer switches private firms**
  - Limitation on lawyer—a lawyer cannot knowingly represent a person in the same or a substantially related matter in which the lawyer's prior firm previously represented a client whose interests are materially adverse to that person if the lawyer acquired material confidential information about the client
  - Limitation on former firm—a lawyer cannot represent a person with interests materially adverse to those of a client represented by the formerly associated lawyer if any lawyer remaining in the firm has material confidential information about the same or substantially related matter
  - Waiver by client—informed consent, confirmed in writing
- **Government lawyers**
  - Former government lawyer:
    - Cannot represent a client in a matter in which the lawyer participated personally and substantially as a government lawyer, unless the government agency gives informed consent, confirmed in writing
    - Cannot represent a private client whose interests are adverse to a person about whom the lawyer acquired confidential information while working for the government
  - Former government lawyer's firm—cannot represent a client in a matter in which the former government lawyer is disqualified unless the lawyer is timely screened from participation in the matter and receives no fee from the matter, and written notice is promptly provided to the government agency
  - Current government lawyer—general conflict rules regarding current and former clients apply

3. **Conflicts involving prospective clients**—a lawyer cannot represent a client with interests materially adverse to a prospective client's in the same or a substantially related matter if the lawyer received information from the prospective client that could be significantly harmful to that person
   - **Exception:** both affected and prospective clients give informed consent, confirmed in writing
   - If the lawyer is disqualified, the lawyer's firm is also disqualified unless the lawyer limited the information acquired, was timely screened, and the prospective client was promptly given written notice
   - Duty of confidentiality applies to information acquired

F. **Influence by person other than clients**
   1. **Responsibility to third party**—a lawyer must not represent a client if there is a significant risk that the representation of the client will be materially limited
      - **Exception:** (i) lawyer reasonably believes he is able to provide competent and diligent representation to the client; (ii) the representation is not prohibited by law; and (iii) clients gives consent after consultation, confirmed in writing
   2. **Payment from third party**—not permitted
      - **Exception:** (i) client gives informed consent, (ii) no interference with lawyer's professional judgment or with lawyer-client relationship, and (iii) lawyer-client confidentiality is preserved

3. **Organization as client**—duties of loyalty/confidentiality owed to the organization
   - Representation of both organization and employee permitted
     - If organization's consent required, consent must be given by someone other than the affected employee
   - **Rectifying misconduct**—upon learning of employee's action (or intent or refusal to act) that will likely cause substantial injury to the organization, the lawyer must act in the organization's best interests

4. **Sarbanes-Oxley Act (SOX) requirements**
   - Securities lawyer must report any evidence of reasonably likely material violations of federal/state securities laws to chief legal officer (CLO) and chief executive officer (CEO)
   - CLO must investigate to determine if material violation may/has/did occur and take reasonable steps to advise corporation to adopt appropriate response
   - Report to corporate officers futile or they fail to respond—securities lawyer must report issue to audit committee of board, independent committee, or entire board
   - Security lawyer may report material violation to SEC without client's consent to prevent client from (i) committing violation that will cause substantial injury to corporation or shareholders, (ii) committing perjury, or (iii) mitigate financial injury
   - Lawyer may be subject to civil penalties and lose ability to practice before SEC for failure to comply with SOX

G. **Imputed disqualification**—if a firm lawyer is unable to represent a client, no lawyer in the firm can represent the client
   1. **Exceptions**
      - Affected client may waive conflict; same rules as conflict between current clients
      - Prohibition on firm's non-lawyer does not extend to firm's lawyers if non-lawyer screened
      - Personal disqualifications of lawyer not imputed to firm if no significant risk of materially limiting the representation of the client by the remaining lawyers in the firm
      - Lawyer who changes firms must be timely screened/no fee and former client given prompt written notice and follow-up certifications of compliance

H. **Conflicts based on service as arbitrator, mediator, or judge**—no representation of anyone in matter in which participated personally and substantially
   1. **Firm**—disqualified unless lawyer screened/no fee and notice given to parties and tribunal
   2. **Exceptions**
      - All parties give informed consent, confirmed in writing
      - Arbitrator selected as partisan of party in multi-member arbitration panel may represent party

V. **Competence, Legal Malpractice, and Civil Liability**

A. **Professional competence**
   1. **Requirements:** Knowledge, skill, thoroughness, and preparation
   2. **Maintaining competence**—a lawyer must meet continuing legal education requirements

3. **Lacking competence**—a lawyer must decline or withdraw from representation unless competence is achievable through reasonable preparation or association with competent counsel

B. **Diligence**—lawyer must act with reasonable diligence and promptness

1. **Dedication to client's interests**—a lawyer is not bound to press for every possible advantage for a client

2. **Controllable workload**—illness, subordinates, personal animosity, or inability to balance other work do not justify lack of diligence

3. **Reasonable promptness**—a lawyer may agree to a postponement that will not prejudice the client

4. **Pursuing matter to completion**

5. **Duty of solo practitioner**—plan that designates competent lawyer to handle matters on disability/death

C. **Malpractice**

1. **Difference between professional discipline and malpractice**

   - **Professional discipline**—a penalty imposed by the state disciplinary authority for violating the MRPC

   - **Malpractice**—civil liability for damages to compensate a client for injury caused by a lawyer

2. **Malpractice theories**—breach of contract, breach of fiduciary duty, intentional tort, and negligence

3. **Malpractice based on negligence**—duty, breach, causation, and damages

4. **Respondeat superior**—a law firm may be civilly liable for damages caused by a principal or employee acting in the ordinary course of the firm's business

5. **Limiting malpractice recovery**—not permitted prospectively, unless the client is represented by an independent lawyer in making the agreement

6. **Settlement of malpractice claims**—not permitted if the other party is unrepresented client or former client, unless advised of the desirability of independent counsel and given reasonable opportunity to seek such advice

D. **Civil liability to non-clients**

1. **Tort liability**

   - A lawyer may owe a duty to a non-client when the non-client has been invited to rely on the opinion or legal services of the lawyer

   - A lawyer may owe a duty to a non-client when the lawyer knows that a client intends the lawyer's services to benefit the non-client

   - Lawyer representing a client in the client's capacity as fiduciary may in some circumstances be liable to beneficiary for failure to use care to protect beneficiary

2. **Liability for contract entered on client's behalf**

   - **Undisclosed principal**—lawyer is subject to liability unless disclaimed at the time of contracting

   - **Contracts for goods and services normally provided to lawyers**—lawyer is subject to liability unless disclaimed at the time of contracting

- **Unauthorized acts**—lawyer is subject to liability if the lawyer tortuously misrepresents to a third person that the lawyer had general authority to act for client

E. **Criminal liability for crime committed in course of representing a client**—guilty to the same extent and on the same basis as a non-lawyer acting in a similar manner

VI. **Litigation and Other Forms of Advocacy**

A. **Impartiality, civility, courtesy, and decorum**

1. **Conduct before tribunal**—no conduct intended to disrupt a tribunal; includes depositions

2. **Civility and courtesy**—must refrain from abusive or hostile conduct

3. **Avoiding improper influence**—must not seek to influence juror, judge, or other official by means prohibited by law

B. **Conduct in the course of litigation**

1. **Duty to avoid frivolous claims**—must be a good faith basis in law for an action, claim, or defense

   - Cannot act if the only purpose is to delay or prolong the proceedings

   - Cannot knowingly assert false material factual statements

   - **Criminal defense**—can defend by requiring sufficient proof of every element of case

2. **Claims brought to embarrass, delay, or burden third party**—not permitted

3. **Duty to expedite litigation consistent with client's interests**—must not (i) routinely delay litigation for own convenience, (ii) frustrate opposing party's attempt to obtain rightful redress, or (iii) improperly delay for financial or other benefit

4. **Duty of candor to tribunal**

   - **No knowing false statement of law or fact**—must correct false statements previously made

   - Controlling adverse legal authority must be disclosed

   - No general duty to disclose unfavorable facts

     - **Exceptions:** to avoid assisting the client in a criminal or fraudulent act; to correct a misrepresentation; in ex parte proceedings

5. **Duty of fairness to opposing party and counsel**

   - **Access to evidence**—must not unlawfully obstruct another party's access to evidence or unlawfully alter/destroy/conceal a document or other material with potential evidentiary value

   - **Inducements to witness**—must not offer inducement prohibited by law

     - Non-expert witness may be reasonably compensated for time spent testifying and assisting counsel

     - Expert witness may also receive a reasonable fee for her professional services

   - No knowing disregard (or advise client to disregard) rules of tribunal, but may test the validity of rules

   - No undermining evidentiary rules by alluding to inadmissible evidence

C. **Client fraud and perjury by client of witness**

1. **Prohibition on falsifying evidence or assisting in witness perjury**

2. **Use of false evidence**

- A lawyer is prohibited from knowingly offering or using false evidence

  o May refuse to admit evidence that the lawyer reasonably believes false

  o If the client is a criminal defendant, the lawyer may not refuse to offer defendant's testimony even if the lawyer reasonably believes it to be false

- A lawyer must take reasonable remedial measures after learning that material evidence offered by lawyer, client, or witness is false

  o If the client refuses to withdraw or correct false evidence, the lawyer must make such disclosure to the tribunal as reasonably necessary to remedy the situation

- A criminal defendant who persists despite the lawyer's attempt to dissuade him—the lawyer must seek the court's permission to withdraw

  o If the court refuses, the lawyer must disclose false testimony to the tribunal

  o May present the defendant's false testimony in narrative form, but the lawyer cannot rely on it in closing argument

D. **Communications in course of representation**

1. **Communicating with client**—must keep the client informed of the status of the matter and respond to client's reasonable requests for information

- May withhold information from client to protect client or comply with court rule/order

2. **Ex parte communications** (all forms) about the merits of a case with persons serving in official capacity (judge) or member of venire/juror or family member

- In general, not permitted in an adversarial proceeding

  o Exceptions for housekeeping matters and emergencies (restraining order)

  o In general, prohibition does not apply after juror discharged

- Applies to communication by any lawyer, even lawyer not connected with the case

3. **Truthfulness in statements to others**

- No knowing false statement of material fact or law to third person

- Must disclose material fact to third person when disclosure is necessary to avoid assisting a client in the commission of criminal or fraudulent act, unless disclosure is prohibited by duty of confidentiality

  o In general, withdrawal from representation of client sufficient

4. **Communication with person known to be represented by counsel**—generally other lawyer's consent needed if matter within scope of representation

- Applies even if represented person initiates or consents to communication

- Lawyer may advise client to communicate with represented party; parties may communicate directly with each other

- Represented organization—communication with constituent (employee) of organization is generally not permitted

  o **Exception:** the prohibition does not apply to former employees of the organization

5. **Dealing with persons unrepresented by counsel**—a lawyer may not state or imply that he is disinterested

   - May negotiate the terms of a transaction or settle a dispute with an unrepresented person as long as the lawyer has explained that he represents the adverse party and is not representing the person

6. **Respects for rights of third parties**

   - Must not represent client by means that have no substantial purpose other than to embarrass, delay, or burden a third person

   - Must not use methods of obtaining evidence that violate a third person's legal rights

   - Must promptly notify the sender of an inadvertently sent document or information if the lawyer knows or reasonably should know of the mistake

7. **Trial publicity**—no extra-judicial statement that lawyer knows or reasonably should know will be disseminated by means of public communication and will have substantial likelihood of materially prejudicing the proceeding

   - **Exception:** statement is required to protect the client from substantial undue prejudicial effect of recent publicity that was not initiated by the lawyer or client

   - Rule applies to any lawyer associated with investigating/litigating lawyer

VII. Different Roles of Lawyer

A. **Advisor**—must exercise independent professional judgment and render candid advice

B. **Evaluator**—may provide an evaluation of a matter affecting a client for use of someone other than the client if the lawyer reasonably believes that making the evaluation is compatible with other aspects of the lawyer's relationship with the client

C. **Negotiator**—must not make a false statement of material fact

D. **Arbitrator, mediator or other third-party neutral**—must inform unrepresented parties that she is not representing them and must explain role if knows or reasonably should know that the parties do not understand role

   - Cannot serve as a lawyer representing a client in the same matter, unless all parties give their informed consent, confirmed in writing

E. **Special obligations of prosecutors**

1. **Representation of a private client**—must avoid if it would result in a conflict with the prosecutor's obligation

2. **No prosecution without probable cause**

3. **Unrepresented defendant**—must make reasonable efforts to assure the defendant is advised of the right to counsel and given reasonable opportunity to obtain counsel; must not seek waiver of pre-trial rights (unless the defendant appears pro se with tribunal's approval)

4. **Any defendant**—must disclose evidence that may help defendant

5. **Subpoenaing lawyer before grand jury**—only if (i) evidence not protected by privilege and essential and (ii) no feasible alternative

6. **Public statements about pending cases**—must refrain from making extrajudicial comments that have a substantial likelihood of heightening public condemnation of the accused unless the statements serve a legitimate law enforcement purpose or are necessary to inform the public

7. **New evidence after conviction**—must disclose to the appropriate authority any new, credible evidence creating a reasonable likelihood that a convicted defendant did not commit the offense for which the defendant was convicted

F. **Appearances before legislative or administrative bodies**—must disclose representative capacity and conform to MR

VIII. Safekeeping Property of Clients and Third Parties

A. **Client's funds**—a lawyer must not commingle his own funds with a client's funds, and the client's funds must be kept in separate client trust account (IOLTA)

B. **Advance payment**—must deposit legal fees and expenses paid in advance by a client into the trust account; must withdraw from the account only as fees are earned or expenses are incurred

C. **Disputed property**—must be kept separate until the dispute is resolved; property not in dispute must be promptly distributed

IX. Communication About Legal Services

A. **Advertising**—widely distributed public statements about a lawyer's services

1. **General rule**—advertising is permitted, but no false or misleading statements

   - Must include name/contact information of at least one lawyer responsible for content
   - Identity of clients only with consent
   - Statements re: fields of practice must comply with MR
     o "Specialist" vs "certified specialist"

2. **Firm names and letterheads**

   - Firm cannot use false or misleading firm name; trade name may be used so long as it does not imply a connection with a government agency or a charitable or public legal services organization and is otherwise not false or misleading
   - Must use the name of one or more lawyers in the firm; name of retired/deceased lawyers of firm/predecessor firm are permitted
     o Name of a lawyer who assumes judicial/legislative/public executive or administrative office cannot be used
   - No false claims of partnership

B. **Restrictions on payment for recommending a lawyer**

   - No payment for recommending a lawyer
   - Payment for certain referrals are permitted—usual charges of a legal service plan/not-for-profit or qualified lawyer referral service
     o Reciprocal referral arrangements—permitted if not exclusive, the client is informed, and the duration is limited

C. **Group legal services**—a lawyer may provide legal services through a prepaid or group legal service plan not owned or operated by the lawyer that uses in-person, telephone, or real time electronic contact to solicit memberships or subscriptions for the plan

D. Solicitation

    1. **Definition**—targeted communications by written, recorded, or electronic communication or by in-person, telephone, or real-time electronic contact, directed at a specific individual or small group for the purpose of securing paid representation of the individual or group

        • Not solicitation:

            ○ Proposal prepared in response to a specific request of prospective client

            ○ Pro bono representation offered

    2. **Prohibition on solicitation by live person-to-person contact**

        • **Exceptions:** another lawyer, family, close personal or prior professional relationship with lawyer

    3. **Other prohibited solicitation**

        • Prospective client has communicated desire not to be solicited

        • Solicitation involves coercion, duress, or harassment

    4. **Professional announcements**—general ones, including personnel or office location, changes are permissible

E. Limitations on specialization—permitted to claim specialization in certain areas, but cannot claim status as a certified specialist unless certified by a state-authorized organization and the certifying organization is identified in the communication

X. Lawyers and the Legal System

A. Voluntary pro bono service—strongly encouraged to provide at least 50 hours annually

B. Membership or leadership role in legal services organization—permitted even if the organization serves persons having interests that are adverse to lawyer's client

    1. **Must not knowingly participate in organization's decision/action if incompatible or material that adverse to client**

C. Law reform activities affecting client interests—permitted even if such reform may affect a client's interests

    1. **Must avoid conflicts of interests and other MR violations**

    2. **Client materially benefited**—must disclose fact but need not disclose client's identity

D. Non-profit and court-annexed limited legal services programs

    1. **Client must give informed consent to limited representation**

    2. **Conflicts**—lawyer only responsible for conflicts of interest of which the lawyer has actual knowledge; conflict does not apply to lawyer's firm

E. Impropriety incident to public service

    1. **Political contributions**—not permitted to accept government legal engagement or an appointment by judge if the lawyer or law firm makes or solicits political contributions for purpose of obtaining engagement

    2. **Judicial and legal officials**—no false statements concerning qualifications or integrity

XI. **Judicial Ethics**—judges are bound by rules of professional conduct for all lawyers, and by special rules of professional conduct (Code of Judicial Conduct (CJC)); CJC applies to all full-time judges

    A. **Duties to uphold integrity and independence of judiciary**—must comply with law, follow precedent and other mandatory authority

    B. **Duty to avoid impropriety or appearance of it**

        1. **Avoiding abuse of the prestige of judicial office**—must not use office to advance personal or economic interest of judge or others

    C. **Duties of impartiality, competence and diligence**

        1. **Precedence of duties of judicial office over personal/extrajudicial activities**

        2. **Impartiality and fairness**—must perform all duties fairly and impartially; must uphold and apply law despite personal views; good faith mistake as to law or facts not a violation

        3. **Bias, prejudice, and harassment**—must perform duties without bias or prejudice; must not engage in harassment

        4. **External influences on judicial conduct**—must not be swayed by public clamor or fear of criticism

        5. **Competence and diligence**—must perform duties with competence and diligence; must devote adequate time to court business

        6. **Administrative cooperation**—must cooperate with other judges and court officials

        7. **Ensuring right to be heard**—can encourage settlement but without using coercion

        8. **Responsibility to decide**—except when disqualification is required by CJC

        9. **Decorum and demeanor**—must be patient, dignified, and courteous

        10. **Communication with jurors**—must not comment or criticize jurors for their verdict other than in a court order or opinion

        11. **Ex parte communications**—must not initiate, permit, or consider ex parte communications, or consider other communications made to the judge outside the presence of the parties or their lawyers for a pending matter

        12. **Statements on pending cases**—must not make if it might reasonably be expected to affect the outcome or impair fairness of a matter

        13. **Disqualification of judge**—must recuse self if impartiality may reasonably be questioned

        14. **Supervisory duties**—must require staff to act in a manner that is consistent with the judge's obligations under CJC

        15. **Administrative appointments**—must exercise power of appointment impartially and on basis of merit; must avoid nepotism, favoritism, and unnecessary appointments

        16. **Disability and impairment of lawyers or other judges**—must take action if reasonable belief that performance of lawyer or another judge impaired by drugs or alcohol, or by mental, emotional, or physical condition

        17. **Responding to judicial and lawyer misconduct**

            • Must inform authorities if judge has knowledge of violation or substantial likelihood that another judge has violated CJC or lawyer has violated the MC

            • Must take appropriate action if judge receives information indicating a substantial likelihood that another judge has committed a violation of the CJC or lawyer has violated the MC

18. **Cooperation with disciplinary authorities**—must cooperate and be candid and honest with judicial and lawyer disciplinary agencies; must not retaliate, directly or indirectly, against a person known or suspected to have assisted or cooperated with an investigation of a judge or a lawyer

D. **Extrajudicial activities**—a judge must conduct the judge's personal and extrajudicial activities to minimize risk of conflict with obligations of judicial office

1. **In general**—a judge is not allowed to:
   - Participate in activities that will interfere with proper performance of judge's judicial duties, lead to frequent disqualification of judge, or would appear to reasonable person to undermine judge's independence, integrity, or impartiality
   - Engage in conduct that would appear to reasonable person to be coercive
   - Make use of court resources except incidental use for activities that concern law

2. **Involvement with governmental bodies and officials**—must not appear voluntarily at a public hearing before, or otherwise consult with, executive or legislative body or official
   - **Exceptions:** Matter concerns law/legal system/administration of justice; matter about which judge acquired knowledge or expertise as a judge; matter in which judge is acting in self-interest or as a fiduciary

3. **Testifying as character witness**—prohibited unless duly summoned

4. **Appointments to governmental positions**—must decline unless relates to law/legal system/administration of justice

5. **Nonpublic information acquired as judge**—must not use for nonjudicial purposes

6. **Affiliation with discriminatory organizations**—prohibited

7. **Participation in organizations and activities**—permitted if related to law/legal system/administration of justice or non-profit

8. **Pro bono legal service**—may encourage lawyers to provide pro bono legal services

9. **Appointments to fiduciary positions**—generally must not serve in fiduciary position unless with regard to estate/trust/person of family member and even then only if it does not interfere judicial duties

10. **Arbitrator or mediator**—must not serve as arbitrator or mediator unless expressly authorized by law

11. **Practice of law**—a full-time judge generally must not practice law, except with regard to self or family members; cannot serve as family member's lawyer

12. **Financial, business, or remunerative activities**—may hold and manage investments of the judge and members of the judge's family; generally must not serve as officer/advisor/employee of a business entity unless a closely-held family business; must divest self of investment or financial interests that might require frequent disqualification or violate CJC

13. **Extrajudicial activities**—may receive reasonable compensation for such activities

14. **Things of value**—must not accept gifts/benefits/other things of value if prohibited by law or would appear to a reasonable person to undermine independence/integrity/impartiality; may accept but must report gifts incident to a public testimonial, invitations to attend event without charge, thing of value from person who is likely to come before judge

15. **Reimbursement of expenses and waivers of fees or charges**—may be accepted if expenses or charges are associated with judge's participation in extrajudicial activities permitted by CJC; must be reported

16. **Reporting requirements**—annually must public report compensation for extrajudicial activities, permitted gift and other things of value, reimbursement of expenses and waiver of fees and charges

E. **Political and campaign activities of judges**

1. **Prohibited political activities**—unless otherwise permitted by law or CJC, judge must not (i) serve as leader/officer of political organization; (ii) publicly endorse/oppose candidate for any political office; (iii) make speeches on behalf of political organizations; (iv) solicit funds for or make contributions to such organizations or to candidate; (v) attend/purchase tickets for events sponsored by political organization or candidate; and (vi) seek/accept/use endorsements from a political organization

2. **Actions by other persons**—must take reasonable measures to ensure that other persons do not undertake prohibited activities on behalf of judge or judicial candidate.

3. **Family members' elections**—must not become involved in, or publicly associated with, a family member's political activity or campaign for public office

4. **Voting and caucus elections**—may participate in caucuses and by voting in elections

5. **False, misleading, or unfair allegations**—may respond to these allegations, but it is preferable for someone else to respond if the allegations relate to a pending case

6. **Pledges, promises, or commitments**—must not make pledges/promises/commitments that are inconsistent with impartial performance of adjudicative duties of judicial office

7. **Political and campaign activities of judicial candidates in public elections**—may (i) speak on behalf of own candidacy through any medium; (ii) publicly endorse/oppose other candidates for same judicial office; (iii) attend/purchase tickets for events sponsored by political organization/candidate; (iv) seek/accept/use endorsements from any person/organization other than partisan political organization; (v) contribute to political organization/candidate; if judicial election is partisan, may (i) identify self as candidate of political organization; and (ii) seek/accept/use endorsements of political organization

8. **Activities of candidates for appointive judicial office**—communicate with appointing or confirming authority; may also seek endorsements for the appointment from any person or organization other than partisan political organization

9. **Judges who become candidates for non-judicial office**—must resign if elective office unless permitted by law; not required to resign if non-elective office

10. **Campaign committees**—may establish a campaign committee to manage and conduct candidate's campaign; may not personally solicit or accept campaign contributions other than through such committee

LEGAL TERMINOLOGY LIST: MPRE

The Multistate Professional Responsibility Exam (MPRE), which is a standardized exam created by the National Conference of Bar Examiners (NCBE), may contain the following terms and phrases. The two main sources of legal principles are contained in the **Model Rules** (i.e., Model Rules of Professional Conduct promulgated by the American Bar Association (ABA)) and the **CJC** (Code of Judicial Conduct, also promulgated by the ABA.

KEY WORDS AND PHRASES USED ON THE MPRE

As used on the MPRE, the following terms and phrases have specific definitions.

Bar, State Bar, or Appropriate Disciplinary Authority	the appropriate agency in the jurisdiction with the authority to administer the standards for admission to practice law and for maintenance of professional competence and integrity
Certified Specialist	a lawyer who has been recognized as proficient in a particular area of law by the appropriate agency in the jurisdiction in which the lawyer practices
May or Proper	conduct that is professionally appropriate (i.e., conduct that is not subject to discipline, not inconsistent with the preamble, comments, or text of the Model Rules or CJC, and not inconsistent with generally accepted principles of the law of lawyering)
Subject to Civil Liability	conduct that would subject the lawyer or the lawyer's law firm to civil liability, such as a claim arising from malpractice, misrepresentation, or breach of fiduciary duty
Subject to Criminal Liability	conduct that would subject the lawyer to criminal liability for participation in or aiding and abetting criminal acts, such as insurance or tax fraud, destruction of evidence, or obstruction of justice
Subject to Discipline	conduct that would subject the lawyer to discipline under the Model Rules or a judge to discipline under the CJC
Subject to Disqualification	conduct that would subject the lawyer or the lawyer's law firm to disqualification as counsel in a civil or criminal matter
Subject to Litigation Sanction	conduct that would subject the lawyer or the lawyer's law firm to a fine, fee forfeiture, disqualification, punishment for contempt, or other sanction by a legal tribunal

KEY WORDS AND PHRASES USED IN MODEL RULES

As used in the Model Rules and the CJC, the following terms and phrases have specific definitions.

Appointment by a Judge	an appointment to a position such as referee, commissioner, special master, receiver, guardian, or other similar position that is made by a judge; excluded— substantially uncompensated services; engagements or appointments made on the basis of experience, expertise, professional qualifications and cost following a request for proposal or other process that is free from influence based upon political contributions; and engagements or appointments made on a rotational basis from a list compiled without regard to political contributions
Belief	a supposition by a person that a fact in question is true; subjective in nature, but may be inferred from the circumstances; contrast with "knowledge"
Confirmed in Writing	a writing that acknowledges the client's informed consent; need not be a document signed by client, but can be prepared by the lawyer after consent is given
Economic Interest	ownership of more than a de minimis legal or equitable interest
Fraud	conduct that is fraudulent under the substantive or procedural law of the applicable jurisdiction and has a purpose to deceive; fraud does not include negligent misrepresentation; for disciplinary purposes, it is not necessary that anyone relied upon or suffered damages from the misrepresentation
Government Legal Engagement	any engagement to provide legal services that a public official has the direct or indirect power to award; excluded—substantially uncompensated services; engagements or appointments made on the basis of experience, expertise, professional qualifications and cost following a request for proposal or other process that is free from influence based upon political contributions; and engagements or appointments made on a rotational basis from a list compiled without regard to political contributions
Informed Consent	consent given after communication of adequate information about the material risks of the proposed course of conduct, as well as reasonably available alternatives; a lawyer is not required to inform a person of facts or implications already known to the person, and can take into account the person's legal knowledge and representation by another lawyer; informed consent generally cannot be assumed from a person's silence, but may be inferred from a person's conduct
Knowledge	actual knowledge of the fact in question; subjective in nature, but may be inferred from the circumstances; contrast with "belief"

Law firm	any association of lawyers authorized to practice law, including a partnership or professional corporation as well as lawyers employed in a legal services organization or the legal department of a corporation or other organization; a lawyer practicing law as a sole proprietorship also falls within the definition of a "law firm"
Partner	a member of a partnership, a shareholder in a law firm organized as a professional corporation, or a member of an association authorized to practice law
Political contribution	any gift, subscription, loan, advance, or deposit of anything of value made directly or indirectly to a candidate, incumbent, political party or campaign committee to influence or provide financial support for election to or retention in judicial or other government office; excluded—uncompensated services and political contributions in initiative and referendum elections
Reasonable	conduct of a reasonably prudent and competent lawyer; an objective standard
Reasonable belief	a lawyer is required to believe the matter in question (a subjective standard) and the circumstances must be such that the belief is reasonable (an objective standard)
Reasonably should know	a lawyer of reasonable prudence and competence would ascertain the matter in question; an objective standard
Screened	isolation of a lawyer from any participation in a matter through the timely imposition of procedures that are reasonably adequate under the circumstances to protect information that the isolated lawyer is obligated to protect
Signed	any means, including an electronic sound, symbol, or process that is attached to or logically associated with the writing and is executed or adopted by a person with the intent to sign the writing
Substantial	a material matter of clear and weighty importance
Tribunal	an entity that acts in an adjudicative capacity (court, arbitrator in a binding arbitration proceeding, and sometimes legislative body or administrative agency); an entity acts in an adjudicative capacity when a neutral official, after the presentation of evidence or legal argument by a party or parties, reaches a binding legal judgment that directly affects a party's interest in a particular matter
Writings	any tangible or electronic record of a communication or representation (e.g., photograph, audio- or video recording, electronic communication)

KEY WORDS AND PHRASES USED IN OUTLINE

As used in the Themis MPRE outline, the following terms and phrases have specific definitions.

Advertising	widely distributed public statements about the services available from a lawyer or law firm
Candor	honesty
Expedite	to speed up a process
Frivolous	lacking a good-faith argument on the merits of the action taken or lacking a good-faith argument for an extension, modification, or reversal of existing law
Impropriety	inappropriate behavior
Impute	to assign a conflict of interest to all lawyers in a law firm based on the conflict of interest of one lawyer in the law firm
Literary or media rights	the legal rights to tell a story relating to the representation of a client through the media (e.g., books, movies, interviews)
Matter	any judicial or other proceeding, application, request for a ruling or other determination, contract, claim, controversy, investigation, charge, accusation, arrest or other particular matter involving a specific party or parties; also any other matter covered by the conflict of interest rules of the appropriate government agency
Pro bono publico	(often shortened to "pro bono") latin, "for the public good"; work done without fee or expectation of fee to persons of limited means or charitable, religious, civic, community, governmental, and educational organizations in matters that are designed primarily to address the needs of persons of limited means
Pro hac vice	latin, "for this turn only"; the permission given to a lawyer not admitted to practice law in a jurisdiction to appear before a tribunal in that jurisdiction
Retainer	money paid to a lawyer solely to ensure the availability of the lawyer
Sarbanes-Oxley Act	a federal law that sets rules for publicly traded corporations on matters including corporate governance and financial disclosures
Solicitation	a targeted communication initiated by the lawyer that is directed to a specific person and that offers to provide, or can reasonably be understood as offering to provide, legal services

| **Substantially related** | matters involving the same transaction or legal dispute, or a substantial risk that confidential factual information as would normally have been obtained in the prior representation would materially advance the client's position in the subsequent matter; not determined by the lawyer's actual knowledge of confidential information, but by whether a lawyer engaged in providing the services provided by the lawyer ordinarily would have learned such information; an objective test |

MPRE
Practice Exam One

PRACTICE EXAM ONE

TIME: 60 MINUTES

Welcome to Practice Exam One. This exam consists of 30 questions and will take 60 minutes. After you have completed this exam, log in to your course to submit your answers, view detailed answer explanations, and compare your performance to other Themis students.

1 ⊏A⊐ ⊏B⊐ ⊏C⊐ ⊏D⊐   21 ⊏A⊐ ⊏B⊐ ⊏C⊐ ⊏D⊐

2 ⊏A⊐ ⊏B⊐ ⊏C⊐ ⊏D⊐   22 ⊏A⊐ ⊏B⊐ ⊏C⊐ ⊏D⊐

3 ⊏A⊐ ⊏B⊐ ⊏C⊐ ⊏D⊐   23 ⊏A⊐ ⊏B⊐ ⊏C⊐ ⊏D⊐

4 ⊏A⊐ ⊏B⊐ ⊏C⊐ ⊏D⊐   24 ⊏A⊐ ⊏B⊐ ⊏C⊐ ⊏D⊐

5 ⊏A⊐ ⊏B⊐ ⊏C⊐ ⊏D⊐   25 ⊏A⊐ ⊏B⊐ ⊏C⊐ ⊏D⊐

6 ⊏A⊐ ⊏B⊐ ⊏C⊐ ⊏D⊐   26 ⊏A⊐ ⊏B⊐ ⊏C⊐ ⊏D⊐

7 ⊏A⊐ ⊏B⊐ ⊏C⊐ ⊏D⊐   27 ⊏A⊐ ⊏B⊐ ⊏C⊐ ⊏D⊐

8 ⊏A⊐ ⊏B⊐ ⊏C⊐ ⊏D⊐   28 ⊏A⊐ ⊏B⊐ ⊏C⊐ ⊏D⊐

9 ⊏A⊐ ⊏B⊐ ⊏C⊐ ⊏D⊐   29 ⊏A⊐ ⊏B⊐ ⊏C⊐ ⊏D⊐

10 ⊏A⊐ ⊏B⊐ ⊏C⊐ ⊏D⊐   30 ⊏A⊐ ⊏B⊐ ⊏C⊐ ⊏D⊐

11 ⊏A⊐ ⊏B⊐ ⊏C⊐ ⊏D⊐

12 ⊏A⊐ ⊏B⊐ ⊏C⊐ ⊏D⊐

13 ⊏A⊐ ⊏B⊐ ⊏C⊐ ⊏D⊐

14 ⊏A⊐ ⊏B⊐ ⊏C⊐ ⊏D⊐

15 ⊏A⊐ ⊏B⊐ ⊏C⊐ ⊏D⊐

16 ⊏A⊐ ⊏B⊐ ⊏C⊐ ⊏D⊐

17 ⊏A⊐ ⊏B⊐ ⊏C⊐ ⊏D⊐

18 ⊏A⊐ ⊏B⊐ ⊏C⊐ ⊏D⊐

19 ⊏A⊐ ⊏B⊐ ⊏C⊐ ⊏D⊐

20 ⊏A⊐ ⊏B⊐ ⊏C⊐ ⊏D⊐

SCORE

1. A toy manufacturer was sued by the parent of a child injured by one of its products. As the manufacturer's attorney was preparing to respond to a discovery request from the plaintiff, the attorney found a document that was very damaging to his client's case. Prior to complying with the discovery request and turning over the document, the attorney called his opposing counsel and offered to settle the case. The attorney stated that although he believed his client was very likely to win a summary judgment motion, they would settle the case for a modest amount to save the costs of litigation. In fact, the attorney believed his client had no chance of winning a summary judgment motion and was also likely to lose at trial based on the document he had found. The opposing counsel declined the attorney's offer. The attorney turned over the document, and the case proceeded to trial, where judgment was awarded to the plaintiff.

Were the attorney's statements to the opposing counsel proper?

(A) No, because the attorney did not believe in the truthfulness of the statement.
(B) No, because the attorney owed a duty of candor to the opposing counsel.
(C) Yes, because the attorney's statement did not constitute a statement of fact.
(D) Yes, because the opposing counsel did not accept the attorney's offer.

2. An attorney was convinced that his client was suffering from dementia. The attorney spoke to his client's family physician and the client's only daughter to determine whether a guardian should be appointed to monitor the client's finances. These were the only discussions the attorney had ever had with either the physician or the daughter. In these discussions, the attorney revealed confidential information about a bank account maintained by the client before learning that the daughter and her mother were estranged because the daughter had stolen from her mother in the past.

Was the attorney's revelation of the confidential information proper?

(A) Yes, because the attorney was trying to determine whether his client needed a guardian.
(B) Yes, because the daughter had relevant information to help determine whether the client needed a guardian.
(C) No, because the attorney should not have disclosed confidential information about a client to others without prior court approval.
(D) No, because the attorney did not first determine whether either the doctor or his client's daughter might act adversely to his client's interests.

3. In representing a client in litigation involving a boundary dispute, an attorney, after consultation with and approval by the client, employed a surveyor. The attorney, who had used and compensated the surveyor in previous, similar situations for other clients, described the purpose of the survey and the party she represented to the surveyor. The retainer agreement between the attorney and the client specified that the client was responsible for payment of all litigation expenses. The surveyor performed a survey of the disputed boundary and submitted an invoice to the attorney for the agreed-upon amount. Prior to payment of this invoice, the client, in direct conversation with his neighbor, reached an agreement over the boundary between their properties. The client paid the attorney her fee as agreed upon in the retainer agreement but refused to pay the attorney for the cost of the survey.

Is the attorney likely subject to civil liability to the surveyor for the unpaid invoice?

(A)   No, because the client was responsible for the payment of all litigation expenses.
(B)   No, because the client was consulted about and approved the hiring of the surveyor.
(C)   Yes, because an attorney is primarily responsible for litigation expenses.
(D)   Yes, because of the nature of the services rendered by the surveyor.

4. A plaintiff filed a personal injury complaint, and the case was assigned to a judge. After the defendant was served, a partner from a large law firm filed an appearance on behalf of the defendant. The judge's niece was a salaried associate in the estate planning department of the law firm representing the plaintiff. At the initial scheduling conference, the judge disclosed this relationship to the parties. Subsequently, the judge also disclosed that a person listed by the plaintiff as a material witness was his wife's nephew. Neither the niece nor the nephew resided in the judge's household. Neither party moved to disqualify the judge. Other than the disclosures made by the judge, there were no grounds upon which the judge's impartiality could be reasonably questioned.

Should the judge disqualify himself from presiding over this action?

(A)   Yes, because of the judge's relationship with a member of the law firm representing the defendant.
(B)   Yes, because of the judge's familial relationship with the material witness.
(C)   No, because neither party moved to disqualify the judge.
(D)   No, because neither the niece nor the nephew were members of the judge's household.

5. An attorney was passionate about civil rights, but the jurisdiction in which he practiced was less progressive than he. The attorney accepted the case of a client whose claim was not supported by law within the jurisdiction. If the client had been able to bring the claim in another state, however, his claim would likely have been successful. The attorney accepted the claim despite his knowledge that the client would lose because he was confident that the media attention would provide momentum for a change of the law. He notified the client of the likelihood of losing, but the client wished to pursue the claim regardless.

Is the attorney subject to discipline for bringing this suit?

(A)   No, because the client wishes to pursue the claim even if it will be unsuccessful.
(B)   No, because the case, even if unsuccessful, might lead to a change in existing law.
(C)   Yes, because he knows the claim will likely lose.
(D)   Yes, because there is no basis of law in the jurisdiction to support the claim.

6. While using the copy machine, a transactional associate overheard two summer interns talking in the next room about a litigation associate in the firm. The interns, who did not see the transactional associate or know he was there, discussed the litigation associate's behavior and speculated that she had been drinking while at work. They said they believed that her drinking had caused her to make several mistakes in active cases. The interns never mentioned the litigation associate by name, but the transactional associate knew that they primarily worked with one attorney. He had never seen the litigation associate drinking and had always heard that her work was satisfactory, so he dismissed the discussion as mere gossip and did not take any action based on the information. Several months later, a client filed a complaint with the disciplinary board against the litigation associate that included allegations related to alcohol abuse. The disciplinary board found that the litigation associate had made errors on the client's case because she was inebriated.

Would the transactional associate be subject to discipline based on his failure to report the litigation associate's alleged misconduct?

(A)   No, because the transactional associate did not have actual knowledge of any misconduct.
(B)   No, because the transactional associate did not personally witness any misconduct.
(C)   Yes, because the transactional associate failed to report another attorney's misconduct.
(D)   Yes, because the misconduct raised a substantial question as to the litigation associate's professional fitness.

7. An attorney represented a corporation in a suit brought by one of its competitors for misappropriation of trade secrets. Shortly before trial but after the discovery deadlines had passed, the corporation's chief engineer told the attorney that he had found a memorandum he had written to himself the previous year. The statements in the memorandum aligned with the chief engineer's version of the events in question and directly contradicted the competitor's claims. The attorney was skeptical of the document's authenticity because it had not been produced during the discovery process, and he believed that it may have been fabricated for trial purposes. Although the chief engineer assured the attorney that the document was authentic, the attorney continued to have doubts. Nonetheless, the attorney offered the document into evidence during his examination of the chief engineer at trial.

Was the attorney's action in offering the document into evidence proper?

(A) No, because the attorney reasonably believed that the evidence was false.
(B) No, because doubts about authenticity should be resolved in favor of protecting the integrity of the judicial process.
(C) Yes, because the attorney did not know the evidence was false.
(D) Yes, because the prohibition on offering false evidence does not apply to a civil action.

8. An attorney represented a father in a custody dispute with his ex-wife regarding their child. As a result of the custody proceeding, the father lost custody of his child. Subsequently, the father sued the attorney, asserting that the attorney failed to diligently represent him in the proceeding because she had taken on too many clients. At trial, the attorney seeks to disclose information she acquired from her client regarding his finances as evidence that he is suing because he is upset about the significant support payments he has to make.

Is the attorney's disclosure of the financial information she acquired from her client proper?

(A) No, because her client's finances are not relevant to the dispute.
(B) No, because the information was acquired during the course of the representation.
(C) Yes, because a dispute between an attorney and a client allows for the disclosure of confidential communications.
(D) Yes, because the client, by filing suit against his attorney, consented to the disclosure of confidential information acquired by the attorney during the representation.

9. An associate in a small law firm represented a property owner in a suit against the former owner, a corporation, for fraud with regard to the sale of the property. The associate has learned that the largest shareholder of a wholly owned subsidiary of the corporation is the managing partner of the law firm. If the property owner is successful in the action, the corporation and its subsidiary would be crippled financially, and the managing partner would likely see a significant decline in the value of his stock, which represents a substantial portion of the managing partner's retirement portfolio.

Must the associate share with the property owner the information regarding the managing partner's relationship to the corporation and seek the property owner's consent in order to continue representing him?

(A)   Yes, because a personal disqualification of a member of a firm is imputed to all other members of the firm.
(B)   Yes, because there is a significant risk of the managing partner's relationship to the opposing party materially limiting the associate's representation of the property owner.
(C)   No, because the associate, not the managing partner, is representing the property owner.
(D)   No, because the associate's duty of confidentiality prevents him from disclosing information about the partner's involvement in the corporation.

10. An attorney represented a shopkeeper who was trying to sell his business, and was approached by an interested buyer. The attorney told the potential buyer that she believed the opportunity to purchase the business would be brief because the business was being offered at a very low price. In fact, the attorney believed that the business was priced too high, and that the shopkeeper would have difficulty selling it for that reason.

Was the attorney's statement to the potential buyer proper?

(A)   No, because the attorney did not believe in the truthfulness of her statement.
(B)   No, because the attorney, as a negotiator, owed a duty of candor to the potential buyer.
(C)   Yes, because as a negotiator, the attorney owes a duty of zealous representation to her client.
(D)   Yes, because the attorney's statement did not constitute a statement of fact.

11. The beneficiary of an estate, who was indigent, met with an attorney about the possibility of representing him in a dispute over his share of the estate. The attorney's secretary attended the meeting to take notes. After discussing the matter with the beneficiary, the attorney stated that she could not take the case because her reasonable fee would exceed the amount of the potential recovery. Later, the attorney learned from another attorney that the second attorney had agreed to represent the beneficiary. The attorney discussed the beneficiary's position with the second attorney, advising the lawyer of what she believed were some weaknesses in the case.

Did the attorney who elected not to represent the beneficiary behave properly?

(A)   No, because she had an obligation to represent the indigent beneficiary on a pro bono basis.

(B)   No, because she breached a duty of confidentiality she owed to the beneficiary.

(C)   Yes, because any duty of confidentiality was destroyed by the presence of her secretary.

(D)   Yes, because she could refuse to represent the beneficiary on the basis of lack of financial benefit to the attorney.

12. An attorney, acting on behalf of a wealthy client, entered into negotiations to purchase land from its owner. Solely in order to forestall the seller from raising the asking price due to the client's financial resources, the client instructed the attorney not to reveal that she was acting on behalf of a client. Adhering to these instructions, the attorney entered into a contract in her own name to purchase the land from its current owner. Prior to the closing date, the client told the attorney that he no longer wanted the land. The attorney informed the owner, who then sold the land to another buyer at a price below the contract price. The seller sued the attorney for expectation damages based on the attorney's breach of the contract.

Is the attorney subject to civil liability to seller?

(A)   Yes, because an attorney acting as a negotiator is nevertheless subject to the Model Rules of Professional Conduct.

(B)   Yes, because the attorney did not reveal that she was acting on behalf of a client.

(C)   No, because the attorney was acting on behalf of her client.

(D)   No, because of the duty of confidentiality.

13. An attorney represented a small business owner in a contract suit. The attorney advised his client that he had a 50 percent chance of winning the case and should accept any settlement offer over $20,000. The client said that he was open to settlement and would think about an acceptable amount. One week before trial, the opposing counsel told the attorney that his client would be willing to pay $25,000 to avoid trial and that the offer would remain open until the end of the day. The attorney could not reach his client to confirm whether the client wished to accept the settlement offer. At the end of the day, the attorney called the opposing counsel and accepted the offer. The attorney did not mention that he had not spoken to his client.

Is the attorney subject to discipline?

(A) No, because the attorney had apparent authority to accept the settlement.

(B) No, because the acceptance of a settlement offer is a tactical decision that falls within the attorney's authority.

(C) Yes, because the attorney did not have apparent authority to accept the settlement.

(D) Yes, because the attorney accepted the settlement offer without his client's consent.

14. An attorney represented a buyer in the purchase of a restaurant. The contract, which was drafted by the seller's lawyer, specified that a portion of the purchase price ($25,000) was to be held in escrow by the attorney until certain conditions were satisfied, including the transfer of a liquor license. The attorney received a check from the buyer for $25,000 of the purchase price. The attorney placed the check in the trust account that he maintained for his clients' funds. Pursuant to the terms of the contract, the attorney timely filed the documents necessary to transfer the liquor license from the seller to the buyer. Upon learning from the proper local authorities that the transfer of the license had been approved, the attorney transferred $25,000 from the trust account to the seller. The seller did not ask and the attorney did not provide the seller with an accounting of the funds.

Were the attorney's actions proper?

(A) Yes, because the attorney performed his duties in a timely fashion.

(B) Yes, because the attorney, as the buyer's legal representative, did not owe a duty to the seller.

(C) No, because the attorney failed to place the $25,000 in a separate escrow account.

(D) No, because the attorney did not provide the seller with an accounting of the retained portion of the purchase price.

15. An attorney represented a client who was sued following a car accident. The attorney and her client discussed the allegations in the complaint, and the client denied the plaintiff's assertion that the client had been speaking on his cell phone at the time of the accident. Relying on this information, the attorney filed a response to the complaint including such a denial. Later, the attorney, in reviewing the client's cell phone records, discovered that a call had been placed from the client's cell phone immediately before the accident. When the attorney confronted the client with this information, the client admitted that he had lied to the attorney. The attorney figured that the information would come out shortly, since the records were being produced to the plaintiff, and did not act upon it.

Were the attorney's actions proper?

(A) No, because the attorney should have taken reasonable steps to confirm the client's factual assertion before including it in a pleading.

(B) No, because the attorney was required to correct any false statement of material fact he made to the court.

(C) Yes, because the attorney did not knowingly include a false statement of fact in a pleading.

(D) Yes, because the attorney was not required to confirm the client's factual assertions before including them in a pleading.

16. A business owner hired an attorney solely to prepare a contract for the sale of the business. Shortly after the sale was completed, the attorney learned from an employee of the business that the owner had falsified the business's records in order to make the business, which had been losing money for several years, appear profitable. When the attorney confronted the owner about the owner's actions, the owner acknowledged the fraud but refused to take any action. The attorney contacted the buyer of the business, who had used his retirement savings to purchase the business, and revealed the owner's fraud.

Is the attorney subject to discipline for this revelation to the buyer of the business?

(A) Yes, because the attorney breached the duty of confidentiality the attorney owed to the business owner.

(B) Yes, because disclosure was not necessary to prevent reasonably certain death or bodily harm.

(C) No, because the attorney did not learn of his client's fraud during the course of a litigation.

(D) No, because the owner had used the attorney's services in the sale of the business.

17. A judge hearing a divorce case appointed an attorney to represent the couple's 12-year-old child. Under state law, the attorney will be compensated by one or both parents at the court's discretion. The child told the attorney that she planned to falsely accuse her father of sexual abuse at the behest of her mother. Although the attorney counseled the child not to make the accusation, the child insisted that she intended to do so. As a result of the attorney's advice, the child indicated that she no longer trusted the attorney, and she wanted the court to appoint another guardian. Disgusted by the child's stated course of action, the attorney sought the judge's permission to withdraw. Both parents object, and the court refuses such permission.

Must the attorney continue to serve as the child's attorney?

(A) No, because a client has the absolute right to discharge an attorney.
(B) No, because the attorney finds the child's course of action repugnant.
(C) Yes, because the child's parents object to the attorney's withdrawal.
(D) Yes, because the court denied the attorney permission to withdraw from the case.

18. An attorney took out an advertisement in a local newspaper, which stated that the cost of his services was "50 percent cheaper than the customary attorney fees in town." The attorney never researched the fees of other attorneys in the area, but he planned to reduce his own fees to half of any such fees if and when a potential client brought them to his attention.

Would the attorney's actions subject him to discipline?

(A) Yes, because the attorney posted an advertisement that mentioned his rates.
(B) Yes, because the attorney's claims regarding his rates were unsubstantiated and specific.
(C) No, because the attorney planned to modify his rates to conform to the advertisement.
(D) No, because the attorney did not state a specific dollar amount for his rate.

19. A family court judge appointed an attorney to represent an indigent father in an action brought by a state agency to terminate the father's parental rights with respect to his only child. Until recently, the attorney was employed as a lawyer by the same state agency to collect court-ordered child support. This agency did attempt unsuccessfully to collect child support from the father, although the attorney was not personally involved in this attempt. Due to his employment with the agency, the attorney has personal knowledge of the father, and honestly believes him to be so repugnant that the attorney's ability to represent the father would be impaired. He also believes that it is in the best interests of the child for the father's parental rights to be terminated. Additionally, since the father is notorious in the community where the attorney practices, the attorney fears that representation of the father could have an adverse effect on the attorney's ability to attract clients.

Which of the following grounds is most likely a proper basis for the attorney to decline the appointment?

(A) The attorney was employed until recently as a lawyer by a state agency that attempted to collect child support from his court-appointed client.

(B) The attorney honestly believes that the father is so repugnant that his ability to represent the father would be impaired.

(C) The attorney believes that it is in the best interests of the child for the father's parental rights to be terminated.

(D) The attorney fears that representation of the father could have an adverse effect on the attorney's ability to attract clients.

20. A defendant is charged with robbery. A police officer received an anonymous tip that a specific individual other than the defendant committed the robbery. The police officer investigated the information, but concluded that the other individual did not commit the robbery. The police officer conveyed this information to the prosecutor. Due to the existence of other evidence that linked the defendant to the robbery, the prosecutor concluded in good faith that the tip, while exculpatory, was not material, and therefore she did not have a constitutional duty to turn the information over to the defense. Consequently, the prosecutor did not reveal the tip to the defendant's lawyer, who failed to make a Brady request for exculpatory evidence. State criminal procedure discovery rules did not require the prosecutor to disclose the anonymous tip.

Is the prosecutor subject to discipline for her failure to inform the defense of the anonymous tip?

(A) Yes, because the prosecutor determined that the anonymous tip was exculpatory information.

(B) Yes, because a prosecutor has a duty to search for exculpatory information.

(C) No, because the defendant's lawyer did not make a Brady request for exculpatory evidence.

(D) No, because the prosecutor acted in good faith in determining that the anonymous tip did not have to be turned over to the defense.

21. An attorney was contacted by a family member of an individual who was near death to prepare a will. After speaking briefly with the individual, the attorney drafted a document and oversaw its execution. After the death of the testator, the validity of the will was successfully challenged. The attorney was then sued for malpractice based on her alleged negligence.

Which of the following standards is applied to determine whether the attorney's conduct complied with the duty of care?

(A) Did her conduct violate the Model Rules of Professional Conduct as adopted in the applicable jurisdiction?

(B) Was her conduct at least average as judged by lawyers with similar skill and knowledge?

(C) Did she act in good faith in light of the emergency situation?

(D) Did she act with the competence and diligence normally exercised by lawyers in similar circumstances?

22. An attorney regularly volunteered as an intake consultant for an established program run by a legal services organization. The program provided indigent individuals with limited short-term legal assistance. If it became apparent that an individual needed long-term representation, the intake consultant would recommend that the individual consult an attorney and would provide a list of legal services organizations in the area. On one occasion, a woman who had received an eviction notice sought help from the program. The attorney gave her some general advice about how to avoid eviction and then recommended that she contact a private attorney or a legal services organization if she needed further assistance. The attorney later learned that the woman's landlord was a corporation represented in unrelated matters by partners in the attorney's law firm.

Did the attorney's actions in providing legal advice to the woman subject him to discipline?

(A) No, because the attorney did not know that his law firm represented the woman's landlord at the time he provided legal advice.

(B) No, because the Model Rules of Professional Conduct regarding conflicts of interest do not apply to programs such as that in which the attorney participated.

(C) Yes, because the attorney had a conflict of interest due to his law firm's representation of the woman's landlord.

(D) Yes, because the attorney did not check to see if he had a conflict of interest before providing the woman with legal advice.

23. An attorney took his grandmother out to dinner. Over dessert, the attorney asked his grandmother if she had updated her will recently. The grandmother stated that she had not, and the attorney offered to draft a new will for her. They met the following day and drafted a will in which she bequeathed to the attorney a rare book collection, which he had always admired, as well as a sizeable monetary gift. She left the remainder of her estate to her son and a charitable organization.

Were the attorney's actions in offering to prepare and preparing a will proper?

(A) No, because an attorney may not prepare a will that gives a substantial gift to the attorney.

(B) No, because an attorney may not solicit an individual to prepare a will that gives a substantial gift to the attorney.

(C) Yes, because an attorney may solicit or prepare a will that gives a substantial gift to the attorney if the client is a family member.

(D) Yes, because an attorney may prepare a will that gives a substantial gift to the attorney as long as the attorney does not exert undue influence over the client.

24. An established law firm located in a state capitol focused mainly on litigation, but it also provided legal services related to lobbying. The firm created a lobbying department and hired a former state legislator, who was not an attorney, to head this department. The former legislator received as compensation a percentage of the fees from all services provided to clients that he brought to the firm, including any legal services, but he did not direct the professional judgment of the attorneys in his department, nor was he made a partner.

Is the law firm's employment of the former legislator proper?

(A) No, because a non-lawyer may not hold a senior position in a law firm.

(B) No, because attorneys may not share fees with non-lawyers, as provided by this agreement.

(C) Yes, because the legislator was not made a partner of the firm.

(D) Yes, because the legislator did not provide legal services.

25. An attorney acting as a mediator in a child custody dispute properly explained his role to each of the parents involved in the dispute, how that role differed from that of a lawyer for a litigant, and that the lawyer-client privilege did not apply. Through the attorney's mediation efforts, the parents settled their dispute and came to a custody agreement that was approved by the court. Subsequently, the mother, wanting to modify the terms of the custody agreement, employed a partner at the attorney's law firm to handle the matter. The partner immediately gave written notice to the father and to the court of her employment by the mother, but she did not seek the approval of either. The attorney who served as a mediator was timely screened from participation in the matter and did not receive any part of the fee from this representation.

Is the partner's representation of the mother proper?

(A)   No, because the father did not give his written consent for the partner to represent the mother.

(B)   No, because another member of the partner's firm had served as mediator with regard to the same matter.

(C)   Yes, because the partner timely notified the father and the court in writing of her representation of the mother, and the firm properly dealt with the attorney who had acted as a mediator.

(D)   Yes, because the attorney who acted as a mediator had properly informed the parents about the difference between a mediator and a lawyer for a litigant.

26. An attorney was appointed to represent a criminal defendant. Prior to trial, the defendant's girlfriend called the attorney without the defendant's knowledge. The girlfriend told him that she had found evidence of the crime at her house and believed the defendant had hidden it there. The defendant's girlfriend asked the attorney whether she should tell the police about the evidence. The attorney, unsure of how to proceed, told the defendant's girlfriend that he would call her back. The attorney called his former law school ethics professor, who agreed to provide confidential legal advice as to the attorney's professional responsibility obligations. The attorney then told the professor about his discussion with the defendant's girlfriend and asked the professor for advice. The attorney did not mention the call to the professor to the defendant.

Was the attorney's action in revealing the discussion with the defendant's girlfriend proper?

(A)   No, because the attorney's discussion with the defendant's girlfriend was protected by attorney-client privilege.

(B)   No, because the attorney failed to secure the defendant's consent before consulting the professor.

(C)   Yes, because the defendant's girlfriend was not the attorney's client.

(D)   Yes, because the attorney was seeking to obtain confidential legal advice about his ethical obligations.

27. A stock clerk employed at a warehouse witnessed, but was otherwise not involved in, an accident between a truck and a car. The accident occurred while the driver of the truck was backing into the loading dock at the warehouse. The driver of the car sued the corporate owner of the warehouse and the truck driver, who was also an employee of the corporation, alleging that the truck driver's negligence was the cause of the accident. The attorney hired to represent the corporation in this lawsuit learned that the stock clerk had witnessed the accident, and he interviewed the clerk. The clerk's version of the accident did not correspond with the truck driver's version, and in several details, it supported the car driver's explanation of the event. The attorney told the clerk not to discuss the accident with anyone, particularly the driver of the car or his attorney, unless contacted by either of them.

Is the attorney subject to discipline for giving the clerk this instruction?

    (A)   No, because the clerk was a warehouse employee.

    (B)   No, because the attorney did not represent the stock clerk.

    (C)   Yes, because a lawyer must not obstruct another party's access to evidence.

    (D)   Yes, because a lawyer owes a duty of candor.

28. A law firm represented residents who were opposed to the rezoning of a nearby undeveloped parcel of land from rural to retail. A newly hired associate was assigned to work on the case. The associate had previously worked for another law firm, where she had participated in the representation of the landowner in securing the environmental permits necessary for the development of the parcel. The associate, after discussing the matter with the supervisory partner at her new firm, accepted the assignment. Even though the associate believed that accepting the assignment violated the conflict-of-interest rules, the partner concluded that there was not a conflict of interest and that, consequently, the consent of the landowner was not required. When the landowner learned that the associate was working with the residents, he notified the appropriate disciplinary authority. Subsequently, the partner was disciplined for violation of the conflict-of-interest rules.

Is the associate also subject to discipline?

    (A)   No, because the associate was acting at the direction of her supervisor.

    (B)   No, because the associate acted in accordance with the partner's resolution of a question of professional duty.

    (C)   Yes, because the associate's participation in the representation of the residents clearly constituted a conflict of interest.

    (D)   Yes, because the associate took actions that she believed violated a professional duty.

29. An attorney received a phone call from a client asking the attorney to represent the client's daughter, a 19-year-old college student, against a drug charge. The father told the attorney that he would pay the attorney's standard hourly rate for the representation, as well as any expenses. The following day, the attorney met with the father and daughter, and the three discussed the matter. When the daughter asked who was paying for the services, the attorney responded that they should simply focus on the case and worry about that later. As the trial date approached, the prosecution offered a plea deal. The attorney brought the deal to the daughter, who accepted it. When the father later learned of this, he was furious with the attorney for failing to include him in the discussion regarding the plea deal.

Were the attorney's actions in representing the daughter proper?

(A) No, because the daughter did not give informed consent for the attorney to be paid by her father.

(B) No, because the father should have been notified of the plea deal.

(C) Yes, because a parent may pay the legal fees for his child.

(D) Yes, because the attorney was not required to inform the father of the plea deal.

30. An attorney and an accountant entered into an agreement providing that each would recommend the other's services. The agreement, which did not specify a termination date, permitted the attorney and the accountant to enter into similar agreements with other parties. The agreement also placed no limitations on the number of clients that could be referred. Both the attorney and the accountant disclosed the nature and existence of this relationship to each client who is referred pursuant to the agreement.

Is the agreement improper?

(A) Yes, because the agreement was of an indefinite duration.

(B) Yes, because the agreement was made with a person who is not an attorney.

(C) No, because such a reciprocal referral agreement is permitted by the Model Rules of Professional Conduct.

(D) No, because the agreement is not exclusive, and each party disclosed the nature of the agreement to clients.

After you have completed this exam, log in to your course to submit your answers, view detailed answer explanations, and compare your performance to other Themis students.

PRACTICE EXAM ONE
ANSWER KEY

Item	Answer
1	C
2	D
3	D
4	B
5	B
6	A
7	C
8	A
9	B
10	D
11	B
12	B
13	D
14	C
15	B
16	D
17	D
18	B
19	B
20	A
21	D
22	A
23	C
24	B
25	C
26	D
27	A
28	C
29	A
30	A

Log in to your online course and upload your answers to view detailed answer explanations.

Themis
Bar Review

PRACTICE EXAM TWO

TIME: 60 MINUTES

Welcome to Practice Exam Two. This exam consists of 30 questions and will take 60 minutes. After you have completed this exam, log in to your course to submit your answers, view detailed answer explanations, and compare your performance to other Themis students.

Name: _____ Date: _____

Start Time: _____ End Time: _____

1 ⊏A⊐ ⊏B⊐ ⊏C⊐ ⊏D⊐　　21 ⊏A⊐ ⊏B⊐ ⊏C⊐ ⊏D⊐

2 ⊏A⊐ ⊏B⊐ ⊏C⊐ ⊏D⊐　　22 ⊏A⊐ ⊏B⊐ ⊏C⊐ ⊏D⊐

3 ⊏A⊐ ⊏B⊐ ⊏C⊐ ⊏D⊐　　23 ⊏A⊐ ⊏B⊐ ⊏C⊐ ⊏D⊐

4 ⊏A⊐ ⊏B⊐ ⊏C⊐ ⊏D⊐　　24 ⊏A⊐ ⊏B⊐ ⊏C⊐ ⊏D⊐

5 ⊏A⊐ ⊏B⊐ ⊏C⊐ ⊏D⊐　　25 ⊏A⊐ ⊏B⊐ ⊏C⊐ ⊏D⊐

6 ⊏A⊐ ⊏B⊐ ⊏C⊐ ⊏D⊐　　26 ⊏A⊐ ⊏B⊐ ⊏C⊐ ⊏D⊐

7 ⊏A⊐ ⊏B⊐ ⊏C⊐ ⊏D⊐　　27 ⊏A⊐ ⊏B⊐ ⊏C⊐ ⊏D⊐

8 ⊏A⊐ ⊏B⊐ ⊏C⊐ ⊏D⊐　　28 ⊏A⊐ ⊏B⊐ ⊏C⊐ ⊏D⊐

9 ⊏A⊐ ⊏B⊐ ⊏C⊐ ⊏D⊐　　29 ⊏A⊐ ⊏B⊐ ⊏C⊐ ⊏D⊐

10 ⊏A⊐ ⊏B⊐ ⊏C⊐ ⊏D⊐　　30 ⊏A⊐ ⊏B⊐ ⊏C⊐ ⊏D⊐

11 ⊏A⊐ ⊏B⊐ ⊏C⊐ ⊏D⊐

12 ⊏A⊐ ⊏B⊐ ⊏C⊐ ⊏D⊐

13 ⊏A⊐ ⊏B⊐ ⊏C⊐ ⊏D⊐

14 ⊏A⊐ ⊏B⊐ ⊏C⊐ ⊏D⊐

15 ⊏A⊐ ⊏B⊐ ⊏C⊐ ⊏D⊐

16 ⊏A⊐ ⊏B⊐ ⊏C⊐ ⊏D⊐

17 ⊏A⊐ ⊏B⊐ ⊏C⊐ ⊏D⊐

18 ⊏A⊐ ⊏B⊐ ⊏C⊐ ⊏D⊐

19 ⊏A⊐ ⊏B⊐ ⊏C⊐ ⊏D⊐

20 ⊏A⊐ ⊏B⊐ ⊏C⊐ ⊏D⊐

SCORE

1. An attorney at a law firm was hired to represent a client involved in a car accident. After reading the police report, the attorney realized that a partner in his law firm was a witness to the accident. The attorney interviewed the partner and concluded that the partner's version of the accident significantly undermined his client's position. Consequently, although the attorney did not plan to call the partner to testify, the attorney anticipated that the opposing party was likely to do so. Had the partner rather than the attorney been asked by the client to represent her, the partner would have been required by the conflict rules to decline.

Is the attorney subject to disqualification from representing the client?

   (A) Yes, because the partner could not have represented the client.
   (B) Yes, because an attorney must withdraw if he or another attorney at his firm may be a witness at a trial in which the attorney acts as an advocate.
   (C) No, because the attorney did not plan to call the partner as a witness.
   (D) No, because an attorney may serve as an advocate in a trial in which another attorney in his firm is likely to testify.

2. An attorney, who was well known in the community for previously representing a celebrity in a high-profile murder case, regularly served as a guest speaker at various legal seminars. At a criminal law seminar, he presented a hypothetical in which he never named his high-profile former client but outlined all the facts relevant to the murder case. Many of the facts he referenced were widely known among the general population, and many of the participants in the seminar rightly assumed that the attorney was talking about his celebrity client.

Were the attorney's actions with regard to disclosure improper?

   (A) No, because the facts were already known to the general public.
   (B) No, because the attorney never named his client.
   (C) Yes, because an attorney may not discuss confidential facts about a client even in the form of a hypothetical.
   (D) Yes, because the attorney presented facts that allowed the participants to identify the client.

3. The owner of real property who entered into a contract to sell the property employed a lawyer to conduct a title search. The lawyer's properly performed search revealed a cloud on the seller's title that rendered the property unmarketable. The lawyer provided this information to the buyer. As a consequence, the buyer refused to complete the sale.

Has the lawyer violated the rules of professional conduct?

- (A) Yes, because the lawyer represented the buyer and the seller in the same transaction.
- (B) Yes, because the lawyer failed to obtain the seller's consent before revealing the information to the buyer.
- (C) No, because the lawyer properly performed the search.
- (D) No, because the information is accurate.

4. An associate at an insurance defense law firm worked on many automobile accident claims on behalf of an insurance company under the supervision of a partner. As part of that work, she performed extensive legal research that was incorporated into memoranda filed by the partner, who attended hearings on the matter. All research projects were based on assignments from the partner, and it was not necessary that the associate reviewed the files, so she never did. After the partner left the firm, the insurance company terminated its relationship with the firm. The firm then agreed to represent a different insurance company in a case involving a dog bite in which the opposing party was insured by the former-client insurance company.

Is it proper for the firm to represent the new insurance company?

- (A) Yes, but only if the new insurance company provides informed consent to the representation.
- (B) Yes, because the dog bite matter is not substantially related to the previous automobile accident cases.
- (C) No, because the associate remains at the firm.
- (D) No, because the old and new clients have adverse interests.

5. A union offered a group legal services plan for its members. An attorney seeking to generate more income contacted the union about becoming a provider of legal services through the plan. The attorney met face-to-face with a plan representative and discussed the attorney's participation in the plan, including the services the attorney would render and the compensation to be received. The union decided not to use the attorney's services.

Is the attorney subject to discipline for this conduct?

(A) Yes, because the attorney initiated the contact with the union about the provision of legal services.

(B) Yes, because the attorney met face-to-face with the plan representative to solicit professional employment for pecuniary gain.

(C) No, because the attorney did not directly contact the union members who would be using the attorney's legal services.

(D) No, because the plan did not utilize the attorney's services.

6. A husband and wife were attorneys who practiced at different law firms. The husband dealt exclusively with estates and trust matters, while his wife was a criminal defense attorney. A decedent's daughter employed the husband to represent her in a dispute with her brother over property owned by her deceased father. The decedent's son contacted the wife about legal representation in this dispute. The wife directed the son to a partner in her firm whose practice was limited to estate and trust matters. The partner agreed to represent the son. Apart from the spousal relationship between the daughter's attorney and the attorney in the partner's firm who referred the decedent's son to the partner, the partner correctly concluded that the arrangement did not create a significant risk of materially limiting the partner's representation of the decedent's son. Accordingly, the partner did not discuss the possibility of a conflict of interest with his client, the decedent's son.

Is the partner subject to disqualification with regard to his representation of the decedent's son in this dispute?

(A) Yes, because the partner came to represent the decedent's son through a referral from another attorney, the wife, who was personally disqualified from representing the son.

(B) Yes, because the partner failed to secure the informed consent of his client with regard to representation of the opposing party by the spouse of a member of his law firm.

(C) No, because the wife's personal disqualification is not imputed to the partner as a member of her firm.

(D) No, because only the husband was personally disqualified from representing the decedent's daughter in this matter.

7. A client met with an attorney about representing her in a divorce proceeding. The attorney informed the client of his hourly rate, specified the litigation expenses and court costs for which the client would be responsible, and stated that these charges would apply regardless of the outcome of the case. The client agreed to the attorney's representation of her in the divorce action and to his terms for doing so, but no documentation of this agreement was prepared or signed by either the client or the attorney. After the divorce was final, the attorney sent to the client a bill, which detailed his fee, the litigation expenses, and court costs, all in accord with the prior oral agreement reached by the attorney and the client. Even though the amounts were reasonable, the client, who was unhappy with the court's allocation of marital property, refused to pay the bill.

Was the attorney's action regarding his fees and other charges related to the divorce proceeding proper?

    (A)   No, because an attorney must offer a client the option of a contingency fee arrangement with regard to representation in a divorce proceeding.

    (B)   No, because a fee arrangement must be in writing and signed by the client.

    (C)   Yes, because the client's refusal to pay the attorney's bill was unjustified.

    (D)   Yes, because the attorney's fees and other charges were reasonable and communicated to the client prior to the commencement of the representation.

8. An attorney was a sole practitioner who confined her practice to family law matters. Her best friend, who was employed as an accountant, was arrested for embezzling from her employer through a series of complex transactions. The friend asked the attorney to represent her. Although the attorney explained that she had no experience in criminal law, and did not understand the transactions at issue, the friend prevailed upon the attorney to represent her. The attorney agreed to this representation free of charge. The friend voluntarily and in writing waived any claims related to the attorney's competence. At trial, the attorney lacked the skills necessary to defend her friend effectively against the embezzlement charges.

Would the attorney be subject to discipline for her representation of the friend?

    (A)   No, because the friend voluntarily and in writing waived any claims related to the attorney's competence.

    (B)   No, because the attorney did not charge the friend for the representation.

    (C)   Yes, because the attorney lacked the legal knowledge and skill necessary for the representation.

    (D)   Yes, because there is an inherent conflict of interest when an attorney represents a friend.

9. An attorney performed all legal matters for a client for nearly 50 years. The client told the attorney that he planned to leave the attorney $10,000 in his will as a thank you for "becoming like a son to [him]." The attorney stated that he could not accept the gift. Unbeknownst to the attorney, the client secured another attorney to help him amend his will to provide the former attorney with a $10,000 gift upon the client's death. When the client died, the trustee of the estate gave this bequest to the attorney, and the attorney accepted.

Is the attorney subject to discipline for his acceptance of the $10,000?

(A) No, because the client considered the attorney to be a son.
(B) No, because the attorney did not draft the will.
(C) Yes, because a gift that stems from an attorney-client relationship is presumed to be fraudulent.
(D) Yes, because an attorney may not receive a substantial gift from a current or former client's will.

10. A defendant was convicted of murder after waiving his right to counsel and representing himself at trial. The defendant's juvenile record showed that he had sustained severe physical abuse during his childhood and adolescence. The prosecutor had a copy of the defendant's juvenile record, which he provided to the defendant before sentencing. Although past physical abuse is recognized as a mitigating factor for sentencing in the jurisdiction, neither party presented evidence of the defendant's past abuse at the defendant's sentencing hearing.

Was the prosecutor's failure to introduce evidence of the defendant's past abuse proper?

(A) No, because a prosecutor must disclose to the court unprivileged mitigating information known to the prosecutor at sentencing.
(B) No, because a prosecutor has a duty to disclose to the court mitigating information if the defendant is not represented by counsel.
(C) Yes, because a prosecutor must disclose only material information that would tend to negate the guilt of the accused.
(D) Yes, because the prosecutor has a duty to disclose mitigating evidence to the defendant only.

11. Johnson, Jackson, and Jones established a law firm in 1950. When Jackson died in 2000, Johnson decided to accept a job as in-house counsel for a local business, while Jones decided to retire; they terminated the practice and sold the firm in 2001. The purchasers renamed the firm, though nearly all of the prior firm's clients retained the services of the attorneys who purchased the firm. In 2004, Jones's son and Johnson purchased the firm back and reestablished the firm as Johnson, Jackson, and Jones, as the name was still well recognized as being one of the most prominent and well-respected firms in the region.

Were the actions in renaming the firm Johnson, Jackson, and Jones proper?

(A)   Yes, because Johnson was one of the original founding partners.
(B)   Yes, because the practice had functioned continuously since before Jackson's death.
(C)   No, because Johnson did not join the new firm after its purchase in 2001.
(D)   No, because the firm was not continuously operated.

12. Looking through a window, a man witnessed an altercation between his adult nephew and another person. The nephew was charged with assault. The nephew's attorney interviewed the man about the incident. The man's version of the events called into question the nephew's version of what had happened. The attorney, aware that only the nephew knew that the man had seen the altercation, requested that the man not talk about the matter to the police or the prosecutor unless questioned by them.

Is the attorney subject to discipline for this request?

(A)   Yes, because a lawyer must not obstruct another party's access to evidence.
(B)   Yes, because a lawyer must not encourage a witness to lie.
(C)   No, because the man was the defendant's uncle.
(D)   No, because the defendant has been charged with a crime.

13. A law firm associate was assigned to work on a plaintiff's tort case with a partner. The associate was charged with the day-to-day management of the case, although the partner checked in with the associate regularly. Despite the associate's solid performance, the client lost the case at trial. After the time for filing an appeal had expired, the associate told the partner for the first time about a settlement offer made by the opposing party that the associate had rejected as too low without consulting the client. The partner scolded the associate for failing to bring the settlement offer to the client's attention, but otherwise took no action.

Is the partner subject to discipline for failure to adequately supervise the associate?

(A) No, because the associate was charged with the day-to-day management of the case.
(B) No, because the partner did not learn of the action until it was too late to avoid the consequences.
(C) Yes, because the partner was the associate's supervising attorney.
(D) Yes, because a partner may be subject to discipline for an associate's misconduct.

14. A client retained an attorney to represent her in a personal injury lawsuit. A written agreement signed by both the client and the attorney provided that the attorney was entitled to a 20 percent contingency fee, plus all litigation expenses. The client later agreed to accept a $100,000 settlement. The defendant sent a check to the attorney for that amount, which the attorney deposited into a client trust account. The attorney notified her client that she had received the funds and that the attorney would be entitled to $25,000, which represented the contingency fee and expenses. The client objected, arguing that the claimed expenses were unreasonable and that she owed the attorney only $20,000. The attorney distributed $75,000 from the account to her client and told the client that the remaining $25,000 would be held in the account until the dispute over the party responsible for the litigation expenses was resolved.

Were the attorney's actions proper?

(A) Yes, because the attorney promptly distributed to the client $75,000, which was the undisputed amount to which the client was entitled.
(B) Yes, because the attorney was not required to distribute any client funds until the dispute was resolved.
(C) No, because the attorney was required to keep all settlement funds in the trust account until the dispute was resolved.
(D) No, because the attorney was required to distribute all undisputed amounts from the account.

15. A prominent local attorney decided to run for the position of city judge. The candidate had been active in a bar association for a number of years and chaired a committee of the bar association. At a meeting of the committee, the vice-chair announced that the candidate was running for office and that the members of the committee should show their support by donating generously. The vice-chair collected checks from the members of the committee and gave them to the candidate. The candidate did not know that the vice-chair planned to make such an announcement but was grateful for the contributions. Shortly thereafter, the candidate formed a campaign committee to manage the contributions to her campaign, and she turned the contributions over to the committee. State law does not address the contribution of funds to the campaigns for judicial office.

Did the candidate's actions subject her to discipline?

(A) No, because a candidate for elective judicial office may personally solicit or accept campaign contributions.

(B) No, because a candidate for elective judicial office may personally accept campaign contributions, provided she did not personally solicit them.

(C) Yes, because a candidate for elective judicial office may not personally solicit or accept campaign funds.

(D) Yes, because a candidate for elective judicial office must form a campaign committee before announcing her candidacy.

16. A sole practitioner and her client, a plaintiff in a products liability case, entered into a proper, written contingency fee agreement. After it became evident that discovery would be voluminous and contain a great deal of technical information, the sole practitioner recommended to her client that they bring in a law firm that specialized in products liability. The client orally agreed, and the lawyer sent a written confirmation of their agreement to the client. The agreement did not specify how the fee would be allocated between the sole practitioner and the firm. Upon the successful conclusion of the lawsuit, the sole practitioner split the contingency fee, which was reasonable, with the other firm in proportion to the services rendered by each.

Was the sole practitioner's action in splitting the contingent fee with the other firm proper?

(A) No, because the client did not agree to the fee-splitting arrangement in writing.

(B) No, because the client did not agree to the shares that the sole practitioner and the law firm were to receive.

(C) Yes, because the contingency fee arrangement was in writing.

(D) Yes, because the fee was shared in proportion to the services rendered by the sole practitioner and the law firm.

17. An attorney, who herself had been the subject of sexual discrimination, represented an employee in a civil sexual discrimination case against her employer. The attorney told the jury, "I believe that sexual discrimination is rampant in this country and should be eliminated. If ever there was a just cause, my client's case is it."

Is it proper for the attorney to make this statement?

(A) Yes, because, in a civil matter, an attorney may state her personal opinion as to the culpability of the defendant.

(B) Yes, because a lawyer is required to zealously represent her client.

(C) No, because the matter is one of personal interest to the attorney.

(D) No, because a lawyer, in addressing the jury, may not give her personal opinion as to the justness of a cause.

18. An attorney was sued by a client for malpractice. The client alleged that the attorney failed to reveal a conflict of interest that arose from the attorney's prior representation of another client. The former client refused to consent to the attorney's disclosure of information about that representation. Nevertheless, at a deposition, the attorney testified about the nature of that representation, revealing information to the extent that it was relevant to the conflict-of-interest issue. The attorney reasonably believed that the disclosure was necessary to his defense of the malpractice charge.

Does such testimony subject the attorney to discipline for breach of the duty of confidentiality?

(A) No, because the attorney reasonably believed that disclosure of the information was necessary to his defense.

(B) No, because the information revealed did not relate to a current client.

(C) Yes, because the litigation was not between the attorney and the client whose confidential information the attorney's testimony revealed.

(D) Yes, because the former client refused to consent to disclosure.

19. A sole practitioner accepted a matter in which he was to represent the potential buyer of a large business. After the attorney accepted the case, he realized that he represented the seller in a separate divorce action. The attorney had already begun working on the sale before he realized this fact and became concerned that the seller would have a problem with this arrangement. He therefore disclosed the issue to the seller and received written confirmation from the seller that the attorney's involvement was not a problem. Months after the attorney began representing these clients, they met in the lobby of the attorney's office, where the buyer learned that the attorney represented the seller in a divorce action. He confronted the attorney about the issue that day. After talking to the attorney about the sale, he grew more confident that the attorney could still successfully represent him, and he told the attorney that he did not have any problem with the arrangement. The attorney continued to work on facilitating the sale of the business.

Is the attorney subject to discipline?

(A) No, because the matters are unrelated.

(B) No, because the attorney was not aware of any conflict at the time he accepted the buyer as a client.

(C) Yes, because an attorney may not represent opposing parties.

(D) Yes, because the attorney did not receive proper consent.

20. A minister who belonged to a religious sect that prohibited the consumption of alcohol was charged with a crime. Shortly before trial, the minister's friend, who was to testify as a character witness on behalf of the minister, revealed to the minister's attorney that, at the time of the crime, the minister was at a bar, and not alone in his study, as the minister had previously told the attorney. When confronted with this information, the minister said that he would rather go to prison than have anyone else find out he was at a bar. The attorney, acting in what she believed was her client's best interests, contacted an investigator employed by her firm and asked the investigator to go to the bar and find out if any of the bar's regular patrons remembered seeing the defendant.

Were the attorney's actions on behalf of her client proper?

(A) No, because the attorney disclosed information protected by the duty of confidentiality to a non-lawyer.

(B) No, because the defendant did not authorize his attorney to disclose the information.

(C) Yes, because the attorney had implied authority to disclose the information to the investigator.

(D) Yes, because the revelation regarding the defendant's whereabouts was not made by the defendant and therefore such information was not subject to the duty of confidentiality.

21. An attorney represented a client in a suit against the client's former employer. Counsel for the employer approached the attorney with a settlement offer. Because the attorney was unable to reach her client despite due diligence before the offer was set to expire, the attorney accepted it on her client's behalf. The attorney honestly believed that the client would have accepted the offer if the client had known about it. When the attorney told her client about the offer the following day, she did not initially mention that she had already accepted the offer on behalf of her client. The client told the attorney that the offer sounded great, and she accepted it. Upon hearing this news, the attorney stated, "Thank goodness, because I already did!"

Is the attorney subject to discipline?

(A) No, because the client ratified the attorney's acceptance of the offer.

(B) No, because an attorney may accept a settlement offer without the client's consent if the attorney acts with due diligence in attempting to inform the client of the offer and honestly believes that the client would have accepted the offer had the client

(C) Yes, because an attorney may be disciplined for a violation of the Model Rules of Professional Conduct regardless of whether the client was harmed by the violation.

(D) Yes, because the attorney committed legal malpractice.

22. A sole practitioner who specialized in family law shared office space with a criminal defense attorney. When the family law attorney's clients required legal representation in a criminal matter, he referred them to the criminal defense attorney. Likewise, when the defense attorney's clients sought counsel for a family law matter, he referred them to the family law attorney. Because this arrangement had been fruitful, both attorneys decided to change their signs and letterhead so that they listed both attorneys' names and read "Specializing in Family Law and Criminal Defense."

Were the attorneys' actions in changing their signs and letterhead proper?

(A) No, because an attorney may not refer to himself as a specialist in a particular field of law.

(B) No, because attorneys may not imply that they practice in a partnership when that is not the case.

(C) Yes, because an attorney may refer to himself as a specialist in a particular field of law.

(D) Yes, because the signs and letterhead do not specifically state that the attorneys are members of the same law firm.

23. A business owner retained an attorney to represent him in a suit against a former employee. The business owner specifically instructed the attorney not to agree to a delay in starting the trial. The former employee's lawyer, unaware of this instruction, approached the business owner's attorney about delaying the start of the trial. Despite his client's contrary instruction, the attorney agreed to the delay.

Is the attorney's agreement to the delay enforceable?

- (A) No, because the client has ultimate control over the conduct of a case.
- (B) No, because the client specifically instructed the attorney not to agree to the delay.
- (C) Yes, because an attorney has control over the means by which a client's objectives are pursued.
- (D) Yes, because the attorney had apparent authority to agree to the delay.

24. An attorney represented an employee in a discrimination action against her employer. The employer filed a motion to dismiss the action as untimely. The attorney, in critically assessing the situation, determined that it was more likely than not that the judge would grant the employer's motion because there was not a current factual basis for the employee's position, but he reasonably believed that critical factual evidence could be developed during discovery in support of the employee's position. The attorney unsuccessfully contested the motion.

Was the attorney's action in contesting the motion improper?

- (A) No, because the attorney expected to develop critical factual evidence that would support the client's position during discovery.
- (B) No, because an attorney must zealously advocate on behalf of his client.
- (C) Yes, because the attorney determined that the employer's motion was likely to be successful.
- (D) Yes, because the judge granted the employer's motion.

25. A defendant was convicted of the murder of a celebrity. One year after the conviction, a man came into a police station in a different state and confessed to the murder of the celebrity. A prosecutor in that jurisdiction questioned the man after obtaining a copy of the case file. The prosecutor determined that the man did not know several details about the murder and that the man seemed mentally unstable. The prosecutor let the man go and did not disclose information about the confession to the convicted defendant or the appropriate authority because he believed that it was a false confession.

Would the prosecutor's action in failing to disclose information about the confession subject him to discipline?

(A)   No, because a prosecutor is not subject to discipline if he makes a good-faith, independent judgment that new evidence does not require action.

(B)   No, because a prosecutor is not subject to discipline for failing to disclose evidence relevant to a conviction obtained in another jurisdiction.

(C)   Yes, because a prosecutor must disclose to the appropriate authority any new evidence relevant to a defendant's conviction.

(D)   Yes, because a prosecutor must disclose to the defendant new evidence creating a reasonable likelihood that a convicted defendant did not commit the offense for which he was convicted.

26. A husband contacted his friend, a lawyer, about obtaining a divorce. The friend was aware that the husband's spouse was a lawyer who served as general counsel for a corporation. During the initial meeting about the divorce at the friend's office, the husband revealed that he and his wife had not filed tax returns for several years. At the conclusion of the meeting, the friend declined to represent the husband. The following week, the friend had a casual conversation with the couple's daughter, during which she confided in the friend, "You know, my parents have not filed tax returns for several years." The friend has not further discussed the couple's failure to file tax returns with either the husband or the wife.

Must the friend report the wife's failure to file tax returns to the bar disciplinary authority?

(A)   Yes, because the failure to file tax returns raises a substantial question as to the wife's honesty.

(B)   Yes, because the couple's daughter revealed that her mother had not filed tax returns for several years.

(C)   No, because the duty of confidentiality applies with regard to information learned from a prospective client.

(D)   No, because the wife's failure to file her own tax returns does not relate to her legal practice.

27. An attorney accepted a client in a medical malpractice action but was nervous that the client was prone to filing malpractice actions. After explaining his apprehension to the client, the client suggested that they enter into a written agreement limiting the attorney's own malpractice liability to a specified amount. They entered into such an agreement after the client sought the counsel of a partner at the attorney's firm who was not involved in the case.

Were the attorney's actions in entering into the agreement with the client proper?

(A) No, because an attorney may not prospectively limit malpractice liability.
(B) No, because the partner who reviewed the agreement is a member of the attorney's firm.
(C) Yes, because another attorney reviewed the agreement.
(D) Yes, because the client suggested entering into the agreement.

28. A recently licensed attorney attended a fundraising event for a local judge running for reelection. The attorney attended the event to network with fellow attorneys and judges in the area. The attorney had a chance to speak with the judge for a long time, and was impressed with her. On his way out of the event, he stopped by the table being staffed by the judge's campaign committee and made a donation to support her reelection efforts. Two weeks later, the judge won her bid for reelection, and her staff posted an opening for a law clerk position. The attorney applied for the position, and when the judge subsequently interviewed candidates to serve as her law clerk, she noted that the attorney she met at the fundraising event was on the shortlist of potential clerks. The judge recalled the great conversation with the attorney that occurred at the fundraising event, and after interviewing him, she offered him the position. The attorney immediately accepted the position for a two-year term.

Is the attorney subject to discipline for accepting the legal appointment?

(A) Yes, because the attorney applied for the clerkship after making the contribution.
(B) Yes, because the attorney attended the fundraising event for networking purposes.
(C) No, because the attorney's contribution was not for the purpose of securing an appointment.
(D) No, because the appointment was only for two years.

29. An attorney represented a small business owner who was sued by a former employee following the employee's termination. After the attorney tried unsuccessfully to engage the opposing counsel in a settlement discussion, the owner told her attorney that she believed the parties could settle the lawsuit if their attorneys were not involved and that she planned to invite the former employee to lunch to discuss a settlement. The attorney tried to dissuade the client from meeting with the opposing party but acquiesced in the face of the client's determination to do so. Neither the attorney nor the owner spoke with the former employee's lawyer about this invitation prior to the lunch. Unfortunately, the lunch meeting did not produce a resolution of the dispute.

Were the attorney's actions proper?

(A)   No, because direct communication with an opposing party who is known to be represented by an attorney is prohibited.

(B)   No, because neither the attorney nor his client sought the permission of the opposing party's lawyer before the client communicated with the opposing party.

(C)   Yes, because an attorney may advise a client with regard to communication by a client directly with an opposing party.

(D)   Yes, because the lunch meeting did not result in a settlement of the case.

30. An established attorney who truthfully advertised that he would only accept estate and trust matters hired a newly licensed attorney as an associate. The proposed employment agreement contained a non-compete provision. This provision would have prohibited the associate, if justifiably discharged, from practicing estates and trusts law within a 25-mile radius of the attorney's office for four months. The state's highest court has upheld a similar non-compete agreement between an architect and an architectural firm. The associate refused to consent to the provision, and the attorney agreed to drop it from the employment agreement that was entered into by the two lawyers.

Is the established attorney subject to discipline?

(A)   Yes, because the attorney advertised that he would only accept estate and trust matters.

(B)   Yes, because the proposed non-compete provision would have restricted the right of the associate to practice law after termination of the associate's employment.

(C)   No, because a similar non-compete provision was upheld by the state's highest court.

(D)   No, because the provision was not ultimately included in the employment agreement entered into by the two lawyers.

After you have completed this exam, log in to your course to submit your answers, view detailed answer explanations, and compare your performance to other Themis students.

PRACTICE EXAM TWO
ANSWER KEY

Item	Answer
1	A
2	D
3	B
4	B
5	C
6	C
7	D
8	C
9	B
10	A
11	D
12	C
13	B
14	D
15	C
16	B
17	D
18	A
19	D
20	B
21	C
22	B
23	D
24	A
25	A
26	C
27	B
28	C
29	C
30	B

Log in to your online course and upload your answers to view detailed answer explanations.